CHILDREN with AUTISM

A Parents' Guide

Edited by Michael D. Powers, Psy.D.

Foreword by Beverly Sills Greenough

WOODBINE HOUSE • 1989

**For information regarding sales of this book please contact:
Woodbine House, 5615 Fishers Lane,
Rockville, MD 20852, 800/843–7323.**

Cover Design & Illustration: Gary A. Mohrmann

Library of Congress Cataloging-in-Publication Data

Children with autism

Bibliography: p.
Includes index
1. Autistic children—Popular works. I. Powers, Michael D.
RJ506.A9C45 1989 618.92'8982 87-51322
ISBN 0-933149-16-6

Manufactured in the United States of America

7 8 9 10

This book could never have been written without the participation of the thousands of families of children and adults with autism whom we—as contributors—have known professionally and personally over the years. They have allowed us into their lives to share their hopes, fears, tough times, and triumphs, enriching our lives and our work. It is to them that we dedicate this book.

TABLE OF CONTENTS

ACKNOWLEDGEMENTS

Many individuals contributed to the development of this book. I have been most fortunate to work with a group of contributors whose commitment to helping children with autism and their families is matched only by their concern for those with whom they work. I owe a special thank you to the parents of children with autism who have shared their expertise: Beverly Sills Greenough and Peter Greenough, Lillian and Joe Tommasone, and Bernard Rimland.

I would also like to thank the many people who supported the preparation of this book: Diane Kelly and Sarah Gossett for their assistance in researching material; Marty Schrecengrost and Barbara Young for their help in preparation of the manuscript; the staff of the New Jersey Council of Organizations and Schools for Autistic Children and Adults, Inc. (COSAC), and especially Nancy G. Richardson, Executive Director, for permission to reprint their Program Checklist; and Dr. Fred Volkmar, Dr. Sandra Harris, Dr. Gina Richman, Susan Goodman, and Herbert Hinkle for their helpful comments on several chapters. (Dr. Harris, in turn, would like to acknowledge the assistance of Jan S. Handleman, Ed.D., who has worked with her these many years in the creation of the Douglass Developmental Disabilities Center, their school for children with autism.) Preparation of chapters one, five, and seven was supported in part by grants from the United States Department of Education (#G008630278 and #G008630423); however no official endorsement is intended or should be implied. Finally, I owe a special debt of gratitude to Dr. David Holmes for his advice and assistance throughout this project.

I am especially indebted to the staff at Woodbine House: Irvin Shapell, publisher; Susan Stokes, editor; and Jim Peters, Robin Dhawan, and Fran Marinaccio. Their dedication, persistence, and good humor have shaped this book immensely and they have been a joy to work with. Of far greater importance, however, is their vision for their "Special Needs Collection," which has guided the development of this book.

Finally, as in each of these endeavors, I owe a most special thanks to my sons, Seth and Evan for their part in keeping the sense of wonder in my life.

FOREWORD

Beverly Sills Greenough*

"I know just how you feel..."

Over the years (some twenty-six now), I wish I could tell you how many times I have heard these words from well-meaning people attempting to empathize with me over the problems of my autistic son.

They don't know. Really, they have *no* idea of what we go through. I say this not in any way as a sob sister. It's just fact. No one knows except those who have undergone the same thing.

However, just as my husband, Pete, and I learned early on, parents of children with autism quickly start saying "Why them?" instead of "Why us?" They also are greatly benefitted by the growing depth of understanding and general knowledge about autism, as is abundantly demonstrated in this new guide.

But let me go back twenty-two years to when I first met this puzzling affliction head-on. These recollections are largely drawn from a recent autobiography of mine.

Bucky was two months old when we summoned a photographer to take pictures of our adorable, perfect, beautiful son (are there any other kinds?).

The photographer startled me when he observed: "There's something wrong with your kid, Mrs. Greenough. He won't follow the birdie" (the fake canary attached to his camera).

We began watching Bucky very closely. He seemed to have spasms and peculiar movements when his eyes crossed badly and when he lost control of his hands. I began worrying that Bucky might have some sort of nerve affliction. But then he'd calm down. Bucky was a cheerful and extraordinarily handsome boy (he still is), but it was impossible to make eye contact with him.

So we took him to Children's Hospital in Boston. A woman doctor there (not exactly tactful, but blunt) told us: "There are so many things wrong with this boy that if I listed what they are today,

---

* Beverly Sills Greenough is an internationally renowned coloratura soprano and the retired General Director of the New York City Opera.

they would be only half of what you're going to be facing."

The first thing she cited was *retardation.*

What did she know about autism? Zilch. *Very* few doctors in the sixties had any notion about it.

That doctor also stated flatly that Bucky would never talk *or* be toilet-trained. And that he'd have to be fed for life. She did not know that he was, or would later become, deaf. Or that he was capable of learning sign language.

Nor did she know that in our household was a wonderful young Irish girl named Ona McCarthy. Purely by instinct and intelligence, Ona just knew how to work with a kid with autism. Through repetition and reward—boy, did we buy a lot of fruit Lifesavers—she not only trained Bucky but she also taught him how to use table utensils. Soon he could feed himself.

We managed, not easily, to keep Bucky at home until 1969. He was able to play outdoors a lot, within the confines of a very large, protected backyard. We also had a trained sheepherding dog—a Welsh corgi—who would steer Bucky back to us when he tried to run away.

Still, there had to be bars on Bucky's windows, a locked gate for his room, and a variety of restraints that hardly fitted well with a home full of normal youngsters.

So Bucky went to a school for the retarded in central Massachusetts, a fine institution in its way. But that was not for a youngster with autism. Again, they knew nothing about autism or how to deal with it.

When Bucky reached twenty-one, we were told that he had to be moved. I won't detail the difficulties we had in finding the right place for him, or the complications thrown in our path by one greedy individual who expected us to build a major part of a group home before Bucky could be accepted.

Happily, we found the Eden Institute in Princeton, New Jersey. In addition to getting Bucky started on sign language, Eden placed him in a sheltered workshop. With the money he earns there, he has been able to pay for a week at a winter camp in the Poconos *and* another week at a summer camp on the Jersey shore. He is developing a sense of self-accomplishment, and the resulting gains in behavior and control have been significant.

When we take him for drives, which he loves, the detached, vague look on his face disappears—to be replaced by a lucid expression. For fleeting moments we see a normal, extraordinarily handsome young man of twenty-six. I swear to you—he *can* display normal intelligence. His brain just gets wrong messages.

Yes, and my husband teases me by saying, "There you go, Beverly, playing doctor without a license."

Bucky cannot climb any mountains (unlike his adventurous sister, Muffy). But he has negotiated some fairly steep hills. And his triumphs will continue to mount, thanks to Eden (which plays a part later in this book, through its wonderful director, Dr. David Holmes).

One last high note (as a prima donna, I was entitled to *that*):

I would not exchange my son for anyone. His triumphs are ours. But those gains only are possible because of the wealth of information now known about autism and how to deal with it. But we can't stop there. The next step is discovering why the many forms of autism occur, and then ways of *prevention*. I am confident we shall live to see that!

INTRODUCTION

Bernard Rimland, Ph.D.*

What a boon this book will be to parents of autistic and autistic-like children. It contains information that will be immensely helpful, not only to the bewildered parents of newly diagnosed youngsters, but also to the bedraggled parents of the older children, adolescents, and adults with autism.

I am pleased that the editor invited me to tell you, in this Introduction, about my personal initiation to the world of autism, over three decades ago, and about my responses to what I found.

It is a great pity this book was not available in the "bad old days" when very little was known about autism, and most of what was known was wrong. Today, thanks to television, movies, innumerable magazine articles, and dozens of books, one scarcely encounters a high school student without at least some idea of what an autistic child is like. It was not always that way, I can assure you.

I did not learn of autism in high school, nor college, or even in graduate school. To the best of my knowledge, the first time I saw the word "autism" was in early 1958, when I was 29 years old, and that was five years after I had earned a Ph.D. in psychology! Granted, my training in psychology had been concentrated in measurement, statistics, experimental design, and similar areas of research, but I had to take courses, and pass examinations, in such areas as child development, abnormal psychology, and clinical psychology, where a student today would run across the term, "autism," scores, it not hundreds, of times.

I clearly remember the occasion, and the eerie feeling it gave me, when, for the first time, I saw the strange words, "early infantile autism," staring up at me from my wife Gloria's old college textbook. But I'm getting ahead of myself. Let me explain why I

---

* Dr. Bernard Rimland received his Ph.D. in experimental psychology and research methodology from the Pennsylvania State University. He is the author of the prize-winning book, *Infantile Autism: The Syndrome and Its Implications for a Neural Theory of Behavior* (Appleton-Century-Croft, 1964), the founder of the Autism Society of America, the editor of *Autism Research Review International*, and the Director of the Institute for Child Behavior Research in San Diego.

had pulled that box of old textbooks off the garage shelf to find the one, the only one, in which autism was mentioned.

Our eagerly awaited son Mark had been born two years earlier, after a picture-perfect pregnancy. Mark was a beautiful, picture-perfect baby, except for the screaming. He started screaming in the hospital nursery and rarely stopped. He screamed so violently that it was difficult to nurse him. The screaming continued, many hours a day, during most of his early childhood. Hard as we tried, we could discern no reason for his crying. Holding him didn't help. He just struggled and cried harder. The only thing that would placate him, we discovered, was placing him face down in his carriage and rolling him back and forth until he fell asleep. I found that by taping a yardstick to the nursery floor and running the carriage back and forth over it, the gentle jouncing would calm him more quickly.

Mark seemed totally oblivious to us, and to others, although he screamed in terror when our kitten approached. He began to rock in his crib constantly, banging his forehead on the headboard until a large, perpetual bruise appeared on his forehead. The crib began to fall apart under the constant banging, so I replaced all the wood screws with nuts and bolts.

During the day he spent hours bouncing incessantly in a jump chair, happily chanting songs in some ancient, unknown tongue, and breaking or wearing out two or three jump chairs over the course of several years. Mark was also extremely intolerant of change, and had violent tantrums when my wife put on a new dress. Only the grandmothers were willing to babysit this extremely difficult child. My wife conceived of a major breakthrough when it occurred to her that she could buy several dresses of the same size and pattern for herself from the Sears Catalog, and buy several larger-sized dresses of the same pattern for my mother, as well as several others, in a smaller size, for her own mother. Mark didn't really care who fed or changed him, just so long as they were wearing that familiar pink-and-gray flowered dress.

Mark began speaking at about eight months, pronouncing, with perfect diction, the words "spoon," "all done," "teddy bear," and "come on, let's play ball." At age two he could repeat anything said to him, with remarkably clear pronunciation. His uncle tried him on "hippopotamus," and Mark replied, "hippopotamus," with no hesitation. (An Italian father once told me a similar event with his two-year-old autistic daughter, involving the word "chrysanthemum." If you think chrysanthemum is hard in English, try it in Italian!)

It soon became evident that Mark's speech was like that of a tape recorder—just repetition of words, phrases, sentences, and even nursery rhymes, without any real idea of what they meant. Our pediatrician, a widely respected physician who had spent 35 years in the field of pediatrics, had never seen nor heard of a child like Mark.

One sunny morning, as Mark was wandering through the house with a vacant, staring-into-space expression, repeating words and phrases he had heard in a hollow, monotone, parrot-like voice, Gloria remembered having read in one of her college textbooks, almost 10 years earlier, about an unusual type of child who walked around the house, staring vacantly into space, while repeating words and phrases in a hollow, monotone, parrot-like voice.

Before long I had hauled the box of textbooks off the garage shelf, found the one she had mentioned, and found myself looking at, for the first time in my life, the words that would dramatically change my life—the words that would never leave my mind for more than a few moments for the next 30 years: *early infantile autism*. At last I knew the name of the unseen foe who had seized my child. I vowed not to rest until this enemy was defeated. If it took the rest of my life—so be it.

The textbook provided some references to the medical literature, and I took these to the nearby university library and began to read. I was startled to find, in Leo Kanner's *Textbook of Child Psychiatry*, case histories of children who were *identical* in every respect to my son Mark. There was the autistic aloneness, the dream world inaccessibility which left him staring into space for hours at a time, taking no notice of those, even his parents, in his environment. There was the insistence upon sameness; the precocious use of words and sentences, without any understanding; the repetitive rocking; the leading of an adult by the hand to the refrigerator, a toy, or another object he wanted; the reversal of pronouns, where he would say "you" where the word "I" should be used; the repetition of a question to indicate "yes," rather than the use of the word "yes" itself. There was the strong preoccupation with mechanical objects, which reminded me of the times his loving grandmother stood in the doorway, staring in dismay as her grandchild rushed past her into her house to find the vacuum cleaner, which he towed from room to room by its cord, while he played with the various hoses and nozzles.

Mark once wandered about our house for months, saying "it's all dark outside," even in broad daylight. We finally figured out that the expression was his "word" for window. Gloria had once held Mark near a window and said, "It's all dark outside." Kanner described this phenomenon and labelled it "metaphorical use of language." The resemblance between the children Kanner described as having early infantile autism and our Mark was extraordinary—truly uncanny.

What caused this strange disorder? I went to the *Psychological Abstracts* and to the *Index Medicus* to see what had been written in recent years on the topic of autism. I found that "autism" was constantly used by professionals in the field as an alternate word for childhood schizophrenia. I read paper after paper by Kanner, who kept insisting that the children he wrote about constituted a small, unique sub-population of the larger group of children who had been called childhood schizophrenics in the past. He insisted that the children to whom he had given the label "infantile autism" or "early infantile autism" were so remarkably similar to each other in their behavior and speech (if they had speech) that they must be regarded as a unique clinical entity. His pleas were ignored by his colleagues (as they are to this day). The word "autism" had a much better sound than the term "childhood schizophrenia," which they had used in the past, and thus they applied the term "willy nilly," to use Kanner's words, in referring to children who resembled only remotely those he had labeled as being truly autistic.

I quickly learned that it was almost uniformly believed by authorities in the field that autism (and thus childhood schizophrenia) were emotional disorders which occurred in children who were biologically normal, when the children realized, in some obscure way, that their mothers really didn't love them enough, or loved them too much, or something. I remembered how Mark had screamed implacably in the nursery, even before he was brought home from the hospital, and wondered why these highly trained professionals, psychiatrists, neurologists, pediatricians, and psychologists, were so convinced that autism was caused by bad parenting rather than by an unknown biological factor. I read books and articles by Bruno Bettelheim, a psychoanalyst who proclaimed that autistic children had been mistreated by their mothers in about the same way in which Nazi concentration camp prisoners had been mistreated by their guards, thus giving the children (or the prisoners) feelings of hopelessness, despair, and apathy, and leading them to withdraw from contact with reality.

The topic fascinated me. I devoured everything I could lay my hands on that had any connection at all with autism. The trail led into biochemistry, genetics, and neurophysiology.

I took voluminous notes as I read, and began to order from libraries copies of papers on autism and related subjects from faraway lands, even though receiving the papers would require that I find someone who would be willing to translate the paper for me from German, Dutch, Czechoslovakian, Polish, etc., into English. By 1962 I had studied just about everything ever published on autism, in any language, except for the possibility that there might be some articles in Japanese, Chinese, or Russian which were not indexed through the National Medical Library.

My search for the reasons why the professionals believed autism to be a psychogenic (psychologically caused) disorder revealed no compelling evidence whatsoever. Ultimately I came to believe that it was nothing but bias, bigotry, and greed on their part that had lead them to the psychogenic conclusion. This angered me greatly, because it was evident that many parents were feeling terrible guilt as a result of these unwarranted professional attitudes. Meanwhile, the professionals were growing richer, and the parents poorer, as the doctors probed, in session after expensive session, for the nonexistent psychic trauma.

By 1962 I had finished a draft manuscript for a book titled *Early Infantile Autism: The Syndrome and Its Implications for a Neural Theory of Behavior.* The book summarized the world literature on autism and related disorders, and presented some sorely needed new ideas on the nature and cause of autism. It also presented some new ideas on how the normal brain might function.

At about this time, a major publisher of college and professional books announced a new manuscript competition for "A Distinguished Contribution to Psychology." I submitted *Early Infantile Autism* and was awarded first place in the competition. As soon as the announcement of my book was released to the press, I began receiving letters from parents of autistic children, first from throughout the U.S., then from throughout the world. Critics published rave reviews about this bold new book that would force people to look at autism in "a new light." They would have to discard their old theories about "refrigerator mothers" causing autism, and view autism as a biological disorder of the brain. Little did I realize what further effects the book would have. Letters started to pour in from throughout the world, from parents, professionals, students and others, and continue to pour in to this day.

At this time, the mid-1960s, there were essentially only two methods used to treat autistic children—psychotherapy and drugs. Both of these methods were universally accepted and deeply entrenched. Autism was viewed as a mental health issue, not an educational problem. When parents brought their autistic children to child psychiatrists or clinical psychologists, they were told, "You caused this problem in your child: your child has only one chance, and that is for you to relinquish control to us, and do as we say." "Treatment" ordinarily involved many years of psychotherapy or play therapy for the children, and weekly sessions with a therapist for the parents. The professional literature was replete with articles discussing the psychoanalysis or psychotherapy of this or that child with autism or childhood schizophrenia (the terms were used interchangeably). The idea that the children suffered from a brain disorder which required specialized methods of teaching was quite foreign.

In the fall of 1965, I decided that the time was ripe for starting a national parents' organization. Without pressure from informed parents, nothing would change. I gathered together the addresses of as many parents of autistic children as I could find. Most were those of parents who had written to me after my book was published. Another list was obtained from Ivar Lovaas, who had received many letters and phone calls from parents as a result of an article on his work that had appeared in *Life* magazine in early 1965. Still more names were gotten from Rosalind Oppenheim, of Chicago, whose article about her autistic son had appeared in *Good Housekeeping* magazine several years earlier.

I was doing a great deal of travelling at the time, some of it as part of my job with the government, but much more as a result of the numerous speaking invitations I received from universities throughout the country, whose students and faculty were very much interested in this strange and little-known childhood disorder called autism, and the (probably) strange fellow who had written a prize-winning book that had revolutionized thinking about the disorder. Whenever I was invited to another city, I would write in advance to all the parents on my list who were within driving distance of that city, tell them I was coming, and ask one or two of them to arrange a meeting at which I could speak to the entire group. At each meeting I gave a talk in which I told the parents how useless were the methods that were now being used to treat their children, and how promising was the new method of teaching—behavior modification—then being pioneered by Ivar Lovaas and a few others. I also told the parents about the new organization we were forming, the National Society for Autistic Children, and suggested that they start a local chapter. This approach proved to be a great success. During the first year about a dozen chapters of the National Society for Autistic Children were formed in various cities. The organization (recently renamed Autism Society of America) has grown to approximately 185 chapters throughout the United States as of this writing (May, 1989).

Many of the letters and phone calls from parents who had read my book contained information, clues, and ideas that might be of critical importance to researchers studying the cause and treatment of autism. No one was compiling this information, correlating it, or studying it. In response, in 1967, shortly after establishing the National Society for Autistic Children, I founded the Institute for Child Behavior Research (ICBR), which is devoted to collecting information about autism from parents, from researchers, from the medical and scientific literature, and from all other sources, analyzing the data, and making it available to parents and others who need it. ICBR started as a desk and two filing cabinets in the side porch of my home. It has expanded and moved four times since then, and now publishes a quarterly newsletter, the *Autism Research Review International*, corresponds with thousands of parents and professionals throughout the world, and maintains the world's largest data base on children with autism.

As an example of the kinds of invaluable information that can be gotten from parents, let me mention our experience with the use of high dosage vitamin B6 and the mineral magnesium in the treatment of autism. In the late 1960s, I learned from a number of parents that their children with autism had improved when given much larger-than-usual amounts of certain vitamins. Although I was skeptical at first, I eventually conducted two scientific experiments. Both turned out positive. Other researchers followed our lead, and a number of studies have since confirmed the value of this approach for many children.* My years of experience with children with autism have taught me that these children vary enormously from one another in numerous ways. It is important for you as a parent to decide for yourself whether this, or any other intervention, is useful for your child.

Before closing, I want to do two things. The first is to provide a brief update on my son Mark, with whose story I started this rather lengthy Introduction. Secondly, I want to give a few words of advice to the parents who will be reading this book.

Mark has just passed his thirty-third birthday. Even though we were told when Mark was four to institutionalize him as a hopeless case, he has come a very long way, and is now a handsome, pleasant, courteous, and reliable young man who, while far from intellectual-

---

* Readers interested in learning more about this research, and other research on autism, are invited to write the author at: ICBR, 4182 Adams Ave., San Diego, CA 92116.

ly gifted, nevertheless has many fine qualities. Behavior modification played a major role in his extraordinary improvement, as did megavitamin B6 therapy. He has been on high doses of vitamin B6 since 1968, when I began working with the vitamins as a means of treating autism. It is clear from the few instances when he has been temporarily taken off the B6 that it helps him immensely. If there is a healthier individual in North America, I would be surprised. (Recently the dentist found a small cavity—Mark's first.) Mark answers the telephone for us and takes accurate messages when we are not at home, does paintings which have sold well at art exhibits for the handicapped, and in general has turned out to be a very fine, if limited, young man. He is the only student in his school for "developmentally disabled" adults who can read and write, and who is capable of using public transportation to get to and from school. We keep experimenting with different nutrients (never drugs) and Mark continues to improve. Recently he has even begun to display rudiments of the guile and manipulation which are second nature to us "normals," but I'm not sure I should call *that* improvement! For example, not long ago I overheard the following exchange: "Mother, do you think the bus driver would let me bring home one of the baby lop-eared rabbits from school?" "No, Mark," my wife said, "we have enough pets already."

As to my words of advice for the parent-readers of this book: although there is much valuable and useful information in the ensuing chapters, take all the advice you get from anyone, including me, with a grain of salt. The field is changing rapidly, and much of what is given as gospel truth today may be passé in a few years.

In particular, be cautious about accepting unquestioningly the diagnoses given to your child. Such designations as PDD (pervasive developmental disorder), ADHD (attention deficit hyperactivity disorder), and similar labels change rapidly. The letters and phone calls we get at ICBR reflect the confusion engendered in parents (and in professionals as well!) by the attempts of the American Psychiatric Association to establish criteria for the diagnosis of autism and related disorders. Until the biological bases of autism are more firmly understood, all diagnostic efforts, except for a few instances of clear-cut subtypes of autism, such as Fragile-

X autism, or Rett syndrome, will inevitably be revised. Masking our lack of a complete understanding of autism with fancy diagnostic labels or acronyms really doesn't help very much. Be patient—the professionals are trying their best—but don't be misguided, either.

We have come a long way since the dark ages of the 1950s and before. One of the most important advances is represented by the publication of this book, devoted as it is to informing parents, as intelligent and concerned advocates for their own children, on the state of current thought in the field. We have made great strides since the years when the parents were treated contemptuously, and were widely regarded as having caused autism and as the enemies of their children. With a little luck, we will make much larger strides in the years to come.

ONE

What Is Autism?

MICHAEL D. POWERS, PSY.D.*

Introduction

Autism is a very puzzling and painful disorder for parents to understand and deal with. You have a beautiful child who seems totally withdrawn—you reach out with love in your heart and get no response. You are bewildered and hurt. You feel helpless. Autism, however, is not an impenetrable wall; there are things you can do to reach your child and to try to help her. But before you can help her, you need to understand what autism is, how it is diagnosed, and how it is treated. The following true story illustrates how one family first encountered autism in their child:

Robbie was a handsome, blonde boy who stopped talking at twenty-one months of age. His parents had been concerned about him before, but now they were really worried.

Robbie was the older of their two children. There had been nothing unusual about his birth or early months. Robbie stood at

---

* Michael D. Powers, Psy.D., is the Director of Community Resources for People with Autism in Springfield, Massachusetts. He received his master's degree in special education from Columbia University and his doctorate in psychology from Rutgers University. Dr. Powers is the author of many articles on the evaluation and treatment of autism and two books, *Behavioral Assessment of Severe Developmental Disabilities* (with J. Handleman, Aspen Press, 1984) and *Expanding Systems of Service Delivery for Persons with Developmental Disabilities* (Paul H. Brookes, 1988).

six months, said his first word at ten months, walked by his first birthday, and could name about thirty-five objects by the time he was a year and a half old. His parents were proud of his progress and tried to excuse his solitary habits. They noticed that although Robbie usually preferred to be left alone to play with his toys and puzzles, he did smile at family members occasionally and seemed to recognize some of them. That first year, Robbie's generally tolerant nature and lack of fussiness led his parents to consider themselves truly lucky. His excellent hand and finger coordination and early words convinced them that Robbie was a very bright little boy—one who just preferred his own company to that of others.

But as Robbie grew older, other puzzling, disturbing behaviors changed his parents' vague concern into outright worry. For example, sometimes he fell down and scraped his knees or hands but showed no reaction to the pain. Other times he would break into tears for no reason, sometimes crying inconsolably for twenty minutes. He spoke less and less, until there were times when he would go for weeks without saying a word. He would, however, babble, shriek, laugh, and cluck his tongue frequently throughout the day. More and more, his parents suspected a hearing problem or even deafness because he no longer responded to his name. They weren't sure about this, though, because sometimes it seemed as if Robbie would stop whatever he was doing to listen to a train whistle blowing ever so faintly in the distance.

His parents bought Robbie toys they thought he would enjoy. But he preferred to be alone with his trucks and cars. He would turn them over and spin their wheels for long periods of time, all the while shaking his hands and babbling as he intently watched them spinning. He would also line up his cars and trucks by size so that they all pointed in the same direction and would become enraged if anyone disturbed the order while he was away. This insistence on routine and sameness was not just limited to cars and trucks. An agile little boy, Robbie soon learned to climb up onto the kitchen counter and open the cabinets to find plates, which he then brought down to the floor to spin. His climbing on the counters was only a preview of more daring feats such as standing on the railing overlooking the stairwell. Unlike other children they had known, Robbie seemed completely unaware of the danger he was in.

Robbie's grandparents were the first to begin to piece together the unusual behavior and lack of social and communication skills. They mentioned the word "autism" for the first time when Robbie was two years old. Their daughter and son-in-law quickly reminded them that many children are slower to talk. Besides, didn't Robbie's uncanny skill with puzzles and mechanical toys seem very advanced for his age? As concerned parents, they had discussed Robbie's behavior with his pediatrician at his last check-up and had been told to forget about it. "It was nothing." Robbie's grandparents were quieted—temporarily.

Several months later, however, when Robbie's language had not improved, his parents took him to a Child Development Center at a nearby university hospital. Robbie's grandparents had been right. Robbie was diagnosed as having autism.

What Is Autism?

Autism is a physical disorder of the brain that causes a lifelong developmental disability. The many different symptoms of autism can occur by themselves or in combination with other conditions such as mental retardation, blindness, deafness, and epilepsy. Because children with autism—like all children—vary widely in their abilities and behavior, each symptom may appear differently in each child. For example, children with autism often exhibit some form of bizarre, repetitive behavior called *stereotyped behavior.* Some, like Robbie, may incessantly spin plates or other objects. Others may lick their fingers immediately after touching a doorknob. The following section introduces the six major symptoms of autism.

The Symptoms of Autism

Failure to Develop Normal Socialization

The inability of children with autism to develop normal social skills is probably the most noticeable characteristic of autism. Children with autism don't interact with others the way most other children do or simply don't interact at all. Like Robbie, they seem to prefer to be alone most of the time. They appear to live a life of extreme isolation. They have great difficulty understanding and expressing emotion, and show few, if any, signs of *attachment*, the emotional bonding that occurs between people who care for each other. This behavior is very different from the social behavior of most infants and young children.

The child with autism may appear to be very uninterested in other people. She may avoid eye-contact or appear to "look through" people. She may seem extremely apathetic and unresponsive, showing no desire to initiate contact or to be held or cuddled. Indeed, when she is held she may stiffen or arch her back as if being held is somehow distressing. The social cues of others—a smile, a wave, a frown—may be meaningless to her. She may not develop a social smile until quite late. In addition, she may not play with others. She may use people mechanically as a "means to an end." For example, your child may approach you and take you by the hand to something she wants—like to the refrigerator for juice—without a word or a glance. You are treated just like any other tool.

Most children with autism have extremely limited social skills and seem to live in a world of their own, separate from and unfathomable to outsiders. This inability to relate to the world of people is often the strongest clue to autism.

Disturbances in Speech, Language, and Communication

Autism's second major symptom is speech, language, and communication problems. Approximately 40 percent of children with autism do not speak at all. Others have what is called *echolalia*, a parrotlike repeating of what has been said to them. Sometimes echolalia is immediate, as when your child says, "Do you want a cookie?" after you have just asked her, "Do you want a cookie?" Sometimes echolalia is delayed, and may involve the recitation of T.V. commercials, advertising jingles, or single words heard several minutes, days, weeks, or even months ago. Your child may have little or no understanding of abstract concepts such as danger, or of symbolic gestures such as waving "bye-bye." She may not understand the proper use of pronouns, particularly "you" and "I," and may reverse them. She may not use speech for communication, and what speech she does use may be repetitive and filled with illogical words or phrases.

Your child's voice may sound flat or monotonous and she may have no apparent control over her pitch or volume. For example, she may speak in a loud, high-pitched voice in response to your questions. In addition, she may rely excessively on jargon or use words or phrases out of context. For example, one child said, "Time to be heading home," with great agitation whenever asked to do something she did not want to do.

Abnormal Relationships to Objects and Events

Children with autism are usually unable to relate normally to objects and events. For example, remember the way Robbie would constantly spin objects. Your child may also interact with things or events in this nonfunctional way.

A great many children with autism have what is called a "need for sameness," and may become very upset if objects in their environment or schedules are changed from their familiar placement or pattern. For example, if you ask your child to brush her teeth before her bath instead of afterwards, she may resist the change mightily. This inflexibility can force families into a very difficult and rigid existence as they attempt to follow their child's "rules."

The way children with autism "play" may be very unusual; sometimes children with autism do not play at all. Your child may have no "pretend" play and may start few, if any, play activities on her own. When she does use toys or play materials, she may use them in unusual ways. For example, she may repeatedly drop

Legos onto a hard surface, or always arrange her blocks in the same pattern based on size, shape, or color.

These unusual responses to people, objects, and events can and do change. Over time, and with appropriate treatment, children with autism can learn to enjoy using various objects appropriately and can learn to tolerate some change in their world.

Abnormal Responses to Sensory Stimulation

Sensory stimuli are the things in the environment that we touch, smell, feel, see, and hear. While we respond to much of what goes on around us, our brains filter out certain unimportant stimuli, allowing our attention to be focused on the most important information in the environment at that moment. For example, many large department stores use a tone signal to alert store employees. For shoppers, these signals are extraneous noises in the environment. Because they do not communicate a meaningful message to shoppers, most people just filter them out. Children with autism have difficulty with this "filtering out" process. They may greatly overreact to sensory stimuli, or have almost no reaction whatsoever. For instance, some children with autism find the tone signals in department stores very distressing. They may cover their ears and throw a tantrum until their parent takes them out of the store. Other children may appear enthralled with sounds they make themselves or with "background" sounds such as distant police sirens. Yet, except for a strong reaction to *only* these sounds, they may appear to have no reaction to any other sounds whatever, and indeed may appear deaf at other times. We do not know exactly why sounds affect children with autism in this way, but it appears to be part of the overall tendency of children with autism to overreact to some stimuli and underreact to others.

As part of her sensory problems, a child with autism may be fascinated with lights, color patterns, logos, shapes, or the configuration of letters and words. She may be preoccupied with scratching or rubbing certain surfaces. She may also furiously avoid certain food textures—for example, "rough" textures like toast. In addition, your child may respond to motion in abnormal ways. Some children with autism enjoy being thrown into the air or spinning themselves around and around, never apparently becoming dizzy. Others have an intense fear of "roughhousing" or the movement of elevators.

Generally speaking, children with autism, especially younger children, appear to use their senses of taste and smell more than their senses of hearing and vision to learn and explore. Their reaction to cold or pain may vary from indifference, to oversensitivity, to unpredictable vacillation between the two.

Developmental Delays and Differences

The fifth symptom of autism is the significantly different way a child with autism develops. Children without special needs develop at a relatively even pace across all of the many areas of development. A child's skills at a given age may be slightly ahead of or behind most other children's and still be well within normal limits. For example, a child may learn to walk sooner than most children, but learn to talk a bit later. For children with autism, however, this development process is not at all even. Their rate of development is quite different, particularly in communication, social, and cognitive skills. In contrast, motor development—the ability to walk, hop, climb stairs, manipulate small objects with the fingers—may be relatively normal or only slightly delayed.

The sequence of development within any one of these areas of development can also be unusual. For example, your child may be able to read complex words and phrases like "Exxon" or "Masters of the Universe" and yet have no understanding of the sounds of particular vowels and consonants.

Sometimes skills will appear in children with autism at the expected time and then disappear. Like Robbie, a child may appear to develop spoken language at the normal time, and then at about age two abruptly stop talking. While a child's abilities in areas such as working puzzles or counting may be normal or even precocious, her language skills may remain far below her age level.

Development is discussed more fully later in this book. Chapter 6 provides an overview of typical child development and explains how you can judge your child's individual development compared to that of most children.

Begins during Infancy or Childhood

The sixth symptom of autism is that it begins during infancy or childhood. Autism is a lifelong disability that one is born with. Generally, parents get a diagnosis before their child is thirty-six months old, but later diagnosis sometimes occurs. Furthermore, for a variety of reasons, some children may not be correctly diagnosed until several years later. In fact, some parents of children diagnosed with mental retardation do not learn until their child's adolescence or adulthood that she actually has autism. Do not rule out autism in your child just because all of the symptoms of autism are not actually observed until after thirty-six months.

Regardless of their age at diagnosis, children with autism almost always exhibit the five other symptoms to some degree throughout their lives. In some children, symptoms become less severe around ages five or six. This change can occur even earlier for some children where highly specialized early intervention programs are available, although the evidence is inconclusive as to exactly which children benefit most from these programs.

Adolescence typically heralds additional changes—some positive, others not—for the child with autism, and the severity of his or her symptoms may increase. Remember that your child's disorder and diagnosis are features of her personality that signify her need for carefully planned, well thought-out services throughout her life.

Types of Autism

Some children with autism are more disabled by their disorder than others. Autism in children can run the gamut from mild to severe, with the majority of children clustering toward the midpoint. However, it is important to remember that with any given child, *each symptom* can also be present in varying degrees of mildness or severity. In other words, some of a child's autistic symptoms may be milder than others. For example, a child with seriously impaired social skills may have normal or near normal cognitive skills—he may be quite aloof socially, but have no trouble learning to read or solve arithmetic problems.

We sometimes say that children most severely disabled in social interactive skills, language, and communication have "classic autism" (sometimes called "Kanner's autism"). These cases are rare, however; most children have a variable assortment of symptoms and severity. Instead of hearing that their child has classic autism, parents are more likely to hear labels like "Pervasive Developmental Disorder," "Atypical Pervasive Developmental Disorder," "Autistic-like," or "Pervasive Developmental Disorder Not Otherwise Specified." *It is important to remember that, regardless of their label, the education and treatment of these children is the same.*

The examples below illustrate the possible range of severity for two of autism's primary symptoms—problems with social interactions and problems with communication. Also listed are behavioral symptoms. The mildest symptoms—those closest to "normal" behavior—come first, followed by the more severe symptoms.

Social Interactions

Shows little or no interest in making friends
Prefers own company to being with others
Does not imitate others' actions (e.g., raising arms for "so big")
Does not interact playfully (e.g., participating in "hide-and-seek" games)
Avoids eye-contact
Does not smile at familiar people
Seems unaware of others' existence; for example, treats family members and strangers interchangeably

Communication

Has difficulty maintaining a conversation despite good speech skills
Reverses pronouns such as "you" and "I"
Has echolalia—repeats others' words, either immediately or after a delay
Lacks imagination or the ability to pretend
Does not use symbolic gestures such as waving "bye-bye"
Cannot communicate with words or gestures

Behavioral Symptoms

Is physically inactive, or passive
Does not respond to requests by familiar people
Has picky eating habits
Throws frequent tantrums, often for no known reason
Behaves aggressively, physically attacking or injuring others
Injures self with behavior such as head-banging or eye-gouging

How Many People Have Autism?

In the United States, there are at least 360,000 people with autism,* one-third of whom are children. Autism is the fourth most common developmental disability; only mental retardation, epilepsy, and cerebral palsy occur more frequently. Autism occurs in about four to five of every ten thousand births. Children with the most severe form of this disorder probably make up only about 2–3 percent of children with autism. Some researchers maintain that autism occurs in fifteen out of ten thousand births, but they include children who have some, but not all, of the symptoms of autism. Again, you must remember that regardless of the number or severity of symptoms, the treatment for all of these children is basically the same.

Do More Boys Than Girls Have Autism?

For reasons we do not yet understand, autism occurs about four times more frequently in boys than in girls. There is some indication that autism is more common in first-born males, but there have been no conclusive studies to date and there is just not enough research available to know for sure. Girls, when affected, are more likely to be more seriously disabled and to have lower IQs.

---

* This includes approximately 110,000 with the full syndrome, and approximately 250,000 who exhibit most, but not all, of the symptoms required for diagnosis.

Why Does My Child Have Autism?

Scientists do not know why some children have autism. The most important thing *you* should know about the causes of autism is that *parents do not cause it.* We do not know for sure what causes autism, nor do we know exactly how autism affects brain structure, brain function, or brain chemistry. One recent study did find that people with autism have differences in the structure of their cerebellums—a part of the brain. It is far too early, however, to draw any conclusions from this finding or from the other promising research conducted in the area of biological and genetic causes.

While the rates are very low, there is some evidence that autism can be inherited. If you have a child with autism, your overall chances of having a second child with autism are between 2–3 percent. While this frequency may seem insignificant, it is actually fifty times higher than for parents who do not have a child with autism. Given the low incidence of autism in the general population, however, the risk of recurrence is still very small.

To date, scientists have only identified one specific genetic connection with autism—a condition called Fragile-X syndrome. Fragile-X syndrome is a recently discovered form of genetically caused mental retardation. Both sexes are affected by Fragile-X syndrome, with males usually more severely affected. The degree of disability caused by Fragile-X syndrome ranges from severe mental retardation to varying degrees of learning disabilities. Children with Fragile-X syndrome also can have behavior problems such as hyperactivity, violent outbursts, and autistic-like behaviors. Severe language delays are common, as are delayed motor development and poor sensory skills.

This condition, in which one part of the X-chromosome has a defect, affects about 7–10 percent of people with autism. It is a good idea to have a geneticist check for Fragile-X syndrome in your child with autism if you are considering having additional children. For unknown reasons, if a child with autism has Fragile-X syndrome, then there is a 1-in-2 chance that boys born to the same parents will also have Fragile-X syndrome.

Getting a Diagnosis

Children with autism have been the subject of considerable research in recent years. Much has been learned about the symptoms your child must have in order to get a diagnosis of autism. This section reviews how professionals arrive at a diagnosis of autism and how you participate in that diagnosis.

When you talk with professionals about diagnosing autism in your child, they probably will refer to the American Psychiatric Association's Revised Third Edition of the *Diagnostic and Statistical Manual of Mental Disorders* (DSM-III-R) (1987). The *DSM-III-R* contains the "official" diagnostic criteria for identifying almost all mental and emotional disorders in children and adults, and is the primary source of this information for medical and mental health professionals throughout the United States.

The *DSM-III-R* outlines the following criteria for diagnosing autism:

1. Severely impaired social interaction;
2. Severely impaired communication and imagination;
3. Extremely limited interests and activities; and
4. First observed in infancy or early childhood.

If you leaf through *DSM-III-R,* you will have the same basic vocabulary as the professionals you are working with. Remember, however, that these professionals are working *for* you, and it is up to them to speak in plain English so that you can understand exactly what is being said. Never feel shy about asking a professional to "say it again, in words I can understand." Professionals say the same thing to each other sometimes!

Differential Diagnosis

When you first became aware that something was different about your child, you probably told your pediatrician about the behaviors that concerned you. Lack of language and a hard-to-describe aloofness were very likely two of those concerns. As various specialists became involved with you and your child, they began the process of deciding what disorder your child has and what disorders she does *not* have. This process is called *differential diagnosis*.

The differential diagnosis of autism involves comparing the behavior of your child with the behavior typical of children with other disorders that might account for the same symptoms—for example, mental retardation or speech-language problems—as well as with medical problems associated with autism such as Phenylketonuria (PKU) or Fragile-X syndrome. In the differential diagnosis of autism, there are two major disorders from which autism must be distinguished:

Mental Retardation. While children with autism have uneven development—delays in some areas and not in others—children who are mentally retarded tend to be slower in all areas. Even though approximately 70 percent of children with autism also have some degree of mental retardation, the diagnosis of autism—not mental retardation—is appropriate if a child fits the diagnostic criteria for autism.

Professionals can decide whether mental retardation or autism is your child's condition by carefully evaluating the "unevenness" of your child's profile of development. Children whose primary disability is mental retardation will show a more generalized developmental delay than a child with autism. Figure 1 shows how developmental patterns may differ between autism and mental retardation.

Figure 1 shows that it is the *pattern* of development that helps to support or rule out a diagnosis of autism.

Language Disorder. The other major condition professionals eliminate in diagnosing autism is a language disorder. They can usually eliminate a language disorder because children who just have a language disorder do not also have the abnormal responses to sensory stimuli that children with autism have. In addition, children with language disorders typically can use gestures or other methods of communication; children with autism have great difficulty doing this. Finally, the child with a language disorder usually can relate appropriately to people, objects, and events—an ability that a child with autism may not have.

Figure 1
Peter, a 3-year-old with autism.

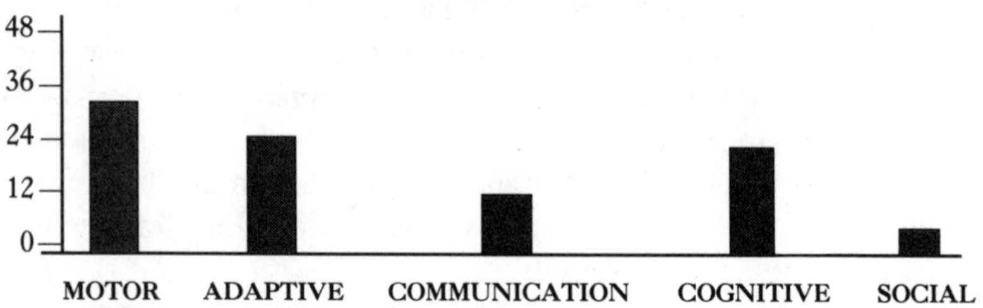

Richard, a 3-year-old with Down Syndrome

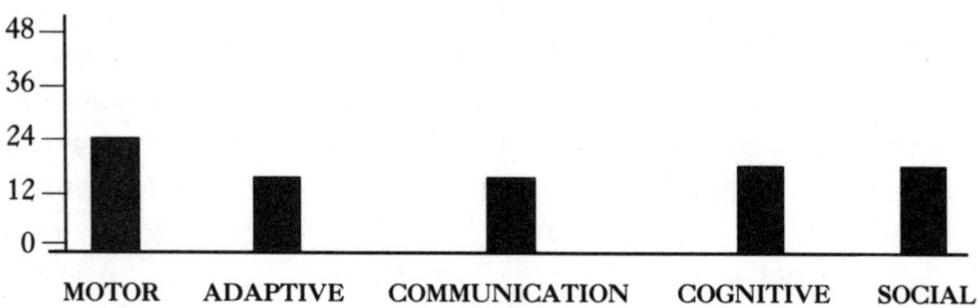

There are two other conditions—each quite rare in childhood—that may be considered in making a differential diagnosis of autism.

Schizophrenia. Schizophrenia, a serious mental disorder, is very rarely diagnosed in infancy or early childhood, whereas autism almost always is. In those rare cases when the disorder does occur in childhood, the young child with schizophrenia has delusions or hallucinations, and uses speech to communicate irrational thoughts. In contrast, the young child with autism does not use speech to communicate.

Degenerative Organic Brain Disorder. In extremely rare cases, children can have Degenerative Organic Brain Syndrome. This condition involves progressive deterioration in one or more areas of development. Although many parents report that their child with autism began to lose words and other early language skills at around eighteen months, this slide eventually stopped and many of these lost skills were regained with appropriate education. This is not the case for children with Degenerative Organic Brain Syndrome.

Finally, a differential diagnosis must eliminate disorders, such as Tic Disorders and visual impairments, that may have symptoms similar to those seen in children with autism. In these disorders, there may be unusual responses to sensory stimuli, apparent deafness, or bizarre, ritualistic body movements (snorting, grunting, hand flapping). Because many children with autism do not respond to sound normally, deafness is often suspected. Deaf children, however, do not show the overwhelming lack of social attachment that children with autism do.

The Evaluation Process

In establishing a diagnosis of autism, you and your child will likely come into contact with a variety of professionals, each with a special area of expertise. Although these professionals do not replace your pediatrician, who is responsible for the routine medical care of your child, they supplement your pediatrician's information. Often it is your pediatrician who will recommend that you consult specialists. Chapter 3 reviews how to select and work with your pediatrician. This section describes the many professionals you may need to consult to get a definitive diagnosis for your child.

There are two different methods you can use to get an evaluation of your child. The first method is to consult a series of professionals, each of whom separately evaluates your child's abilities and needs in the area of his or her expertise. The biggest drawback to this method is that many times these specialists conduct their evaluations in something of a vacuum. While they may have read previous evaluations of your child, they may design and perform their evaluation without any actual contact with the other professionals involved with your child. The net result is a series of evaluations, each of which addresses one aspect of your child. This method often fails to provide a unified, comprehensive picture of the "whole child."

The better method of evaluating a child with autism is the *interdisciplinary team approach*. Here, a group of professionals, each representing a specialty area—psychology, speech, medicine, special education—develops the assessment. While team members each conduct their evaluations independently, they usually maintain close contact with one another throughout the course of the evaluation. This contact fosters closer collaboration and information-sharing during the evaluation, as well as a more unified interpretation of the team's findings in the final report. While each specialist writes his or her own report, an assigned *case manager* serves as your link to the entire team. The case manager summarizes the team's findings for you in a special report which you are encouraged to share with others working with your child, as appropriate. The case manager also oversees implementation of the team's recommendations. If you can use the interdisciplinary team method, do so. It is a better way to get an evaluation of your child.

Interdisciplinary teams come in many shapes and sizes, depending upon the resources of the organization or agency supporting them. For the evaluation of a child with autism, a team should contain at least a *psychologist, pediatrician, speech pathologist, and educational diagnostician*. Other specialists, such as audiologists, community health nurses, geneticists, social workers, psychiatrists, and nutritionists, may be included, or available, for referrals in particular cases.

Locating an interdisciplinary team is not always easy. One important resource is the American Association of University Affiliated Programs (AAUAP) in Mental Retardation and Developmental Disabilities. There are fifty-five members of the AAUAP network in thirty-eight states and the District of Columbia. The addresses and phone numbers for the executive offices of the AAUAP network and the location of each AAUAP facility are listed in the Resource Guide in the back of this book. You can also call the national office or your local University Affiliated Program.

In addition to the AAUAP network, private interdisciplinary teams are sometimes organized by groups of professionals who share an interest in autism and other developmental disabilities. Your pediatrician, local public health (or mental health) department, or local chapter of the Autism Society of America can help you find the private team nearest you. Whether you choose a private team or a hospital-, university-, or clinic-based team, a major factor in your decision should be the recommendations of other parents and professionals and the type of response you get from a team member when making your initial phone inquiry.

The different evaluations of your child may take two to three days to complete. Usually you will get an explanation of the results several days to a few weeks later. You will probably meet with the professionals in what is called a *parent interpretive*, during which the results of the evaluation will be explained to you. At this meeting, the evaluation team should give you its recommendations, and you should have the chance to ask questions. It is crucial that you understand what the evaluation means. Ask as many questions as you want. You probably won't have too many chances to get so much information from so many sources at once. Use this opportunity.

Learning all you can at a parent interpretive is very important because most children with autism require an interdisciplinary evaluation only a few times in their lives, usually at key transition points: once for an initial diagnosis; once after a couple of years of formal schooling; once in adolescence; and once in early adulthood. Of course, some children may require more frequent evaluations, especially if there is a special problem requiring close follow-up.

One of the most important things you can do for your child and your family is to find a professional you trust who has special expertise in the diagnosis and treatment of children with autism. Use this person as your child's case manager and have all reports and evaluations forwarded to him or her. As your child grows older, you will become more and more effective in advocating for your child, locating necessary services, and moving systems and organizations on your own. But having a trusted expert to help you locate resources, to bounce ideas off of, and to provide reassurance can be a great comfort along the way.

Professionals on the Evaluation Team

When you bring your child for an evaluation, you should be aware of what each of the specialists will do, and what information each will contribute to forming the picture of the "whole child." You might encounter a number of professionals, each performing a different part of the evaluation. Which professionals you see will ultimately be based on the needs of your child and family and on your community resources.

Psychologist. A psychologist, a professional trained in understanding human behavior, learning, and how the human mind works, is usually part of the evaluation team. The psychologist will collect a great deal of information about your child, including information about your child's emotional growth, her developmental strengths and weaknesses, her IQ, and her ability to function socially. The psychologist's goal is to get a complete picture of your child with autism. Once the psychologist has this information, he will recommend educational and family intervention plans to capitalize on your child's strengths and address her special needs.

In order to get the information he needs, the psychologist will give your child one or more intelligence tests. He will observe your child's behavior and ask you a seemingly endless list of questions on your child's development. He will conduct a behavioral assessment on your child's special problems—such as severe tantrums—to try to determine their cause. The psychologist also will measure the kinds of "real-world" things your child can do, such as eating with a spoon or using the toilet appropriately. Finally, the psychologist may wish to review any evaluations of other professionals to get clues about other areas of concern.

Pediatrician with a Special Interest in Autism. The pediatrician, a medical doctor who specializes in treating children, will usually gather information on your child in four main areas:

1. Her general state of physical health;
2. The way she reacts to structured and unstructured situations during the evaluation session;
3. The way she reacts to attempts at social interaction and her ability to initiate social interactions; and

4. Her general developmental status.

Your pediatrician should review the records of your child's previous evaluations. During the initial office visit, she should take a detailed family history and review how your child is progressing developmentally—with language, social, self-help, and motor skills. Some pediatricians perform developmental evaluations using a formal standardized test, while others gather the information informally by direct observation and parent report. The pediatrician will observe your child's response to the office environment, as well as to you and to various structured and unstructured tasks and demands like playing with toys in different ways. Development is discussed further in Chapter 6.

During the physical examination, the pediatrician will check your child's medication history. She will look for the presence or absence of seizures and for signs of problems in the function of your child's brain—including motor coordination problems and clumsiness.

Depending on where you live, the medical evaluation may be conducted by a child psychiatrist rather than a pediatrician. Regardless of your physician's specific medical specialty, the most important factor is choosing a physician who has expertise in autism and the medical and health concerns associated with it.

Speech/Language Pathologist. A speech and language pathologist is an essential member of the diagnostic team. Speech and language pathologists can oberve your child and evaluate whether her particular speech and language problems are associated with autism or some other condition. The speech/language pathologist assesses your child's skills in the following areas:

1. *Receptive language*, or the ability to understand communication.
2. *Expressive language*, or the ability to communicate using words, gestures, or written symbols. This area includes word usage and word combinations—verb-object combinations like "want juice"—and nonverbal communication.

3. *Pragmatics,* which is the function of words and gestures in social situations. For example, some children express their desire for something by whining or having a tantrum. Others point to the object, or lead their parent by the hand. Still others may use words, either appropriately or inappropriately.
4. Play behaviors.
5. Articulation of sounds.
6. *Oral-motor functioning*—how well your child can control her tongue, lips, and jaw.
7. *Voice*—resonance, pitch, and loudness—and *fluency*—how smoothly speech flows.
8. *Auditory memory*—your child's ability to immediately recall information she hears.
9. Attention.

The speech/language pathologist will observe you and your child together; work directly with your child; give her tests; and review her records. If your child has some language, the speech/language pathologist will probably use more standardized tests than she would use if she were nonverbal. Some children are very resistant to testing. With these children, the professional relies more on direct observations—both yours and hers. These observations can give her an estimate of your child's abilities and needs.

Audiologist. Since hearing impairment is one of the conditions that must be eliminated in diagnosing autism, an audiologist—a professional trained in evaluating hearing—is often a member of the interdisciplinary diagnostic team. Before getting a diagnosis of autism, parents frequently suspect their child has trouble hearing because she is uncommunicative and unresponsive to sound. In reality, children with autism are no more likely to have hearing problems than the general population. The audiologist on your team will assess your child's hearing using a wide variety of tests. She can use tests that require your child's active participation and she can use passive tests. Most importantly, the audiologist will observe your child and ask you about your own observations. Often parents are able to supply the clue that demonstrates that there is no hearing loss. At home, for example, parents may notice their child listening to faint, distant sounds that are not present in the audiologist's office.

Audiologists may be found by contacting the American Speech-Language-Hearing Association, listed in the Resource Guide in this book, by checking with local agencies and organizations, and by asking other parents.

Nurse. The nurse plays an important role in your child's evaluation. Working either with the pediatrician or alone, she looks at any health problems your child may have and observes her behavioral strengths and weaknesses. She attempts to develop a picture of your child as she functions in your family and community.

To get this picture, the nurse will first review records of your child's previous evaluations so that she can note the concerns of other health professionals and family members and pay special attention to these issues in the current evaluation. Next, the nurse will probably observe your child at home so she can assess your child's behavior in a familiar setting. The nurse will also want to note your complaints, your interactions with your child, your child's play behavior, your disciplinary strategies, and the organization of your home environment. Finally, the nurse will interview you to learn about a typical day at home for your child; her sleep and play patterns; the degree of structure in her daily life; safety issues; your child's self-care skills such as dressing, toileting, and feeding; and her current state of health. With information from the interview and observation, the nurse can develop a list of major areas of concern to your family and to health professionals.

Social Worker. Interdisciplinary evaluation teams often include a social worker who works to obtain an overall picture of how your family functions. Through interviews with both your immediate and extended family, the social worker will gather information on the roles family members fill within your family, the quality of family relationships, your family's ability to cope with challenges, the support of your extended family, the commitment of family members to solving family problems, and your family's problem-solving style.

After developing a picture of your family's strengths and needs both as individuals and as a group, the social worker will direct you to helpful resources such as parent support groups, parent training, and respite care. The social worker may also serve as a service coordinator and liaison with other professionals working with your family.

Many other professionals may also participate in the diagnosis of autism, depending on the resources in your area. For example, educational specialists or nutritionists may be part of the diagnostic team. Because these professionals have responsibility for the ongoing care and education of your child, they are described in detail in later chapters. These later chapters also provide information about the treatment of autism that you will find helpful as you prepare now to move from the diagnosis stage to the treatment stage. Chapter 3 discusses the medical conditions associated with autism and the medications that are sometimes used to treat the symptoms of autism. Chapter 7 explains how an appropriate educational program can help to minimize your child's autistic symptoms and maximize her potential.

A Brief History of Autism

Autism has a long past but a short history. As early as the late eighteenth century, medical texts described cases of children who did not speak, were extremely aloof, and who possessed unusual memory skills. But it was not until 1943 that the condition was given a name. In that year, Dr. Leo Kanner, a child psychiatrist at Johns Hopkins University Medical School, described the common characteristics of eleven children he had seen between 1938 and 1943. These children shared several features, the most notable of which was extreme isolation or withdrawal from human contact beginning as early as the first year of life. So convinced was Kanner that autism was present from birth or shortly thereafter that he adopted the term *early infantile autism.* Even today, some professionals use the terms "infantile autism," and "early infantile autism."

In naming this condition, Kanner borrowed the term *autism* from Eugen Bleuler, a Swiss psychiatrist who had coined the term in 1911. In many ways, this borrowing proved to be an unfortunate choice. In his writings, Bleuler used the term "autism" to describe the *active* withdrawal of adult schizophrenic patients into fantasy away from social interaction. From the 1940s through the 1960s, many professionals believed that the child with autism made a *conscious* decision to withdraw from a hostile, unnurturing human world and was afflicted with a disorder similar to schizophrenia.

Today we know that this is not true. Children with autism do not withdraw because they feel rejected. Unfortunately, however, many parents—and particularly mothers—were labelled cold, ungiving, unnurturing "refrigerator parents" who had in large part caused their child's autism. There were also persistent notions that autism was more common in families of higher socioeconomic status. Needless to say, we now know this is wrong; autism affects children of all classes, nationalities, and races.

Early incorrect beliefs about the causes of autism led to the treatment strategy of removing the child from her family for residential treatment, with psychotherapy for the parents. Fortunately, new ways of thinking based on solid research have evolved. Nowadays the crucial help that parents can give as part of their child's team is fostered. Families are counseled that the best place for their child with autism is almost always with the family. Where circumstances make this option impossible and residential placement is in the best interest of all concerned, placement within the community in a supervised group home or similar alternative living arrangement is often best. Throughout, the family's *continuing* involvement with their child is encouraged and supported.

Starting in the 1960s, advances in the diagnosis and treatment of autism were made. Researchers identified the particular symptoms of autism that separate it from other conditions and concluded that autism is likely a result of neurological and biochemical causes. Teachers and therapists also began to use more advanced techniques—including applied behavior analysis or behavior modification—to teach important school and life skills to children with autism. Research demonstrated that the techniques of applied behavior analysis were successful in teaching skills to children, and these techniques have become the treatment of choice today. Applied behavior analysis is explained more in Chapters 4 and 7.

Although autism still remains somewhat of a mystery, much progress has been made in understanding how it affects children. More work remains to be done, but today the stereotypes and myths of the past that so hurt parents and families are being replaced by facts.

Your Child's Future

Just as children with autism have a very wide range of abilities and skills, so, too, do adults with autism. Generally, children with less severe cases of autism will have less disability as adults. A few achieve almost normal functioning. Most children with autism, however, continue as adults to be significantly affected by autism, some severely so.

Certain factors—notably the level of intelligence and the presence of language—are important indicators of a more favorable future. While there is some disagreement as to the exact cutoff, it appears that children with an initial IQ over 60–70 tend to have a better long-term outlook. Children with some spontaneous speech by age five or six also appear to fare better as they grow older. Additional positive indicators include less severe symptoms of autism and a more passive behavioral style.

Other considerations which may improve your child's outlook include her participation in early intervention programs or in mainstreamed school settings. These opportunities are fairly recent and will certainly improve the futures of many children with autism. At this point, however, there is some controversy over which children will benefit most, and how those benefits will affect adolescents and adults with autism.

There are now many more educational and vocational options for children with autism than existed even ten years ago. Part of the reason is the information gathered from research, part has to do with new laws mandating an appropriate education for children with autism, and part has to do with society's increased acceptance of children with special needs. Parent involvement, community integration, early identification and intervention, and systematic teaching all will contribute to a favorable future for your child.

It is impossible to define "favorable future" except to say that more and more children with autism will be growing up with less and less of a disability thanks to constantly improving educational services and a greater understanding of autism. As a result, the future will continue to get better; opportunities for growth and accomplishment will continue to expand. At this time, however, certain limitations *are* lifelong. In most cases, an adult with autism will always require some degree of supervision. Fully independent living and economic self-sufficiency is possible only for a very few. Even when the severity of the symptoms of autism decreases over time, these symptoms usually don't disappear altogether. For example, the adult with autism may appear extremely shy, reclusive, or rigid when faced with variation in routines.

Children more severely affected by autism face an even less independent future. In addition, children with autism who develop a seizure disorder by adolescence, who do not develop the ability to play appropriately with toys, or who live in an unstable home environment will likely require more supervision throughout their lives. However, just as the future for those with less severe autism has improved with recent social, political, and educational mandates, so too should the future for those more severely disabled.

Conclusion

Your child's autism is probably due to a combination of neurological and biochemical disorders that she was born with. Today, with improved testing, more enlightened professionals, and more effective teaching techniques, the future of children with autism is far more promising than in the past.

Right now, most children with autism will need supervision on a continuing basis all their lives. But research continues and as the possibilities expand—through research and social acceptance—so do the boundaries expand for people with autism.

Your child's autism is not her sole characteristic. She is a multi-faceted personality like all the rest of us. Keep this in mind when planning her future. You must insist that your child be treated as a learner *first,* and as a child whose learning is impaired by the symptoms of autism second. You should always work for the best possible educational placement for your child. To do otherwise risks her future life in your community. Remember, the future for those with autism is constantly getting brighter. There is every reason for you to work for, and expect, the brightest possible future for your child.

Parent Statements

The pediatrician said, "Have you thought about autism?" He was the first one who had mentioned the word. And we said, "No, she's too outgoing. It can't be autism. She's too affectionate, too outgoing."

We knew about the stereotype of autism—you know, the self-destruction, the withdrawal—so at first we said, "That couldn't be it; she's just slow." And then we began to see that maybe the pediatrician did have a point. That's when we started looking more into the possibility.

We took him to a day care center and the people there said, "Why did you bring us this problem child?" And that's when the wheels started turning. We took him to a doctor first of all, and she said that there was some mental disorder but she couldn't diagnose what it was. We went to a psychologist, and he said that Billy was severely retarded. And then we took him to the diagnostic center, and they diagnosed him as having mild to moderate retardation. Finally, we went to another psychologist, who diagnosed Billy as having autistic tendencies. That was when he was about four and a half.

We noticed there was something wrong, but we expected the pediatrician to say, "You need to start this process." We asked the questions, but we didn't get any answers.

We didn't know what steps to take, or what type of evaluations Scott needed, or what was necessary to see exactly what was going on.

He went through all kinds of tests to see if he was allergic to different things, but never mental-type tests.

People look at him, and I'm torn between making a sign to hang on him, "I can't help it—I'm autistic," and then handing out little pamphlets, or just screaming obscenities at these people, telling them to mind their own business.

I took him to our pediatrician, who said, "Yes, there is a problem. Take him to this speech pathologist who works for the state." Our son was not quite two and a half at that point. The speech pathologist seemed to understand things about him that nobody else had ever understood.

I can't look at him as a case study. I can't look at him as an interesting thing. I can't look for a different common cause, because I see potential.

I look at Tommy and I treat him as if he's got a label. I don't treat him like a normal kid. I mean, I see his problem and make allowances, or I exert myself more because I figure that something is part of his handicapping condition.

I don't care what you call him, just do what's appropriate.

If I see the kid get off the bus and he's shaking his head like this for no apparent reason, I wonder why. Is this just a tic, or what's going on with him?

I'm defensive about the diagnosis, although I don't have problems with people saying the child's got problems—he's got learning problems, he's got speech problems. But he's done so wonderfully.

My husband thinks of it like this: he says, "Good thing that they don't look at the world as we do, because they would be miserable. They're in their own little sphere and everything is happy-go-lucky, and that's it."

Ray's whole outlook on life seems to be: "I'm in my own little world. I have a sister here and I have a brother there, and I love my parents," and that's all there is to life. As long as they don't know any bad things, they're as happy as a peach.

One of the doctors we took Gary to told us, "Well, if he's autistic, he could just snap out of it, like amnesia." I thought to myself, don't hold my breath.

When you first understand that your child's been diagnosed with autism, part of the frustration is that people always ask you, "Well, what causes that? What's the cure?" There are no answers. And it's frustrating for us to have to know that initially, but even harder for us to try to explain it.

A girl I was going to school with had just about completed her degree in psychology, and when I was explaining different behaviors of Tommy's, she said, "That sounds like he's autistic." So then I went and read up on autism on my own. Then when they gave me the diagnosis, I could see where they were coming from.

If I had known that there was a diagnostic center right down the street, we would have taken him there after six months or so.

TWO

═══ ❖ ═══

Adjusting to Your Child's Diagnosis

LILLIAN AND JOE TOMMASONE*

You probably spent the first years of your child's life walking an emotional tightrope between hope and despair. On the one hand, you wanted so much to believe the encouraging signs that your baby was perfectly healthy and was making normal progress. On the other hand, you couldn't quite squelch the worry that *something* about him—something you couldn't pinpoint—was a little bit off. In the beginning, you were probably able to explain away some of the fears, but as new fears kept materializing to take the place of old ones, you likely found yourself coming perilously close to losing your emotional balance. I think our experience was fairly typical:

My husband and I came home from the hospital with a beautiful baby. Mike had an impish grin and a mischievous gleam in his eyes. He gurgled and cooed and was fat and healthy. But we held our breaths as our picture-perfect son began to develop. You see, our first child was born with a developmental disability, so we waited anxiously to see if Mike would reach his developmental

---

* Joe and Lillian Tommasone are the parents of Michael, a thirteen-year-old with autism, and Jon, a sixteen-year-old with multiple handicaps. Joe works for a major airline as a jet mechanic and Lillian is a parent educator for the Statewide Parent Advocacy Network (S.P.A.N.) in New Jersey. Lillian holds a master's degree in special education from Kean College (NJ) and writes frequently on the subjects of respite care and advocacy.

milestones on schedule. We knew what to look for—or at least we thought we did.

I remember coming home from the monthly pediatrician visits during Mike's first year and putting him to the test. I'd make him do all the simple exercises the doctor had done in his office. And Mike could do them. He followed an object with his eyes, reached out to us, looked at our faces, and laughed when we tickled him. He rolled over, sat up, and crawled. Just as you probably did with your son or daughter, we had a sense that all was well.

When Mike was about a year old, however, doubts began to surface. Our child, who had once been so full of expression, now seldom looked at us. Instead he seemed to be looking through us—beyond us—absorbed in his own thoughts. Despite our encouragement, Mike refused to walk, but was content to sit and rock. We rationalized that he was too chubby and was a thinker rather than a doer. Mike also didn't play with toys the way they were meant to be played with; instead he chose to collect them and carry them around. We decided he was feeling insecure. Most worrisome of all, Mike wouldn't respond when we called his name. We knew he didn't have a hearing problem, though, because he always came quickly whenever he heard the rustling of a candy wrapper.

What finally forced us to admit that Mike's problems were not just part of some stage he'd outgrow was his failure to talk. Although Mike whined and made other sounds, he still had not developed any purposeful language by about twenty-four months. His way of communicating was to throw a tantrum.

Although Joe and I could tolerate and understand an occasional tantrum from our toddler when he didn't get his way, it seemed as if Mike lashed out constantly. He'd throw a tantrum if we tried to read him a story or build a tower of blocks with him. He'd throw a tantrum if we interrupted a favorite pastime such as sitting and rocking, fondling the fringe on his blanket, or looking at his hands. And he'd throw tantrums for reasons known only to him.

Mike's temper tantrums were constant, lengthy, intense, and violent. He'd bang his head against the floor or wall, scream at the top of his lungs, kick and thrash about, and even bite himself. In desperation, I'd rattle off a list of things I thought Mike might want.

Sometimes I'd name what he wanted immediately, but more often than not I wouldn't, and the tantrum would go on and on.

Puzzled, distressed, and frustrated, we made an appointment with a neurologist at a large metropolitan hospital. Surely modern medicine and the scientific community could give us some answers and help. Surely *someone* could fling us an emotional safety net.

Getting the News

The sequence of events that led *you* to seek medical help for your son or daughter may have been somewhat different than the one I've just described. For example, you may have been most concerned because your child never smiled or continually flapped his hands, or because he learned to talk, but then mysteriously seemed to forget how. But whatever your worries, nothing could have prepared you for your child's actual diagnosis.

In our case, we were informed after a week of intensive testing that our son was autistic-like. You may have been told that your child is autistic or that he has early infantile autism or a pervasive developmental disorder. However the news is phrased, it is usually a devastating shock to parents already buffeted by months of worry and foreboding. For many parents, this pain is so searing that even years later, the memory automatically causes tears. Very few things indeed are worse than learning that your child has autism. You want to go back in time—to change things somehow. You think that if you could just hold your child and squeeze him, maybe he could be okay. You feel so desperately helpless and overwhelmed that you can't imagine ever laughing or feeling good about anything ever again.

No one would ever claim that adjusting to a diagnosis of autism is easy. There are no secret coping formulas; no magic words that can take away the pain. Still, parents sometimes find that learning to understand and work through their feelings helps get them started back on the path to a manageable, enjoyable family life. This chapter will help you sort out your feelings and then turn your attention to helping your child and the rest of your family.

Coping with Your Feelings

Unless you have a background in special education or in medicine, the word "autism" probably meant very little to you the first time you heard it. And in my case, that one word, "autistic-like," was just about all I heard—that and the neurologist's pronouncement that there was nothing the medical profession could do for autism. I remember listening to the doctor explain the disorder afterwards, but I never heard his words.

Usually, it is not until after the seriousness of your child's diagnosis sinks in that your emotions really become overwhelming. While you are floundering toward acceptance, you are likely to be bombarded with feelings that range from rage and resentment to guilt, helplessness, and sorrow. To make matters worse, you may worry that some of your reactions are bad and shameful, and that you must be a terrible person to be having them.

Believe me, you have nothing to be ashamed of. Both your feelings about your child's autism and your feelings *about* these feelings are completely normal. You are going through the same emotions that most parents of children newly diagnosed with autism experience.

Shock

Shock is often the first reaction parents have when their child is diagnosed with autism. You might have felt, as I did, that you had somehow stepped outside of yourself and had physically removed yourself from what was actually happening. Inside, I felt nothing at all, although I do recall thinking that tragedies like this happen only in the movies—not in real life, and certainly not to *us*. This inner numbness is a built-in defense mechanism our bodies have for insulating us from traumatic situations. Our minds just naturally shut down until we can begin to come to grips with the reality we face.

Helplessness

Once the shock wears off, you may be paralyzed by a new emotion—helplessness. In the beginning, you feel powerless because you know absolutely nothing about autism or what to expect for your child. You don't have the first idea what you should do, and doubt that you'd have the physical or emotional strength to do it even if you did. Like Joe did, you may feel as if you are falling into a deep, dark hole and that you have to reach the bottom of the pit before you can think of getting up again. And even if you have had experience teaching or working with young children as I had, you may feel completely incompetent to deal with your own child's problems. In desperation, you turn to your doctor for guidance, but each new fact you learn only increases your feelings of helplessness. Eventually, the sheer enormity of your child's disability seems to weigh on you like a boulder. You feel defeated and immobilized, even before you've begun.

Guilt

Another emotion parents of children with autism frequently must grapple with is guilt. Each spouse may secretly worry that he or she is somehow responsible for their child's disability. Was it the aspirin I took when I was pregnant? Should I have dropped out of aerobics class sooner? Could it be my genes? Your anguish may become even more acute if you happen to come across an out-of-date book written when autism was thought to be caused by cold, unfeeling, "refrigerator" parents.

Soon after Mike was diagnosed, Joe and I read just such a book—Bruno Bettleheim's *Empty Fortress*. According to Bettleheim, parents of children with autism did not give their children either enough love or the right kind of love. His book made us feel that our personalities, parenting skills, and home environment were so defective that they had made Mike autistic-like. His theory made it sound as if we had the problems, not Mike.

I admit that we needed direction in bringing up Mike. And we didn't always understand him as well as we should have. But Mike was our child and there was nothing we wanted more than to love him and to watch him grow, learn, and be happy. I knew in my heart that there was nothing wrong with our love for Mike. Eventually, my good common sense made me reject the idea that we were to blame for Mike's autism.

No matter what your feelings now, sooner or later your common sense will also help you overcome any guilt you might have. As Chapter 1 explains, your behavior—either before or after your child's birth—could not possibly have caused your child's autism. And even if a genetic cause is eventually proven, there is currently no test that could have predicted with any surety that you and your spouse would have a child with autism.

Anger

Anger is a natural outgrowth of guilt. You are convinced your child's autism has to be *somebody's* fault—if not yours, then somebody else's. You can't believe that something so unspeakable could just happen to a helpless little kid without someone being to blame.

When Mike was diagnosed, my husband and I were angry with everyone. We were angry first of all at God for allowing this to happen. Our first child was developmentally delayed; hadn't we suffered enough? We were angry with the doctors and medical profession for not finding a cure. We were angry with the educators for not knowing how to make Mike catch up. And we were angry with family and friends whose words of comfort couldn't make the pain go away.

At the time, it just seemed as if no one else in the world understood what we were going through. You may feel the same way now, but believe me, it's not true. I understand your agony, and so do thousands of other parents of children with autism.

Grief

Underlying and complicating your other emotions, you are likely to have a heart-wrenching, bottomless sense of grief. You have lost the ideal, perfect child you once thought you had, along with many of the hopes and dreams you cherished for his future. The idyllic family life you'd once imagined for yourself lies in ruins around you and you don't know where to begin picking up the pieces.

For us, the pain and grief of realizing our children had permanent disabilities was shared and separate. Many a night Joe and I would stay up late and talk and cry and talk and cry, trying to find some answer to the question, "Why us?" This only led us to the next question, "Why our sons?" We had many questions, but few answers.

I dealt with my grief in an outward, vocal way. I would cry, yell, moan, groan, and complain until I was wallowing in my own self-pity. I was hurting and I wanted the *world* to know it.

Joe grieved in a more controlled, quieter way. He'd get very quiet, serious, and somber. He wanted to be alone to think. These were the days he needed to go fishing.

There were times we wished our children had not been born—not so much because of who or what they were, but rather because of the problems their conditions posed for them. We worried about the quality of their lives because it seemed there would be so many empty holes that could never be filled. Our older son, Jon, would never know the thrill of hitting a home run or the anticipation of his first date. Mike would never feel compassion for another person or develop lasting friendships. He would always be a taker, never a giver.

At times, you may feel such profound emptiness inside that you may wonder if it might be better if you—or your child—had never been born. Contemptible as feelings like these may seem to you, they are normal, common reactions. They are just a way we have of trying to avoid the reality of our children's autism. With time, your grief, too, will become more bearable.

Resentment

On top of everything else, you may harbor terrific resentment. Why were you, out of all people, singled out to have a child with autism? What did you ever do to deserve this burden? It's just not fair.

Often parents of children with autism find themselves resenting other parents who take the normalcy of their children for granted. For instance, I remember feeling consumed with jealousy as I listened to friends recount stories of their children's latest accomplishments. They just seemed to have it all. I would wish some terrible misfortune would befall their families so they would have a chance to stand in my shoes and feel the pain I felt.

Afterwards, I hated myself for feeling this way. How could I wish misfortune on my friends? How could I be so cruel?

Some parents also resent their children for having been born with autism. Even though they know their child has no control over his condition, sometimes they can't help thinking that if only he would *try* a little harder to be normal, everything would be all right. For example, there was a time we thought Mike was acting autistic-like on purpose. We may have felt this way because we were still denying Mike's disability. After all, Mike had a hidden handicap. He was normal in so many ways. He had no physical limitations or distinctions, seemed aware, and was developing within normal limits. Yet sometimes he acted so bizarre in social situations. Couldn't he see that other children were not flapping their hands or getting undressed in public? Why did he act this way? Was it a maneuver to get our attention?

Not until we got a better understanding of the disorder did we realize that Mike's perception of the world was distorted. He doesn't perceive things the way most people do. His view of the world is mixed-up and fragmented. I imagine it's like listening to a static-filled phone conversation. You hear only parts of words and conversations, so you can't understand the total message. As a result, you get a different message than originally intended.

Your resentment of your child's autism and behavior, although understandable, will only build a wall between you and your child if you cling to it too long. Let your resentment go, and you will be able to use your emotional energy to fight your child's disorder in more constructive ways.

Shock, helplessness, guilt, anger, grief, and resentment are all normal reactions to the diagnosis of autism in a loved one. You will probably experience these emotions many times—not only in the beginning, but also later, after you think you have finally adjusted to your child's condition. For example, I still occasionally feel guilty if we're out somewhere in public and a minor inconvenience like waiting in line sets Mike off into a rash of uncontrollable behaviors. I blame myself, even though I know in my heart that I've set the stage for success and have prepared well. It is an unfortunate fact of life, but the healing process is slow and you will always have more stresses and emotions to cope with than other parents will. What is important to remember, though, is that you *will* deal with them. You *will* adjust.

How to Adjust

Address Your Emotions

No matter how strongly you may have suspected that something was wrong with your child, it is still devastating to have your worst fears confirmed. After all, your world has just been turned upside down—it is humanly impossible for you to know which way is up right now.

At first it can be like living in a pressure cooker. All the stresses and strains of everyday life and those worrisome feelings about your child can build to the point where you are ready to explode. You have to release that pent-up emotion somehow. Often the way I coped was to go out into the garden and furiously yank away at the weeds, pulling up flowers and vegetables in the process. Other times I'd go on a shopping spree. I'd buy every toy in sight, reasoning that educational toys were what I needed to "fix" Mike. Sometimes I stored the toys away, thinking that next month he'd catch up and play with them and everything would be okay. Other times I would realize the toys were completely beyond Mike's abilities and interests, so I would return them in despair.

Whatever *you* do, don't try to deny what you are feeling. If you feel like crying, cry. You have a right to cry. If you feel like pulling your hair and screaming at the top of your lungs, pull your hair and scream. You have a right to express whatever emotions you are feeling in whatever fashion seems right to you. Indeed, you *must* come to terms with everything you are feeling before you will be able to accept your child's condition. After all, if you back away from your emotions now, how will you ever regain enough mental composure to be able to make the best decisions for your child?

Take Time to Heal

This will probably seem like small consolation, but most parents of children with autism go through what you are experiencing, and most eventually come to terms with their feelings. The key word here is eventually. Don't rush the healing process. If the house is a mess and you don't feel like straightening it out, don't. If you don't feel up to going back to work yet, then stay home—another day, week, month—whatever it takes. And by all means, don't try to solve all of your child's problems at once. Even if you could, you don't know nearly enough about autism yet to know where to start.

It may take a while, but someday you will wake up and realize that something has changed. Your mind will be clearer and you will feel more optimistic. Without really knowing when, you will have accepted your child's autism and also another momentous fact—namely, that your child is exactly the same person he was before you got a label for his condition. He hasn't lost a single one of the qualities that endeared him to you before his diagnosis; only your perceptions of them have been temporarily distorted. To illustrate, here is how Mike's label made us see him in a different light:

As a baby, Mike was very expressive. His entire face would light up when he was happy. If he saw an airplane in flight, for instance, he just bubbled with excitement. He'd jump up and down, flapping his hands and squealing with delight. He'd follow the plane's path until it was out of sight, screeching and toddling from one end of the yard to the other. For my husband and me, Mike's enthusiasm almost made up for the noisy flight pattern over our home.

Then we learned Mike was autistic-like. Almost at once, we began to see his enthusiasm as a weakness rather than a strength. It worried us that we could never quite predict Mike's response or the intensity of his reaction in any given situation. We felt we always had to be on guard. Now in place of a spirited, alert, happy child, we saw a loud, demanding child who was out of control. Our focus had shifted from Mike to his autism.

Since then, time, training, experience, and exposure have helped Mike get a better handle on his emotions and reactions. And Joe and I have learned to rediscover Mike as a child. Now, although Mike still challenges us, we can once again see him as a happy, lively, vivacious child.

On the day you are able to see your child for himself again, you will be ready to take positive steps to cope with your child's autism. You will be ready to start educating yourself. You will want to reach out to other parents. You will begin to trust yourself and your instincts again. And most importantly, your early feelings of helplessness, anger, grief, and resentment will begin to loosen their stranglehold on you.

Get the Facts

Once you have begun to cope with your emotions, you will recognize that you can never go back, only forward. And to move forward, you need facts about autism and about disabilities in general. Everyone absorbs information in their own way and at different rates, but be careful not to move too quickly or you may find yourself overwhelmed by the sheer amount of information out there. It is also important to bear in mind that, although you will eventually have to make quite a few decisions about your child's future, you do not have to make these decisions as soon as you read about them. You will likely discover—as my husband and I did—that measured doses of information, as needed, will sustain you best.

The Reading List in the back of this book can help get you started in the right direction. The Autism Society of America (ASA) can suggest books and articles for you to read and provide you with brochures and other information. Your local chapter of the Association for Retarded Citizens (ARC) can also recommend reading matter if your child has mental retardation in addition to autism. Finally, to learn more about special education and other issues confronting parents of all special-needs children, you may wish to read some of the journals and magazines listed in the Resource Guide.

Your Family and Friends

There is no getting around it. Everyone who is close to you and your child will experience the same emotions that you did when they learn that your child has autism. Brothers and sisters may not yet be able to articulate their feelings and older friends and relatives may not know how to do so in a tactful manner, but the feelings, whether expressed or unexpressed, will be there.

Brothers and Sisters

Most parents find it difficult to break the news of their child's autism to their other children. To begin with, it can be hard to come up with just the right words with which to explain such a complex disorder to young children. Sometimes it helps if you can explain the disorder using experiences your children can identify with. For instance, to explain why your child with autism flaps his hands or bangs his head, you might ask your children to remember the last time they felt like crying, and then tell them that their sibling can't help flapping his hands any more than they could keep from crying. Do not talk down to your children, but do not overwhelm them with an overly technical explanation, either.

Once your children understand that there is something wrong with their sibling, you should be prepared to help them adjust to their feelings. Your children will probably need to cope with the same emotions that you did. They may wonder, for example, whether they caused their sibling to get sick. They may resent the disruption of their lives and wish that their brother or sister would die. Because your children will not know how normal and acceptable their feelings are, it is up to you to reassure them.

One way to help small children express their feelings is to use play therapy. Using a doll, a television show, or a book to begin the discussion, zero in on the emotions you think your children are struggling with: "Wow, Kelly sure was mad at her brother. I wonder why. Do you know why Kelly was so mad?" Whatever reasons your children give you, reassure them that it is all right to feel that way.

To further help your children understand that they—and their feelings—are normal, you may want to introduce them to other siblings of special-needs children. Just as you and your spouse do, your children need to be reassured that there are others in the same boat as they are. Chapter 5 explains how to get your children involved in a siblings' group and also provides additional suggestions to help your children adjust to their sibling's autism.

Grandparents

Most parents of children with autism approach telling their own parents about their child's disability with painfully mixed emotions. They desperately want their parents' support and understanding, but at the same time they worry about how their parents will take the news. And it's true your parents likely *will* go through the same range of emotions you did. In their guilt, they may wonder if they passed along defective genes. In their anger, they may try to fix the blame on their son- or daughter-in-law. In their grief, they may mourn the loss of the ideal, super-achieving grandchild they'd had their hearts set on.

Whatever your parents' first reactions, bear in mind that they *are* grandparents. Your child's label no more changes the relationship they had with him before his diagnosis than it changes yours. Chances are that once they have adjusted to your child's diagnosis, their natural grandparents' urge to dote on, and brag about, their grandchild will return in full force. This was certainly the case in my family, although there is no doubt that both grandmothers have felt the strain of Mike's (and his brother's) disability. In fact, in the beginning, they seemed to have double the grief. They grieved over their grandchild's handicap *and* their own child's pain. We talked a lot and cried a lot and were open and honest about our feelings. Now both grandmothers have a special relationship with Mike and are our much-needed extra pair of hands.

To help your parents comprehend and adapt to your child's situation, you will probably need to assure them that their reactions, doubts, and fears are normal and should be discussed openly. You will also have to provide them all the information they need and give them the opportunity to ask questions. Finally, let them help you respond to their grandchild's needs. Then give them time to come around.

Friends

It is all too easy to let your child's autism come between you and your friends. For your part, you may unconsciously push friends away because you feel they cannot possibly understand your pain or because you resent their normal family home life. For their part, friends may avoid you for fear of saying the wrong thing or avoid the subject of your child's autism for fear of seeming impolite. Most friendships that run into trouble probably do so because of actions (or inactions) on both sides.

From my own experience, I know that it's just about impossible not to feel isolated from friends—at least in the beginning. As a young mother, I felt cut off from my close friends who had had normal babies. Their babies learned, grew, and changed every day. My baby seemed to be frozen in time. My friends would chatter and chuckle about the cute and darling things their toddlers were doing. I'd feel so alone and sad because I couldn't contribute to the conversation. I felt that even if I did share one of Mike's achievements, it would have been one that their children had mastered long ago.

I recall an incident when a group of mothers had come together for an evening social. One of my friends shared a story about how her child answered the telephone saying, "She can't talk right now," and hung up quite abruptly. I felt so alienated from this mother; my child had no idea the phone could even ring.

When it comes to friends, have patience and try not to judge the value of their friendship by how they respond to you and your child in the beginning. Give friends time to adjust, to come visit, and to cope with having a friend whose life has just changed. Friends can often help you enormously if you just give them the chance. In my case, it was my sister and her gentle yet forthright pep talks that roused me out of my self-pity and made me do what I had to do. From the start, she helped me steer my anger and pain into more positive directions such as advocacy. With time, she has become the fulcrum that balances my subjective feelings with the realities of the situation. She strengthens me and helps me grow. In short, she is my best friend and my harshest critic.

Although you, too, may find that autism draws you closer to some friends, don't be surprised if it also drives others away. Maybe your friends can't understand autism or are afraid of illness. No matter. You are bound to make new friends—friends who can sympathize with you and give you advice on how to deal with your problems. You will find these friends at parents' groups and elsewhere in the autism community, and they will do wonders for you and for your perceptions of autism.

Your Marriage

Friends and family are important in helping parents cope with their child's autism, but most parents find that their strongest ally is their spouse. My husband and I have discovered that teamwork is vital to both our emotional and our physical survival. Just keeping up with a child with autism can drain you of so much energy that you've got to have a great backup player ready and able to take over if you falter. You and your spouse can also shield each other from some of the pain and sorrow and rally each other's spirits when everything seems to be falling apart. I don't know how many nights there were back in the early days when all my husband and I could do was hold each other and cry. I don't know what I would have done if we hadn't been able to share our anguish with one another.

Before you and your spouse will be able to work as a team, you will both need to come to terms with your feelings in your own way and in your own time. Don't try to hurry your spouse if he or she does not adjust to your child's autism as quickly as you do. Sooner or later, you will both reach the point where you feel yourselves ready to go on with your own lives, as well as your family's.

Once you reach this point, your next step is to find out what your spouse has been going through. Both of you need to get your feelings off your chests and to confess your darkest fears. You must try to discuss all issues, especially the big decisions. As Chapter 5 explains, communication is probably the single most important factor in adapting your marriage to the stress of raising a child with autism. Although you and your spouse may occasionally be at a loss as to how to help one another, if you can talk about your uncertainty, you can at least be assured that you both still consider your relationship a top priority.

Some parents suffer from chronic fatigue. Because of their tendency to injure themselves or others if not constantly supervised, many children with autism run their parents ragged during the daytime. Mike, for example, needs constant supervision because he is so impulsive and unpredictable. His high activity level and unpredictability not only wear us down, but on occasion have caused our hearts to stop. For example, one day Mike gave me the slip and wandered out of our fenced-in yard. In my frantic search for him, I suddenly remembered his current preoccupation with swimming pools. I was horrified when I found him walking on the pool cover of a neighbor's in-ground pool. He didn't realize that if the cover gave way, he would drown.

Many children with autism also go through periods when they keep the family up all night by throwing tantrum after tantrum or by repeatedly getting out of bed. Mike went through a stage when he wouldn't stay in his room and would get up every two hours. Naturally, he wanted company dragging out his toys and turning on all the household lights. Since fatigue has a way of robbing you of your ability to cope, try to share night duties equally so that you and your spouse each have a chance to get some rest.

To keep your child's autism from becoming the sole focus of your marriage, try to take some time out for yourselves at least once a week. If at all possible, you should find a reliable babysitter and get out of the house to talk or just to have fun. Don't just go to parent support meetings, either. Go out to dinner or to see a movie. Doing things for yourself—by yourself—can also be very therapeutic. Over the years, I have done craft work, sold cosmetics, and become active in church work. I have also returned to college for my special education teaching certificate, and to graduate school for an M.A. in special education. Like all mothers, I have learned that you have to balance your time and energies between family and self. I have also learned that just knowing that you are going to get out of the house or that you have a special outing coming up can boost your spirits tremendously.

Sometimes in spite of all you do, you and your spouse cannot quite manage to cope as a couple. Chapter 5 discusses reasons this may happen and strategies for resolving some typical problems. Whatever your difficulties, however, it is important to realize that your spouse needs you more than ever now, and so do all your children. And believe it or not, having a child with autism just may help you forge a stronger, better marriage than you had before.

Reaching Out

Reading books and pamphlets about autism is helpful and necessary, but there's nothing like getting the facts firsthand. By connecting with a parent support group, you can trade questions, concerns, and feelings with other parents who have been there. You learn that you are not alone in your sorrow, anger, and pain, and you also pick up practical advice about meeting the day-to-day challenge of raising a special-needs child. You may even meet someone who is willing to swap babysitting chores with you and allow you some much-needed respite.

To make contact, call your local ASA chapter, ARC, or any of the other parent organizations listed in the Resource Guide at the back of this book. Explain that you have a child with autism and that you would like to talk to someone who can give you some basic information. You won't have to say more—they'll understand. If you don't feel quite ready to share your emotions, nobody in a parent support group will force you to talk. Often just listening to the stories of other parents of children with disabilities can help to dilute your loneliness. It's only a phone call; what do you have to lose?

Don't Despair

As later chapters of this book emphasize, it is impossible to predict at an early age just how much your child with autism will achieve. Like all children, children with autism are born with varying abilities and potentials—there is no such thing as a typical child with autism. Do not rule out any long-term goals for your child at present; rather, concentrate on the small steps that may eventually help your child reach those goals.

Above all, try to keep your perspective and a sense of humor. Inevitably, raising a child with autism is going to lead you into some potentially embarrassing situations. If you can somehow manage to see the funny side of these incidents, however, you can often disperse a great deal of tension.

I remember an occasion when my family had gone out to lunch at a fast food restaurant. We were waiting in line to order, when

Mike bolted away and sat down with another family. Without a word, he reached across the table, snatched a stranger's hamburger, and took an enormous bite out of it. Needless to say, neither my husband nor I particularly wanted to claim Mike as our child. After we'd made our apologies, replaced the hamburger, and were driving home, however, the humor of the situation hit us. "Did you see the look on that guy's face?" my husband asked. The more we chuckled over the stranger's surprise, the less we felt like haggling over whose fault it was that Mike hadn't behaved quite properly.

On another occasion, when Mike was in his shoe fetish stage, he took a fancy to an elderly woman's shoes. As she was walking along the sidewalk, Mike began tugging at her heel, trying to remove her shoe. Fortunately, I was able to intervene in time to keep the startled woman from falling. Fortunately, too, she had a good sense of humor and was able to laugh with me over my young son's penchant for women's orthopedic shoes.

I'd be the last person to recommend that you laugh off every awkward situation that your child with autism gets into. Remember, though, that your child *is* a child and all children do funny things. Laughter may not be the best medicine for autism, but it can certainly help to ease some of the pain.

Conclusion

Right now, the knowledge that your child has autism may color everything you do. For example, perhaps you can't fully enjoy a good novel or a get-together with your friends without the specter of your child's autism intruding on your pleasure. Maybe you can't even buy a newspaper without wondering if your child will ever learn to read. With time, however, your child's problems will become more of an element in your life and less its main focus. You may still have busy and bad times, but they will no longer seem to swallow you up.

Mike is thirteen now. He is a teen in every sense of the word. He loves loud music, junk food, hanging out, and going out. He doesn't care much for fashion, keeping his room neat, or listening to his mom nag at him. Over the years, there have been ups and downs, good days and bad days, triumphs and tribulations. But Mike has made painstaking strides toward goals Joe and I never dreamed he could reach.

It is really hard to measure what impact Mike and his brother have had on our family life and on our personal growth, but here are a few lessons we have learned:

We have learned to appreciate and treasure the everyday miracles in life—Mike's first word, his older brother's first step, the way both boys roar with laughter when Daddy imitates animal sounds. We have learned to value another human being despite his problems—to look at our children's strengths, not just their weaknesses. We have learned to be givers as well as takers by helping other families through hard times and pain, by advocating for those with disabilities, and by giving our time, energy, and talents—whether it be chaperoning a teen dance, baking cupcakes for a class party, or giving testimony at a national conference on disabilities. And we have learned we can be happy despite our children's disabilities. We can still laugh at each other's mistakes, lean on one another, and love and care for each other every day.

Eventually, you may find that being the parent of a child with autism has completely altered your perception of what matters in life. Most importantly, you may discover that you have developed an appreciation for simple things you once took for granted. Former priorities—career advancement, making a killing in the stock market, bowling a perfect game—may pale in importance compared to enjoying the season's first snow, a hug, or an afternoon together with your family. Sometimes just getting your child with autism to smile at a joke and actually *enjoy* an experience is enough to make you feel like King Midas. If raising your son or daughter with autism does nothing more than deepen your appreciation of such simple things, your child will enrich your life many times over.

Your child has autism, and you cannot change that fact. But the autism is not the end of his life, or of yours. There is no denying it: autism *will* affect his life. But it is your challenge to see through the autism to the child underneath, and not to let autism be all you see. I can promise you that there will be days when you glimpse your child at work, at play, or busy with some activity and see just a child...your child.

Parent Statements

There is nothing more devastating than finding out that your physically beautiful child is mentally handicapped.

When Scott was first diagnosed, a friend of ours read some articles—not encouraging articles—and I read them and got very depressed. I started seeing Scott in a different light than I had seen him before. I just saw him differently; I had a different attitude, and it was very, very depressing. I developed an object attitude—"There's a Down syndrome kid"; "There's an autistic kid." It was as if he was a thing now—not even a human being.

It took me about a week and then I said to myself, "Look, Scott hasn't changed. He's still the same person he was a week ago. I can't do this. I can't look at him in that light. He's a complicated kid and there's a lot wrong, but he's not these critical studies." His humanness, I think, brought me around and I realized that I can't look at him that way. I have to look at him as him.

I think possibly, getting real philosophical about it, that denial is one of the results of lack of support.

I read articles about how it was the parents' fault.

I kept thinking I must have done something to deserve this.

I knew I did everything right during my pregnancy. I knew people who drank and took drugs and everything else and had normal kids, and I thought, "What a slap in the face! I did everything right, and I'm the one with the problem."

I went to the priest and I said, "What is this? Why me?" And he said, "Well, think of it the other way—why not you?" I said, "Because I don't deserve it. I did everything right." Yes, I felt real guilty. I still think about it sometimes.

I wondered whether she got enough oxygen when she was being delivered. I was dehydrated when she was delivered. I had a 101 temperature when she was born. I asked the pediatrician whether that was a cause, and he said, "No."

I share things I learn about autism with my group, or I go and read different things about autism, or I talk to my intimate friends. But my husband and family don't want to hear these kinds of details because they don't want to deal with that term. They want to hear about Tommy's progress.

I went home and I told my husband what they told me and his reaction was, "No way. He's language delayed."

I called up my in-laws and my parents, and my Mom said, "Okay." My Dad said, "Well, he'll grow out of it." My in-laws said, "Oh, no, that's not right. What is that?"

At a year or year and a half, if you see something wrong, or if somebody says there's something going on with your kid, it's devastating. But you love that child already.

When you find out, your reaction is that he's still your child. Whatever's wrong with that kid, there are still all these good things—and there's always good stuff going on with them. You've already accepted those things. You've already loved them.

I just consider him part of me. When they told me something's wrong with him, it was like they were telling me there was something wrong with myself. It was really hard to deal with.

I knew down deep in my gut that there was something wrong with Scott, but I just couldn't really believe it.

I think the shock was what made the final diagnosis so hard. We'd known in our hearts that something was wrong, but here it was from professionals, saying, "Hey, this is it." And, oh, my God—it's like a ton of bricks hitting you or something.

I felt grateful that Scott had been diagnosed in a couple of stages, and that it wasn't all an instant thing.

I think we were all secretly hoping that somewhere along the line somebody was going to say, "He's not really autistic. He has a problem and here's a pill that will make it go away."

The strain on our marriage was a lot worse before we knew what was wrong. Even though we didn't say anything, we were always trying to put blame on each other. Once we knew that we didn't cause the problem, it was easier.

One of our neighbors said, "Well, just be grateful she's not autistic!" And I said, "Well, she is autistic-like; it's pretty close." Then my neighbor didn't know what to say, so I said, "Well, don't feel bad."

The number one piece of advice I'd give to another parent is to get support. I could not go it alone.

I've got to talk to somebody and I've got to talk to somebody who can relate to the boat I'm in. Somebody who's there. And the people with kids who are older that are not in my boat, but who are right across the creek—they can be very helpful and supportive, too.

My sister and her family love Donny very much. They celebrate his successes and accomplishments and accept him unconditionally.

THREE

Medical Problems, Treatments, and Professionals

FRED R. VOLKMAR, M.D.*

Raising a healthy child is one of the most difficult—and rewarding—challenges any parent can tackle. For parents of children with autism, the rewards are just as great as for other parents. The difficulties, however, can be more daunting because you have to take autism into account in almost all decisions you make about your child's medical well-being. For example, how will your child react to having her teeth cleaned? Can she handle a flu shot? Is it more important to take care of these problems now, or is it better to avoid any additional stress for the present?

All children have a chance of developing any number of diseases or conditions. Parents of "normal" children are rarely informed of all the possible diseases their children *might* get. But when your child has autism, doctors often tell you the statistics for your special child. This may seem insensitive and unfair, but the fact is, children with autism are simply more likely to develop

---

* Fred Volkmar, M.D., is the Harris Associate Professor of Child Psychiatry, Pediatrics, and Psychology at Yale University School of Medicine. He received his M.D. from Stanford University School of Medicine. Dr. Volkmar is the author of the section on autism in the 1986 edition of the *World Book Encyclopedia* and of a chapter on autism in *Child and Adolescent Psychiatry: A Comprehensive Textbook* (Williams and Wilkins, 1989).

certain medical problems. And because these medical problems can sometimes cause developmental delays and behavior problems, early detection and treatment are crucial.

As a parent, you can help your child by learning the basic facts about medical conditions so that you can spot problems in the early stages. You can also help your child by learning to ask the right questions and to communicate well with doctors so that you can jointly make important decisions about your child's medical care.

This chapter outlines some of the common medical conditions and potential problem areas you should look out for, and also includes tips on how best to work with medical professionals to ensure optimal care for your child. First, though, because your child's autism and the medications sometimes used to treat its symptoms can contribute to other medical problems or affect the way your child interacts with medical professionals, this chapter discusses the medical treatment of autism itself. It reviews the medications occasionally prescribed to reduce behaviors common in children with autism, and explains their benefits and risks.

Medical Treatment of Autism

Although we do not yet know the causes of autism, medicine has made important strides in treating some of its symptoms. Medications can sometimes be very helpful in reducing or eliminating problem behaviors. Because medications may also produce harmful side effects, though, it is essential to weigh their risks against their benefits. In addition, you should be aware that some treatments are still new or experimental and carefully consider any controversy surrounding them in discussions with your doctor. This section reviews the medications most commonly prescribed for children with autism and the important considerations involved in selecting and using medications.

Medications

The medications used to treat children with autism, like all medications, have their benefits as well as their limitations. Unfortunately, no medications have yet been developed that "cure" autism. Rather, medications are sometimes used to treat specific symptoms when they interfere with education or pose a potential danger to the child. For example, medication may be prescribed to treat a self-abusive behavior like severe head banging or to treat behavior like continual hand flapping which can interfere with education.

The medications most often prescribed to treat autism are called *neuroleptics*, or "major" tranquilizers, and include a number of medications which affect the brain in specific ways. Among the most commonly used major tranquilizers are thioridazine (Mellaril ™), chlorpromazine (Thorazine™), and haloperidol (Haldol™).

Do not confuse these major tranquilizers with the "minor" tranquilizers such as Valium™ and Librium™, which adults commonly take to manage anxiety. The "major" tranquilizers act in a different way, and are most frequently used for adults with severe psychiatric illnesses. One of the ways they work is by reducing the activity of *dopamine*, a chemical in the brain that acts as a *neurotransmitter*, or messenger, between nerve cells. In children with autism, dopamine appears to regulate certain problem behaviors—for example, self-injury and *stereotyped*, or purposeless, repetitive movements. Major tranquilizers may increase the attention span of children with autism and make them more able to learn.

Because each medication has a range of side effects, it is important to balance the potential benefit of the medication against its risks and to be prepared for any side effects you may observe. Whenever medication is prescribed, your child's doctor should review the possible benefits, risks, and side effects with you, other people who help care for your child, and the school staff.

Probably the most common side effect of the major tranquilizers is sedation or sleepiness. A child may become overly sedated after the medication is used and may be unable to benefit from her educational program. In that case, there is little point to using the medications in the first place. Other side effects of the medications include problems in movement. Sometimes children will develop peculiar postures or muscle spasms around the head and neck; these side effects can often be controlled by the addition of another type of medication. To some extent, all major tranquilizers produce dry mouth, constipation, blurred vision, and other effects most commonly associated with allergy medications or over-the-counter cold preparations. Less common side effects include changes in the function of the liver, effects on blood cells, restlessness or agitation, sensitivity of the skin to the sun, and true allergic reactions. Often side effects are dose related—that is, they are more common with higher doses of medication—but sometimes individuals have side effects even on low doses of medication.

After a drug is stopped or has been administered for a long period of time, other side effects may emerge. For example, a child may develop unusual head and body movements, which usually disappear some weeks or months after the drug is stopped. The most worrisome side effect of these drugs, however, is a condition known as *tardive dyskinesia*. Tardive dyskinesia typically occurs only after very long periods of treatment. In tardive dyskinesia, movements of the face—grimaces or tongue protrusion—are accompanied by unusual movements of the body and hands. Probably such movement problems reflect changes in brain sensitivity to neurotransmitters. Because this condition is sometimes irreversible, it is important that the doctor prescribing the medications continue to see your child periodically to monitor the medication.

Given the potential side effects of these medications, it is important that they be used only when necessary. Before starting your child on medications for behavior problems, you and her teachers should review your child's educational and behavioral program to determine whether changes in the environment or program might produce enough improvement to make medication unnecessary. For example, sometimes a change in classroom activities or daily routine may help reduce behavior problems.

When medications are unavoidable, it is essential that they be used sensibly, in the lowest effective dose, and for the shortest possible period of time. This means that your child must be monitored closely while she is taking medication. To make monitoring easier, the prescribing doctor—who may be a psychiatrist, developmental pediatrician, or other specialist—may want to do a physical examination and laboratory studies before starting medication. This enables the doctor to compare behavior before and after medication and to get a "baseline" against which any adverse effects of the medications can be measured. As a parent, you can help monitor your child by providing the doctor with behavioral records from the school and by continuing to observe your child closely.

The choice of medications and dosages depends on several factors. For example, children who are more agitated do better with a more sedating medication. Otherwise less sedating medication is generally used. Typically a low dose of medication is prescribed to begin with, and then adjusted depending on the child's response. Sometimes children have trouble with one medication, but do well on another. Because of the risk of long-term side effects and the need to monitor the usefulness of the medications, you and your physician may decide to reduce or stop the medication during certain periods. In some emergency situations, such as when the child's head banging is so severe as to pose the risk of serious injury, higher doses of medications may be prescribed. Once the behavior is under control, the medication can be gradually reduced.

The use of these medications should not be undertaken lightly. Often, though, these medications can greatly help your child adjust and respond well to an educational program. A good working relationship between you, your child's physician, and the school staff will help to ensure that your child is treated for the shortest period of time with the lowest possible dose of medication.

Aside from the major tranquilizers, there are other drugs available for children with autism, but their usefulness has not been proven as conclusively. In addition, the response of children with autism to other types of medications is more unpredictable than their response to the major tranquilizers or in comparison to the responses of children without autism. For example, stimulant medications are sometimes used for children with attention span problems and "hyperactivity," but when these same medications are prescribed for children with autism with similar behaviors, their behavioral problems often become worse, not better.

Minor tranquilizers such as Valium™ and Librium™ may sometimes make children with autism more agitated. The usefulness of some experimental medications remains to proven conclusively. Some researchers have suggested that special diets or large doses of vitamins and minerals (particularly Vitamin B6 and magnesium) may improve the behavior and functioning of the child with autism. These treatments remain controversial, however, since the results of research studies have been rather mixed. At present, it seems possible that some children do respond positively to these treatments, while others respond negatively. Probably the majority of children have little response to them.

In general, it is important to realize that education, rather than medication, offers the best chance for improving problem behaviors in children with autism. Parents should not engage in new or experimental treatments if their child's education is adversely affected.

Medical Problems Associated with Autism

As you read about the medical problems that children with autism can have, remember that not every child with autism has the medical problems covered in this section. These conditions are mentioned because of the special difficulties they present for children with autism or because children with autism have higher chances of developing them than children in the general population. It does not mean that your child *will* have these problems, but that she *might.* And remember, also, that in medicine, forewarned is forearmed.

The most common medical problems and issues linked with autism are: 1) seizures; 2) accidents and injuries; 3) infections; 4) dental problems; and 5) nutrition problems. This section describes these problems and explains their treatment.

Seizures

For reasons which are unclear, children with autism are more likely than other children to have seizures. Seizures occur in about one in four children with autism, more commonly in those who are mute or have lower IQs. Often, but not always, these seizures do not develop until adolescence.

Seizures are caused by abnormal electrical activity in the brain and disturb the normal functioning of the nervous system. They can produce a temporary loss of consciousness or temporary changes in behavior such as unusual movements, loss of bladder or bowel control, or staring spells. Children with autism can have several of the various types of seizures, depending on the area of the brain where the abnormal activity occurs.

Seizures can sometimes be triggered by environmental factors, or *stimuli*—for example, by rapidly blinking lights. They may also be more common in certain situations—for example, when a child has not had enough sleep. In addition, younger children sometimes develop seizures in connection with high fevers, but these seizures usually do not persist.

Seizure disorders are diagnosed by taking a detailed medical history and by doctor examination, as well as by use of an EEG (electroencephalogram). EEGs record electrical activity in the brain and help the doctor pinpoint where the seizures are originating. Their results are not always conclusive, however. Sometimes people with obvious seizures may have normal EEGs between episodes. Similarly, some people with autism who do not have seizures may have abnormal EEG patterns.

Medicine has advanced a great deal in treating seizure disorders, but cannot always entirely eliminate seizures in every child. In treating seizures, a number of different *anticonvulsant* medications are prescribed. Depending on the type of seizure, one or more medications may be used. The level of the medication in the blood often is monitored carefully and the dosage adjusted so that as little medication as is effective is used. Since these medications sometimes produce side effects such as drowsiness, changes in the blood, and gum swelling, it is important to work closely with your doctor or a neurologist. It is also important that all medical professionals involved in your child's care know exactly which medications he or she receives.

Accidents and Injuries

Even if your child did not have autism, you would probably take care to accident-proof your home as soon as she was able to get around by herself. You would cover electrical sockets, put locks on cabinets containing poisonous cleaning supplies, and store knives and scissors where prying fingers could not reach them. As the parent of a child with autism, you will need to take these precautions and more. Children with autism—and especially younger children with autism—sometimes have a combination of poor judgment and good motor skills which can lead them into dangerous situations or places.

To provide a safe environment for your child, you should periodically check both your home and your child's school for hazards. Check not only for obvious hazards like open stairwells, but also for less obvious hazards like ill-fitting window screens that could easily be jarred loose. In addition, try to keep your child's habits in mind. For example, if your child tends to mouth objects indiscriminately, as many children with autism do, make sure that lead-based paint is not used anywhere at home or at school. In addition, some of the precautions you might take with small children without disabilities make good sense for your child with autism. This can include installing plug covers, door latches, and stair gates; placing cleaning supplies and medicines out of reach; and using an intercom to listen to your child when she is in her room.

Because accidents do happen, keep a well-stocked first-aid kit in your home and make sure that you, your family members, and your babysitter all know how to use it. As further insurance, post emergency numbers prominently near every phone.

Besides protecting children with autism from unsafe environments, sometimes you must also protect them from their own self-injury. Although self-injury occurs infrequently, when these behaviors are severe they can cause physical injury or interfere with your child's education. Self-injury is most common in children with autism who are more severely retarded.

Among children with autism, self-injury can range from repeated scratching or gouging of skin and eyes, to self-inflicted bites or severe head banging. Serious damage can result either from the injury itself or from complications like infections. Head banging, for example, can result directly in serious injuries such as skull fractures, while scratching or biting may lead to infections.

Sometimes these behaviors may actually be connected with other medical problems. For instance, head banging may reflect the presence of pain from an ear infection. For this reason, you and your child's doctor should search carefully for any underlying problem that may be contributing to your child's behavior. Unfortunately, these problems can sometimes be difficult to treat. A minor skin problem, for example, may lead to scratching, which results in infection, which causes further irritation and more scratching.

As Chapters 1 and 4 explain, a variety of methods, including medicine, protective equipment, or applied behavior analysis (behavior modification) can be used to control self-injury. Often two or more of these methods are used together. These methods call for the involvement of parents, school personnel, and physicians.

Treatment of Injuries

The treatment of your child's injuries is much the same as for other children, with a few exceptions. For example, children with autism may sometimes require casts rather than bandages when it is important that an injury be protected from further damage and when the child is unable to leave the injury alone. On the other hand, when an injury is minor, sometimes it may make more sense to avoid extensive treatment; for example, avoiding sutures (stitches) for a wound if they are not really needed. You always need to consider that your child may not do what is in her own best self-interest.

Infections

Infections are a natural part of growing up. In children with autism, these illnesses can be harder to diagnose correctly, because your child may not cooperate with the doctor, particularly when she is ill. Furthermore, infections may go unrecognized for some time unless your child is able to complain of pain or discomfort or a dramatic change in her behavior suggests a medical problem. Accordingly, your observations of your child can often be invaluable in helping the physician reach a diagnosis. Signs of infection can include marked changes in your child's behavior or her appearing ill.

Repeated ear or tonsil infections can be a problem. Decisions regarding possible treatments depend on the particular circumstances. For example, with chronic ear infections, tubes can be placed in the eardrum to reduce further infections, but you must decide whether the potential benefits outweigh the risks and stress involved in hospitalization and anesthesia. In general, you will have to weigh the potential benefits of any medical procedure against the risks to your child's emotional well-being. Usually, it is best to make these decisions jointly with a physician who knows your child very well and who understands his or her special needs.

Sometimes medical procedures must be done. You really have little choice, but as this chapter explains later on, you can try to make the procedure as simple as possible. Your child, like every child, needs her childhood immunizations, periodic laboratory studies of blood and urine, and other aspects of "routine" medical care. In addition, immunization against one type of hepatitis, a form of liver infection common in institutional settings such as residential centers for the mentally retarded, may be appropriate. Ask your pediatrician for his advice.

Dental Care

All children need to take care of their teeth in order to avoid serious problems such as infected teeth and gum disease. Proper dental care may be even more important for *your* child if she is on one of the seizure medications like Phenytoin (Dilantin™) which sometimes cause gum changes. Unfortunately, achieving good dental hygiene for your child can be especially difficult. She may not be interested in toothbrushing or other aspects of routine dental care. For example, she may not like having things put in her mouth or may resist when you try to brush her teeth. In addition, she may become panicky when visiting a dentist's office.

If your child does not cooperate with the dentist, you may have to interview potential dentists to find one willing to adapt his procedures to your child's special needs. In choosing a dentist, you may find it helpful to follow the suggestions for selecting a pediatrician given later in this chapter. You can also take steps to minimize your child's anxiety and discomfort—chiefly by helping your child to become familiar with the professionals involved. In rare instances when you child is very uncooperative and has significant dental problems, general anesthesia may have to be used.

At home, you should take care to teach good dental hygiene along with other skills of daily living. And just as you would with any child, you should use fluoride in the drinking water or in the toothpaste to help prevent tooth decay in your child.

Nutrition

Children with autism often have eating habits and other problems than can jeopardize good nutrition. Some are extremely fussy about the foods they will eat. They may eat the same foods over and over again and resist new foods, or may not tolerate certain food textures. In addition, they may have frequent mealtime temper tantrums. Sometimes these problems can approach a self-inflicted malnutrition that causes other health and development problems. For example, a child who refuses to eat dairy products may not develop strong bones and teeth.

In contrast, other children with autism are compulsive overeaters. Since children with autism may also be less physically active than other children, they may gain excessive amounts of weight. In addition, some medications, particularly certain of the major tranquilizers described previously, may encourage weight gain.

Whatever your child's problems with food are, you may want to have a nutritionist do a complete nutritional assessment of your child. By talking with you, observing your child, and analyzing tests and medical records, the nutritionist can often uncover behavioral and medical reasons, as well as dietary reasons, for your child's nutrition problems. The nutritionist can also evaluate your child's need for vitamin and mineral supplements, and determine whether she is taking any medication that might affect her appetite or nutritional needs.

After completing the assessment, the nutritionist will develop a plan to improve your child's diet and her independent feeding skills. By following this plan and the behavior modification suggestions in Chapter 4, you can help to ensure that your child's nutritional needs are met.

Balancing Costs and Benefits

Obviously, you want your child to be as healthy as possible. Whenever practical, her childhood illnesses and medical conditions should be treated thoroughly. Because children with autism have special needs, though, intensive treatment of relatively minor problems may not always be appropriate. For example, the treatment of allergies should depend not only on the severity of the allergic symptoms, but also on the degree to which your child tolerates or resists the treatment. If your doctor proposes desensitizing your child by using multiple injections over a long period of time, but you know that your child finds shots particularly traumatic, the risks involved may well outweigh the potential benefits. In other words, you must sometimes decide whether your child would be better off suffering the symptoms of a medical condition than suffering the cure. To the extent possible and appropriate, your child should always be involved in discussions and decisions about her treatment.

Because medical treatment of children with autism is *not* always cut-and-dried, it is vital that you make informed decisions about your child's care. You can best do this by building a strong working relationship with the medical professionals treating your child and by becoming part of the professional team. As the next section explains, your first step is to select professionals who are sensitive to your child's special needs and who value your input and opinions.

Dealing with Medical Professionals

Dealing with medical professionals can be complicated for any parent. It's even more complicated for parents of a child with autism. While most parents occasionally have trouble getting their children to cooperate with routine medical procedures like examination of the ears, even the most minor procedures can pose major difficulties for the parents of a child with autism. For example, just sitting in the waiting room for a long time can be very stressful for both you and your child. Then, too, because children with autism often need extra time to get used to the doctor, the examining room, and the medical procedures, the usual rather rapid pace of medical care may be inappropriate for your child.

It is crucial to find health care professionals who understand your child's special needs and who sympathize with your anxiety about bringing your child to the doctor's office. If you have a good relationship with your child's pediatrician, you can often work together to anticipate problems and keep them to a minimum. For example, to reduce the stress of waiting, you could call ahead to see if the doctor is running late, or have an arrangement where you could wait in an examining room rather than with the other parents and children. And if you develop a particularly strong parent-professional relationship, you may want to ask the pediatrician to be your child's case manager—that is, to gather information from all the members of your child's health care team and coordinate the various services she needs.

Selecting a Pediatrician

You will probably not be able to pick a pediatrician for your child right out of the phone book. Since autism is relatively rare, many doctors are unfamiliar with the disorder; some, unfortunately, may even harbor misconceptions about it. To find out which pediatricians in your area have experience in treating children with severe developmental problems, you will probably have to ask around. Good sources of names are other parents of children with autism, teachers, and school staff, as well as members of your interdisciplinary evaluation team, local Association of Retarded Citizens, or ASA chapter.

Once you have the names of several potential pediatricians, your first step is to call one and request an initial visit. You may or may not wish to bring your child along; discuss this with the doctor or his staff when you set up the appointment. Whether you go alone or take your child, your main objectives should be the same: to find out how much the physician knows about autism, to get a sense of how comfortable you are with the physician and his office, and to review your child's medical history.

Do not be shy about asking the pediatrician about his experience with children with autism. Ask him whether he has cared for other children with autism or what he knows about autism. If he has not had firsthand experience with children with autism, try to get a sense of whether he is interested in learning more about the condition. Also bring up special issues—such as the use of medications for behavior modification—to see how the pediatrician's position compares with yours. Pediatricians are usually willing to discuss these issues with you. If communication problems arise during the initial interview, though, chances are you should continue your search.

Just as important as the pediatrician's knowledge of autism is the way he treats you and your child during the child's first visit. If he is rushed, your child will likely feel more anxious or frightened. If he is prepared to take an appropriate amount of time, particularly during an initial interview, future visits to his office may be less traumatic. The pediatrician's sensitivity and tact during the first visit will also provide important clues about his suitability as your child's doctor.

While you are interviewing the pediatrician, he will most likely be interviewing *you* about your child's medical history. Bring any copies of previous evaluations that you have. Be prepared also to discuss your child's past medical problems, family history, and responses to medications. Depending on your child's age, medical conditions, and the extent of previous evaluations, the pediatrician may suggest additional laboratory tests or consultations with other medical or nonmedical professionals. For example, the pediatrician may request hearing tests, special kinds of psychological tests, or communication skills tests.

You should always feel free to ask why a specific test or procedure is needed. As a matter of course, your pediatrician should discuss with you why he feels another physician should be involved. For example, if he is considering prescribing behavior-modifying medication, your child's pediatrician might wish to have the opinion of a psychiatrist or child psychiatrist. Similarly, if your child has seizures, your pediatrician might suggest a consultation with a neurologist. Generally, your pediatrician will supply you with the names of specialists he feels would be appropriate.

Specialists may be located in your area or you may have to travel some distance. The first time you meet with a specialist, your pediatrician will probably send copies of medical records or a letter acquainting the specialist with your child. You should also bring your own copies of past evaluations and other records. And just as your do with your pediatrician, feel free to ask the specialist questions—particularly if he prescribes any medications. Be sure that he provides you and your pediatrician with a report of his recommendations and that your pediatrician is kept informed of any new medicine, since it is the pediatrician who will be most involved in your child's care.

The Attitude to Look for in a Pediatrician

The most important quality to look for in a doctor for your child is a desire to try to make your visits easier for everyone. A willingness to make an effort is the key. Because children with autism typically have severe problems in communication, the doctor should spend the first part of every visit asking you about the history of your child's illness and symptoms. The doctor should also try to reduce your child's anxiety by approaching and examining her gradually and slowly. Whenever possible, he should start with the least stressful procedures and move on to the harder ones as he gains your child's confidence. For example, looking into the ears or mouth may be done after listening to the lungs or heart. This can be very difficult, but it is important that your pediatrician at least *try*.

Even the best pediatrician may occasionally have to examine or treat your child without her cooperation—for instance, in an emergency, or when your child is too upset to cooperate. Parents sometimes feel uncomfortable being with their child in such cases. If you can be present to reassure your child, then stay. If it is too hard for you to watch, explain your feelings to the physician, and wait outside.

Dealing with Hospitals and Medical Procedures

Hospital stays can be stressful for any child. For children with autism, hospitalization is especially traumatic because of the unfamiliar people, new and highly stimulating environment, and often uncomfortable tests or procedures. Accordingly, my first advice is to avoid unnecessary hospitalizations. Try to treat medical problems in an environment that is less stressful to your child. For certain minor surgical or dental procedures, such as having wisdom teeth removed, you can also sometimes arrange a one-day admission for your child so that overnight hospitalization is not necessary. Explore this possibility with your child's doctor.

Sometimes, hospitalization is simply unavoidable. For instance, if your child has acute appendicitis or has an illness that requires administration of medications by vein (IV), then she must be treated in a hospital. In these instances, you can take several steps to ease the stress of hospitalization on your child. For example, to help your child feel more comfortable, you can bring a favorite stuffed toy and see if she can wear her own pajamas. You should also stay with your child as much as possible, or arrange for friends, relatives, or school staff to take shifts with her, too. Finally, make sure you discuss your child's special needs and problems with members of the nursing and medical staff. In larger hospitals, a number of physicians and nurses may be involved; if so, find out which physician and nurse have primary responsibility for your child, then introduce yourself and acquaint them with your child's special needs. As with your pediatrician, do not hesitate to ask questions. You should feel that you are working with the staff as part of the team to provide your child with quality health care.

Teamwork is especially important in helping your child cope with unfamiliar hospital procedures like blood tests. To help prevent a crisis, you or the staff should explain to your child in simple terms what will be done. Be honest: well-meaning lies ("it won't hurt") usually cause more trouble in the long run than the truth. If your child can, and does, ask whether it will hurt, tell the truth, that it may hurt. You don't have to go overboard with this. Be honest and straightforward. Try to keep your child's mind off the procedure by suggesting an activity such as counting or listening to a favorite story. Often if you stay calm, your child will also be able to stay calm.

If your child cannot cooperate, she may have to be restrained. When this happens, having a number of people on hand helps the procedure go as quickly as possible. Occasionally, although you generally want to avoid sedation or anesthesia since there are risks associated with this, it, too, may be necessary. If so, ask that your pediatrician be involved in selecting medications appropriate for your child.

What Can You Do?

As this chapter has emphasized, the quality of your child's medical care depends a great deal on you. You can often control not only *who* cares for your child, but also *how*, *when*, and *where* that care is given. You should keep in mind that you are the person who knows your child best and the person who must make sure that your child receives good medical care. The guidelines below summarize the most important ways you can take part in the health care process.

1. **Be a careful observer.** You are often the primary source of information about your child's health. If your child has very limited communication skills, the doctor or nurse will have to rely on you for information. Frequently, some change in your child's behavior will be a clue to the beginning of an illness. By being a careful observer, you can provide the physician invaluable information.
2. **Ask questions and get information.** While you provide information to your child's doctor, the doctor can provide you with valuable information. Most physicians are sym-

pathetic to your need—and right—to know. They should be able to explain medical terms, issues, and procedures in plain English, but if you do not understand something, ask. Unless you understand your child's medical needs and problems, you cannot be sure she is receiving the most appropriate care.

You may want to keep a notebook with copies of previous evaluations and past reports from specialists. This information can be helpful to physicians who are unfamiliar with your child. You should feel comfortable talking about the results of past evaluations even if you disagree with some parts of them. By showing the physician that you can discuss differences of opinion reasonably, you encourage him to communicate openly with you. If, for some reason, the doctor resists open discussions with you, however, you should probably consider switching to another physician.

3. **Discuss and anticipate your child's special needs.** You should never hesitate to discuss any special needs your child has. For example, if your child does not do well in an unfamiliar waiting room, ask if you can arrange to be seen as promptly as possible. Keep in mind, however, that physicians take care of many children and that emergencies and unanticipated problems will happen. By calling ahead you can sometimes schedule the first appointment of the morning or afternoon. Anticipate how you can make your child as comfortable as possible. Bring activities along for your child, for instance, or coax her to play a favorite game. If you suspect that a visit may be difficult, bring other people who can help keep your child calm.
4. **Get to know the physician.** In general, your child will be less anxious about visits to the doctor's office the more familiar she is with everyone who works there. Consequently, it is best to look for a smaller practice where your child can get to know each of the doctors and nurses individually. It is also a good idea to take your child to the doctor for routine checkups when she is not ill so she can get acquainted with her pediatrician under less stressful

circumstances. While excessive visits to the physician's office should be avoided, occasional routine visits can also be helpful to you and the physician. They give you a chance to talk with the physician in a situation that is less pressured than during sick or emergency visits, and allow the physician to observe your child when she is not ill.

Conclusion

Although autism is not yet as well understood as we could wish, the disorder is steadily receiving more attention from the professional community. It is now quite possible for parents of children with autism to find medical professionals who are willing and able to work with parents as partners on a team. As a parent, you are still the person who is ultimately responsible for your child's medical well-being, but this is a responsibility you can share with competent, compassionate professionals. You need to select them carefully, then work together towards the best possible medical care and the healthiest, happiest future for your child. I hope the guidelines in this chapter will help you do just that.

Parent Statements

The problem with medication is that about half the professionals I deal with insist that I try different drugs to control Lawrence's hyperactivity and self-stimulating. The other half just as adamantly oppose drugs. I find myself leaning this direction one day and that direction the next—depending mostly on how Lawrence is acting at the time.

═❖═

Well, maybe the doctor will tell you something, and maybe he won't. He might just say, "I have another patient—excuse me." And that's nice—that's real, real nice.

I think the parent should research his understanding of autism and say to the professional, "This is what I understand. Am I on the right track?"

Parents should listen to the professionals, but they should believe in themselves. You should believe in yourself.

It's important to have support from professionals who know the field. Sometimes you have to look to someone who knows what he's talking about.

Of all the frustrations in dealing with a child with special needs, I think having to be the middle man between the medical community and the insurance companies is the worst. We've had three different companies since Doug was born, and they are all equally bad. I've spent two years trying to convince one company that they should reimburse me $125 for an equipment use fee that was part of a brain test, but I can't get the hospital to tell me specifically what kind of equipment they used.

I remember going to see a psychiatrist once, and he was late to begin with, and then when he finally came in, he said, "I haven't had a chance to look at Janet's records yet." Then we went in, and he was just kind of looking at Janet, and she was trying to read the words off books and boxes and things that were in the office. And I said, "Gosh, she's trying to read." And he said, "Well, she may read, but she doesn't understand a word she's reading." He'd only looked at her for two minutes.

I said, "Could it be that he's just a late bloomer?" My pediatrician said, "It could be, but I don't think it is." To me that was going out on a limb—saying there was something wrong with my kid. For a pediatrician, that's a very hard thing to do. He steered me, and he steered me in the right direction, and whenever I see him, I always thank him again.

Because our children have special needs, we are often advised to take them to doctors who are the best in their fields—and, consequently, who charge much more than the insurance companies want to pay for. Some doctors are wonderful when you explain the situation; I've had two that reduced their fees substantially so that they coincided with what the insurance company paid for.

One of Doug's doctors kept ordering all these tests not covered by our insurance. When I objected that they weren't necessary and would cause additional, unneeded trauma to my child, the doctor wrote my pediatrician that I had become "frantic" over the cost of these necessary procedures. Now the name of the game for me is to use my common sense. I know what tests Doug needs—how often—and which doctors will deal openly and honestly with me.

Pediatricians are different than neurologists and psychologists and psychiatrists, but pediatricians have to see the whole gamut. Pediatricians have to deal with parents on a regular basis, and to me that means that they should give you more emotional support than someone you go to once every two years for a review or something.

We had a psychiatrist who developed a real relationship with Alan. Then he had to relocate and the child started going downhill. He came back to the area and Alan started coming back up, and then it happened again, and it's been downhill ever since. We saw Alan's condition getting better, and then, bap, all the progress stopped.

We put our son on a major tranquilizer on the advice of a psychiatrist. It was a disaster. The one positive thing he's always had going for him was his speech, but after he went on medication, nobody could understand anything he said. It took us four months to withdraw him.

All medications, household cleaners, and toiletries must be kept under lock and key. There was a time when I felt I had a direct line to Poison Control. Our son has eaten plant leaves, tea bags, crayons, cough medicine, and dog biscuits.

For the first two years of Lawrence's life, he would throw up every time I tried to get him to eat anything with texture. He was turning orange from eating so much pureed baby food. He's better now, but he still has a terrible diet.

Doug simply could not handle any food with texture—he gagged, turned blue, threw up—from six months on. Yogurt became a god-send to us. When we ate out in public, it was something he could handle, and was a "normal" food. I never gave up. Now that he's three and a half, we've just started going to fast food restaurants and he happily sits in a high chair eating french fries, chicken nuggets, and milk shakes.

Once Donny got into his medicine and ate five of the pills we give him for his hyperactivity and seizure disorder. It was necessary to admit him to the hospital because he began to experience severe drunkenness symptoms and his vital signs had to be monitored. (We thought that having a special-needs kid, we would escape the horrors of substance abuse.) We concluded later how very similar in shape, color, smell, and taste the medication was to the bits of candy we were using for reinforcing good behavior.

The seizures are just one small part of his overall condition, but managing them is a major stress and financial burden.

Sometimes it's better for the kid to have a seizure once in a while than to be totally zonked out on medication all the time. You and the neurologist have to agree on the amount of seizure control that's best.

Putting him on medication for his high activity level and his seizures was tough—the side effects seemed so frightening. We talked about it and decided that if it would affect the quality of his life and learning we should try it. If he would have fifty good viable years as opposed to seventy so-so years, then it was worth the risk of side effects. Fortunately, to date he hasn't experienced any detrimental side effects from his medication.

I don't understand how insurance companies can exclude pre-existing conditions. I'm always trying to figure out what to write next to "diagnosis" so that it sounds new.

═❖═

FOUR

Daily Life with Your Child

CAROLYN THORWARTH BRUEY, PSY.D.*

When you have a child with autism, every day is a challenge. Every day you must face dealing with a child who has enormous difficulty communicating with you. Every day you must prepare yourself to reach out to a child who seems emotionally untouchable. Every day you must try again to teach your child a few more of the skills he needs.

At times the challenges you face in the daily care and teaching of your child may seem never ending. This is because of the way autism affects children. Unlike children with other types of developmental disabilities, children with autism have *disturbances* rather than delays in their development. While they may show relative skills in some areas, they will be quite behind in others. Consequently, typical how-to books on child care are difficult to apply to a child with autism. This chapter is a mini how-to book on taking care of your child with autism.

It may seem out of the question right now, but your goal should always be to make your child *part* of the family, not the *center* of it. In other words, do not allow your child's special needs to dominate your life. No child benefits from the exclusive attention of his

---

* Carolyn Thorwarth Bruey, Psy.D., is a psychologist in private practice in Lancaster, PA. She received her doctorate in psychology from Rutgers University. She is the author or co-author of chapters in several books, including *Handbook of Behavioral Family Therapy* (Guilford, 1988) and *Expanding Systems of Service Delivery for Persons with Developmental Disabilities* (Paul H. Brookes, 1988).

parents, and the rest of the family suffers if this happens. Part of your job of caring for your special child and for your family is balancing everyone's needs, including your own. It won't be easy for him, but your child with autism will have to learn to accept this balancing.

Predictability, Structure, and Routine

All children need routine in their lives. If the events of each day were different and unpredictable, almost any child would become anxious and insecure. For children with autism, routine is especially important. In fact, many children with autism have what is called an "insistence on sameness." They become quite upset about even minor changes in their routine or environment. Although this inflexibility can be highly frustrating to parents, it can reveal your child's heightened anxiety and his need for predictability. You must try to give your child the structure he or she needs, but do not let that need dominate your life.

Providing Structure and Consistency

Establishing a household routine is the first step in providing structure for your child with autism. Regardless of how much juggling of family schedules and commitments it takes, you must try to develop a routine that everyone in the family feels comfortable with, and can follow consistently. If you feel disorganized and flustered, it is likely that your child with autism is feeling the same. Unfortunately, the way your child responds to this confusion may involve a variety of bizarre behaviors such as self-injury and toileting accidents. Therefore, you need to come up with an overall "game plan" for how each family day will proceed, and then incorporate each day's requirements into it. For example, have relatively set times for when you do shopping, formal teaching, and cleaning.

If there is one word to stress regarding child care for children with autism, it is *consistency*. Many children with autism have great difficulty learning from the environment. They do not learn well from experience. One way to help them is to make the environment as consistent as possible. This rule applies to almost every interaction you have with your child, ranging from the words you choose when praising his good behavior to how you work to eliminate a behavior problem.

One reason that children with autism need consistency is that they have trouble using the same skills with different people, places, or situations. This inability to use the same skills in different areas is called "poor generalization." For example, although your child may demonstrate wonderful table manners at home, he may be a terror in restaurants. Another child might never have a tantrum when alone with his mother, but may have an average of three tantrums per hour when he is with his father.

Rather than blame anyone or resolve never to go out to eat, you should realize that poor generalization is a characteristic of autism which can be minimized if everyone responds to your child in *exactly* the same way. For example, make sure that every family member uses the same phrases when teaching your child, as well as similar verbal and tangible rewards. If everyone is consistent, then your child's behavior will be more reliable regardless of location or others in the environment.

You can introduce the concept of consistency to other people involved with your child by having them read this chapter. Then sit down together and decide how you want to respond to your child. You can set up hypothetical situations and practice on each other. You can discuss past situations and how they could have been handled better. Working together, you should be able to come up with an outline of how you want to act—both individually and as a group.

Discipline and Behavior Management

Many parents of children with autism find it difficult to discipline their child. They simply are not prepared to respond to their child's unusual behavior. One reason for this difficulty is that most child care books that cover discipline recommend strategies that would be completely ineffective on a child with autism. To make matters worse, parents must also deal diplomatically with unwanted and uninformed advice from friends, relatives, and even strangers.

There is no magic formula that will ensure that your child always behaves well. But the combined experience of other parents has shown that *behavior modification* (sometimes called *applied behavior analysis*) techniques are the most effective means of changing the behavior of children with autism. These strategies basically assume that all behavior is learned through consequences which follow the behavior. If your child likes the consequences following his behavior, he will demonstrate that behavior again. If he does not like the consequences, he will not exhibit the behavior again. Therefore, problem behaviors can be "unlearned" and appropriate skills can be substituted for them through the systematic use of rewards for good behaviors and punishment for undesirable behaviors.

The following techniques and examples should help to clarify these learning principles and increase your effectiveness in managing your child's behavior.

Catch Your Child Being Good

One strategy that is often effective is noticing and rewarding desirable behavior. Most parents feel that their job is to "catch their child being bad," when, in reality, their goal should be to "catch their child being good." This strategy requires a heightened attention on your part. After all, it is easier to notice when your child is screaming than when he is being quiet. The rule of thumb is to provide ten praise statements—"Terrific, you made your bed!"—for every one corrective statement—"Stop throwing toys."

Studies of children with autism also suggest that parents should be specific when praising their children. Use specific language—"Good, you put on your coat"—rather than general statements such as "Good job." Being specific helps your child understand the exact behavior that is being rewarded. It often helps to provide tangible rewards like food or toys in addition to praise, particularly in the early phases of teaching. Because children with autism do not find social interactions rewarding, using more tangible rewards helps to increase their motivation.

Nip It in the Bud

When your child is misbehaving, you have an immediate problem on your hands. Sometimes it is difficult to decide what to do about misbehavior once it is occurring. For example, it is natural to feel flustered and helpless when your child begins to have a loud tantrum in the middle of the supermarket. Sometimes, however, you can stop the behavior before it really starts. Often parents do not realize that they can plan ahead and develop preventive measures rather than continue to react to each crisis as it occurs. It's easier to prevent problems than to react to problems once they have already begun. Here are some preventive strategies you may find useful:

Change the Environment. There are many ways of changing your child's environment in order to prevent problem behaviors. For example, if your child tears pictures off the wall, you can put up laminated posters or paint a mural instead. If your child has toileting accidents because he cannot unsnap his pants, you can buy him elastic-waist pants.

Although these ideas may sound like common sense, take some time and evaluate your own environment and your own daily routine. With all you have to do each day, it is sometimes easy to lose sight of the simple solution. Ask yourself questions like "How is the furniture placed?" "How accessible are necessities?" "Which breakable items are an 'accident waiting to happen'?" Make changes you think might help, and evaluate whether or not the number of problems decreases. If so, congratulate yourself on having prevented some possible crises.

Notice Your Child's Cues. All children give subtle clues when they are about to begin misbehaving. Some children with autism whine, others tighten their muscles, while still others increase the intensity of hand flapping. Others may actually be extra quiet. Parents tend to assume that escalation—worsening or intensifying of behaviors—is inevitable and actually begin incorporating the "inevitable" upcoming behaviors into their plans: "Let's see, if she begins to scream in five minutes, and her tantrum is over within thirty minutes, I can still get dinner on the table."

Instead of assuming the escalation is inevitable, heed your child's warning signals and redirect him before he escalates. One strategy is to slowly begin giving him basic, simple instructions: for example, "Please hand me the book"; "Put your hands down." If your child does as you ask, praise him enthusiastically. If he does not follow your instructions, guide him through the task in a nonchalant manner. After your child has followed five to ten instructions independently, an escalation of behavior is unlikely to occur. After all, it is impossible to be "out of control" while following instructions. By providing simple instructions to follow, you stand a fair chance of successfully defusing the situation.

Describe What Is Happening. One factor that often escalates the behaviors of children with autism is confusion. Therefore, you need to explain to your child exactly what is going on in concrete, simple terms. Many parents describe the upcoming activities throughout the day in order to help their child understand. "Okay, now we are on the way to the drug store. That's the big red store near Grandma's. We will only be there for a few minutes." By telling your child what to expect in the near future, he will often feel less anxious and will be less likely to start problem behaviors.

Set Up Clear Consequences. Parents often say that the hardest part about trips into the community is the ever-present fear that their child's behavior will become a problem. In fact, that fear is often more stressful than the dreaded behavior itself.

To prevent problem behaviors from occurring, it sometimes helps to describe to your child the consequences of misbehavior before placing him in a potentially problematic situation. For example, if your child usually makes loud demands at the supermarket, talk to him before entering the store. Describe what he will earn if he speaks softly and what he will lose if he screams his demands. It is a good idea to actually have the tangible rewards easily visible during this talk. Then, if your child begins to show signs of misbehaving, you can point to the desired reward and say, "What are you working for?" Or, you can remind him what he is working for by holding up a picture of the desired reward.

These discipline techniques may not work for every child in all situations. Because every child with autism is unique, there are simply no guarantees. Although preventive strategies are not always effective, using them will at least decrease the frequency of crisis situations. You can significantly improve your home life by preventing, rather than reacting to, poor behavior. Remember, it is always harder to change a habit than to prevent one from starting.

How to Change Behavior

If you are faced with behavior that is already a habit, then you have to decide whether it is acceptable behavior. If it is not, then it is up to you to try to change it. It will take a lot of work and you may not always succeed, but in many cases you will. A complete review of each behavior reduction strategy is beyond the scope of this chapter; however, the following is a summary of some procedures that have proven effective in eliminating problem behavior. The strategies are listed in order from least to most punishing. Unless your child has a problem behavior which places him or others in significant danger, try less punitive techniques first before going on to harsher ones.

Rewards

As discussed earlier, one method of changing behavior is to systematically reward your child for any and all appropriate behaviors. That is, make sure that you praise your child every time you notice him doing well. Another method is to reward him for a *specific* appropriate behavior which is incompatible, or the opposite of, the undesirable behavior. For example, you can reward your child for being quiet if you are trying to break him of the habit of screaming, or you can reward him for playing with his toys instead of flapping his hands. As your child is rewarded for substitute behaviors, he will be more likely to show them in the future and less likely to exhibit the undesirable problem behavior. In contrast to merely "catching your child being good," you should carry out these strategies in a formalized manner—for example, by setting up a schedule of how often your child will be rewarded or by making a chart with stars earned for substitute behaviors.

Extinction

An "extinction procedure" is the technical term for the strategy of ignoring your child completely when he misbehaves. When you try this technique, you should consciously remove all of your attention whenever your child shows the problem behavior. Avoid letting your child know that you are even aware that he has displayed the problem behavior. Look away, appear distracted by something else, and make no reference whatsoever to the fact that the behavior occurred. Take care that you are not responding to his behavior in subtle ways like tightening your muscles or sighing.

Extinction is used for behaviors which are primarily attention-getting. It is based on the assumption that if you remove your attention, your child will be less motivated to display the behavior in the future. An example of using an extinction procedure would be as follows: If you have determined that your child screams to get your attention, begin to ignore each and every scream. Do not make eye contact or in any other way acknowledge that the behavior is occurring.

When trying an extinction procedure, remember that children's behavior often gets worse before it gets better. Your child will often escalate his behavior to try to get your attention. For example, if you decide to ignore your child when he whines, "Mommy, Mommy!" he may begin to scream or cry very loudly. Your job is to continue to ignore the behavior, giving the strong message, "I'm really not going to pay attention, no matter how high you 'up the ante.'" After a while, your child may finally realize that his efforts are in vain, and may find more appropriate ways of getting your attention.

Time-Out

If your child is misbehaving and your attempts to change his behavior have not worked, then try a Time-Out. Physically remove your child from the problem situation. For example, you can put him in his room whenever he has a tantrum. Or, you can have your child sit in a chair facing the wall whenever he hits someone.

Sometimes your child will misbehave because he wants to get out of something you have asked him to do. In this case, Time-Out would be the wrong response, because it just gives your child what he wants: escape from your request. (In these situations, you should first require that your child comply with your request.)

It is important to plan ahead by making sure the Time-Out room is nearby; you do not want to make things worse by having to drag your child to the Time-Out area. Be sure to watch your child unobtrusively during Time-Out, but do not talk to him or even make eye contact. You can watch him through a peep-hole to make sure he is safe. Time-Outs should not be prolonged nor should they be used when the problem behavior is potentially dangerous. For small children, the Time-Out should not last more than five minutes; for adolescents, the Time-Out should not last more than fifteen minutes.

Response Cost

In the response cost method, your child earns desired treats like stickers or pennies when he behaves well, and he loses some of these items when he misbehaves. Sometimes it helps to have your child earn items like tokens or points which can be exchanged for tangible rewards like food or toys. When using a response cost, make the give-and-take procedure as simple as possible to make sure that your child clearly understands how the system works. Also, provide plenty of rewards so that you never reach the point where your child misbehaves but has no more tokens, points, or other rewards to lose.

Aside from the methods discussed above, there are other common ways to change behavior. The publications in the Reading List in the back of this book provide a more comprehensive review of the strategies you may find useful in eliminating your child's problem behaviors. Should a dangerous or disruptive behavior persist, even with your best efforts, it is best to seek out a professional who has expertise in treating behavior problems in children with autism. You can ask your pediatrician or case manager for the names of appropriate professionals.

General Rules When Using Behavior Reduction Procedures

Children with autism often have unusual responses to discipline techniques. Regardless of the particular behavior reduction procedure you use or the specific problem behavior you are attempting to eliminate, keep the following suggestions in mind:

1. Ask yourself, "What Do I Want to See Instead?" Rather than focus exclusively on decreasing a problem behavior, you also need to choose and teach an appropriate behavior to take the place of the problem behavior. For example, if your child hits you to get your attention, it is important to eliminate the hitting and spend time formally teaching appropriate ways of getting your attention. For instance, you can teach your child to say, "Watch, please," to sign "Help," or to tap you lightly on the shoulder.

If you do not teach a substitute, appropriate skill, your child may stop the problem behavior but begin a new inappropriate behavior which serves the same function for him as the original one. For instance, in the example above, using a behavior reduction procedure alone may help your child stop hitting; however, if he is never taught an appropriate way of gaining attention, he may then begin to scream loudly for attention. Rather than continually eliminating a series of problem behaviors, teach alternative, appropriate behaviors to take their place.

2. Do Not Assume That Your Child Feels Punished. One characteristic of autism that especially frustrates parents is that many children do not find traditional "punishments" to be punishing. For example, although most children dislike being sent to their room, many children with autism prefer being alone. Therefore, using a Time-Out procedure where a child is sent to his room every time he has a tantrum may decrease tantrums in most children, but may actually increase the frequency of tantrums for some children with autism. Unfortunately, parents often inadvertently reward their child when they think they are punishing him.

The only way to determine if your discipline technique is effective is to notice its effect on the particular misbehavior. If that behavior decreases or is eliminated, then the technique is a punishment for your child. If the behavior increases in frequency, however, then you should develop a new strategy because the technique may actually be encouraging the problem behavior. For example, if your child loses a snack each time he tears paper, and his paper tearing subsequently decreases, you have chosen an effective punishment. However, if the tearing stays at the same level or increases in frequency, then, for whatever reason, your child finds losing a snack to be pleasurable. If you determine that you have chosen the wrong punishment, do not give up; instead consult professionals or the Reading List for some new ideas.

3. Ignore It If You Can. Unless your child's inappropriate behavior places him or others in danger, it is usually best to pretend that the behavior never occurred. Your child with autism will often display unusual behaviors as a way of getting your attention. Rather than inadvertently rewarding your child by paying attention to him, simply ignore the behavior and try to wait for an appropriate behavior to occur. As soon as your child behaves appropriately, praise him enthusiastically. That way, your child learns, "I get attention for appropriate behavior and not for inappropriate behavior."

4. Watch Your Own Behavior. Because children learn by imitating other people's behavior, it is important to monitor your own behavior. Do you show, or "model," behaviors you do not wish to see in your child? Picture a parent screaming, "Stop yelling!" Or another parent spanking his child while saying, "No hitting!" While all children have trouble accepting the concept, "Do as I say, not as I do," children with autism are especially confused by contradictions. Therefore, be cautious when choosing behavior reduction procedures and make sure you do not accidentally model behaviors you do not want your child to imitate.

Teaching throughout the Day

The thought may seem overwhelming, but every interaction you have with your child is a teaching situation. Even the briefest encounters can provide learning experiences. For example, when you give in to your child's demands, he is learning that he is capable of manipulating you. When you only give him what he wants when he asks for it in a clearly articulated manner, he learns that he only gets desirable items through speech. Therefore, try to interact with your child in ways that best help him learn. The guidelines below will help you capitalize on these learning situations.

Make Your Instructions Clear and Simple

Clear and simple instructions help your child understand what you want from him. Phrase your instructions according to the following guidelines:

1. Allow at least three seconds of silence before beginning the command.
2. Use brief phrasing. Give enough information for your child to understand what you expect, but do not overload him with too many words. For example, you should say, "Look at me," not, "Look" or "Lookee-lookee at mommy with your big blue eyes."
3. Use familiar phrases. In other words, use the exact wording that has proven effective in the past rather than change how you speak. If "Hands down" has worked in the past, do not switch to "Place your hands at your side."
4. Be specific. Tell your child exactly what you want him to do. Using vague phrases such as "Cut it out," or "Be a good boy" will only confuse him.

Prompt As Needed

If your child does not respond to your instructions, you must prompt, or guide, him to try to at least approximate the desired response. There are four major types of prompts. First, you can prompt through *environmental prompts*. For example, you can place an empty cup immediately in front of your child as a way to get him to say "I want milk, please." You can also use *gestural prompts*—nonverbal signals such as pointing. At times it may be necessary to provide *verbal prompts* such as saying "Start with the sheets" when you have asked your child to make the bed. Finally, if other more subtle prompts fail to produce a response, you may want to attempt a *physical prompt* and physically guide your child to respond.

To provide effective prompts, keep the following in mind:

1. Prompt after one command. Do not keep repeating yourself over and over again, waiting for your child to respond. If you do, he will learn to ignore your initial commands.
2. All prompts should be effective. Once you prompt your child, he must at least approximate the desired behavior even if you have to guide him through the entire action. If not, your child will learn to avoid your prompts—for instance, by pulling away.
3. Provide as little guidance as possible. If you can get a correct response by merely gesturing, this is better than providing hand-over-hand guidance. Graduated guidance is especially important with children with autism because they tend to become what is called "prompt-dependent"; that is, they will rely on prompts rather than respond independently. For example, your child may not respond to a command, but wait for you to guide him through the use of gestures, verbalizations, or physical prompts.
4. Don't prompt too soon. Give your child five or six seconds to begin to respond before prompting.
5. Phase out prompts as soon as possible. You can do this by gradually making your guidance more and more subtle. For example, you may begin to teach speech by pronouncing the entire word; in time you can reduce your guidance until you only vocalize the first syllable of the desired word, then the first sound. Finally, merely shape your mouth as if you were going to say the word.

Provide Corrective Feedback

At times your child may attempt a response but still respond incorrectly. At that point you need to explain both what was wrong with his response and what the correct response is. In providing corrective feedback, remember:

1. Be specific. Tell your child exactly what he did wrong. "No, that's putting the bread on the chair. Put it on the table."
2. Use a neutral tone of voice. Yelling only serves to let your child know he has "pushed your button."
3. Be brief. Do not give lengthy explanations. A short sentence rather than a long-winded correction is best.

Reinforce Appropriate Behavior

It is essential that you reward your child for appropriate behavior. Unfortunately, parents often have a hard time deciding what to use as rewards for their child because "traditional" rewards are often ineffective. Although choosing rewards for some children is more difficult, it is never impossible. All children are "reinforceable."

To determine what is rewarding for your own child, watch him closely. What does he make an effort to obtain? What items or activities interest him for longer periods of time? Consider the sensations (e.g., sight, sound, taste, touch) your child seems to prefer. Choose items or activities that provide feedback to those sensory channels. You can set up a smorgasbord of foods, toys, and household items on the table and then make a list of what piques your child's interest. It may turn out that you need to use relatively unusual objects like string and pieces of lint as rewards.

Regardless of what you actually provide as a reward, remember the following:

1. Reinforce all correct behavior with praise. Whenever possible, provide physical contact—hugs or pats on the back—as well. Even if you use tangible reinforcers such as food, pair it with praise so that your child learns to appreciate praise alone.
2. Give behavior-specific praise. Tell your child exactly what he did to earn the reward: "Good, you said your address" or "Great, you picked up the red block."

3. Be enthusiastic. When praising, make sure your tone of voice is significantly different from other times. Sometimes your child will be able to identify praise simply by the change in tone alone.
4. Give praise first, then tangible rewards, if necessary. This makes it easier for you to phase out the tangible reward in the future. For example, while you may initially have to provide food each time your child uses full sentences, make sure that you say, "Good talking in sentences!" *before* you provide the food. By having the praise so closely linked with the correct speech, your child will eventually learn to talk in full sentences merely to gain your praise.
5. Provide reinforcement immediately after your child's response so that he can easily associate the two.
6. Allow your child to choose the reward. This will help him be more interested in earning the reward. For example, you can offer your child two toys. When he chooses one, offer it to him *after* you see the behavior you are trying to teach.

Being told that every interaction with your child is a potential learning situation can be intimidating. With time and practice, however, you will be able to both teach your child and get on with the rest of your life. You goal should be to "teach wittingly," not unwittingly—to control your life with your child, rather than to be controlled by him. By incorporating the above suggestions into your daily life, your child's skills will improve through your teaching and your daily life will be more manageable.

Mealtimes

Mealtimes can be very discouraging to parents of children with autism—especially if their child's food preferences are very limited. Although not all children with autism demonstrate limited food preferences, it is not uncommon for children to insist on eating only a small variety of food. If the only foods your child will eat are bananas and pancakes, it is difficult to feel creative during meal preparation. In addition, parents often respond to this problem by allowing their child to eat his preferred foods in order to prevent any escalation of problem behaviors. Unfortunately, this only prompts new worries about nutrition.

To help your child eat a balanced diet, slowly introduce new foods during meals. At first, you may include a tiny piece of cheese on the plate. Once your child gets used to it and eats it, you can gradually increase the type and quantity of foods. Whenever your child eats something outside the "preferred list," praise and reward him enthusiastically. Encouraging a balanced diet can be a complicated process. For professional help consult a nutritionist as described in Chapter 3.

Another potential problem at mealtimes may be your child's inability to sit still for the entire meal. Parents sometimes resort to feeding their child through many "mini-meals" rather than expecting him to sit through a full-length meal. Sooner or later, however, your child will have to learn to sit at a table and finish a meal; otherwise, he will greatly limit family life and outside activities such as visits to restaurants or Thanksgiving dinner at Grandma's.

It may be helpful to teach the concept of "sitting still" first. Spend twenty to thirty minutes per day instructing your child to sit still during a seated activity like eating a snack or playing with toys. Initially, reward your child when he sits for a few seconds. Then, gradually increase the length of time he must sit still in order to receive a reward and praise. As he learns to sit still during these "formal" teaching sessions, you can begin to expect longer sitting at the mealtime table.

Toilet Training

It is common for children with autism to be delayed in toilet training. Approximately 70 percent of children with autism are also mentally retarded and therefore may learn toilet training more slowly. It is also often much more difficult for your child to understand the toileting behavior that is required or for you to find suitable rewards for proper toileting. Despite the challenges, however, toilet training cannot be put off; changing diapers when your child is five or six years old can be tiring as well as expensive.

Your major tool in toilet training is knowledge of the times your child normally relieves himself. Although some books recommend taking your child to the bathroom every five minutes throughout the day, this can be exhausting, if not impossible, for many families. Therefore, first try to mark down every time that you notice your child has soiled or wet his diaper.

After a few days of charting, you may have a relatively clear idea of your child's toileting pattern. When you have found a stable pattern, set up a rigorous toileting schedule during the times when your child is most likely to require toileting. For example, if you find your child usually has an accident during the hour after dinner, take him to the toilet every ten minutes during that hour. The rest of the day, merely encourage visits to the toilet on a less rigorous schedule.

During visits to the toilet, praise your child for remaining seated, and reward him with tangible items and praise whenever he urinates or has a bowel movement in the toilet. If he has a toileting accident during other times of the day, guide him in cleaning up the mess. As your child begins to use the toilet reliably, you can gradually begin to lengthen the intervals between visits to the toilet to every fifteen minutes, then twenty minutes, thirty minutes, and more. Most importantly, create and follow a predictable routine for toileting that includes eliminating, wiping, flushing, pulling up clothing, and washing up.

Another problem which sometimes arises when teaching toileting skills to children with autism is smearing or eating feces. This can be especially distressing to parents from both a health standpoint and the inconvenience involved. Yet many parents accept the mess and repeatedly clean up after their child. Guide your child through verbal or physical prompts to clean up his own toileting messes. Otherwise, *you* are penalized for his inappropriate behaviors, and he does not learn that the natural consequence of his behavior is to clean up the mess. At times your toilet prompting may involve hand-over-hand guidance; regardless, it is better that your child realize that there are unpleasant consequences to smearing feces. If your child eats feces, it may be necessary to monitor him during toileting, while reinforcing him frequently if he doesn't eat feces.

When it comes to toileting, many parents put off the inevitable rather than focus on their child's needs. However, with consistent effort and energy, toilet training can be accomplished. It may help to read the "how-to" books in the Reading List or to seek professional help.

Bedtime

Many children with autism have unusual sleeping patterns, such as staying up very late or wandering around the house during the night. Parents are often up half the night chasing their child or listening for any signs that their child has awakened. Such nighttime activities can only leave the parents feeling exhausted and discouraged. Consequently, the very word, "bedtime," can become anxiety-provoking.

Various strategies can help lessen this problem. First, decide what time to designate as bedtime and then stick to this decision. Your child may scream, cry, or rock in bed for hours when you insist that he go to bed on time, but do not allow this to convince you that it would be easier to let your child decide when to go to bed. Otherwise, you may inadvertently teach your child to scream, cry, or rock whenever he wishes to have his own way.

When enforcing a consistent bedtime, remember that you can force your child to go to bed, but you cannot force him to go to sleep. Therefore, your only goal is to teach your child to stay quietly in his bedroom during the night. If he tends to wake up in the middle of the night, provide toys next to his bedside. Or, buy a mat which sets off a buzzer whenever your child goes through the doorway. It is essential that he learn that wandering around the house is forbidden. If this lesson is not learned, you will have trouble sleeping at night for fear that he is drinking drain cleaner, turning on the stove, or placing himself in other potentially dangerous situations.

Regardless of periodic nighttime wandering, set a daily sleep schedule and do not allow your child to benefit from sleepless nights. For instance, allowing your child to stay home from school because he is tired only encourages more sleepless nights. Stick to your schedule regardless of how little he has slept the night before. It may also be useful to contact teachers to let them know that they should not lower their demands just because your child would not sleep the night before.

Babysitting and Respite Care

Getting time away from your child is difficult, but essential. You have a life, too. You have many roles—not just the role of parent to your child with autism. For your own sanity, you must find ways to get some time off.

Unfortunately, it can be very difficult to find a competent, loving babysitter for children with autism. Consequently, many parents either never leave their child or only leave him with relatives. This limits their lifestyles unnecessarily.

Fortunately, more and more agencies and organizations are realizing the need for specialized babysitting for children with developmental disabilities. Some agencies provide training for babysitters in specific techniques that are effective with children with autism. Contact your local resource centers—chapters of the Autism Society of America or the Association for Retarded Citizens—to find out if these kind of services are available in your area.

If there are no specialized babysitting services in your area, there are various solutions nonetheless. Do not assume that you will never be able to go off on your own. Although it may be difficult at first to leave your child with someone else, you need to do so for your own mental health.

If you cannot find a specialized babysitting service, one possible solution is to contact teachers at local special education schools which serve children with autism and other developmental disabilities. Local college students who are studying to be special education teachers also make good babysitters. Not only are they not distressed by any unusual behaviors, they are often trained in behavior management strategies. It is essential that you feel confident in your child's babysitter so that you do not worry the entire time you are out of the house. Special education students can give you that confidence.

In addition to specialized babysitting services, respite programs have been developed in various states. Although the programs differ from state to state, many pay for up to forty hours per month of respite care. The service goes beyond babysitting, however; many programs provide parent training as a part of the service. Therefore, not only do you gain time to do things without your child, you also learn strategies which will help you feel more competent when the respite worker is not in your home. Ask your local chapters of the Autism Society of America or state agencies about the respite programs that are available in your area.

Whether or not your community provides respite programs, specialized babysitting, or any other type of child care, you should set aside time for yourself. Focusing only on your child with autism while limiting your own experiences and relationships can only be detrimental to yourself, your child, and your family.

Conclusion

Having a child with autism is a tremendous challenge. Never forget, however, to treat him as a *child* first and as a child with autism second. Providing clear routines, expectations, and standards will help your child reach his full potential and enable him to become a part—and not the center—of your family's life.

Remember to take time for yourself. If you are exhausted or stressed, you will be unable to notice the little bits of progress that your child demonstrates. It is through the awareness of these tiny improvements—and the knowledge that *your* teaching helped to bring them about—that you will find true enjoyment in your child.

Parent Statements

We never feel like we can sit back and relax. We can't just sit back and relax and give up.

═❖═

When I see what he can't do, I try to go through all the different techniques. I give him a reward—I do all that good stuff—and when he still won't do it, it's frustrating.

A lot of energy is necessary.

We used to give Benjamin what he wanted when he screamed. It got him quiet. But lo and behold, when we stopped giving him what he wanted, he stopped screaming in the first place. He learned that that kind of behavior didn't work for him anymore.

He likes to run around and roll on the ground—he has to do that. I can't tell him not to do that. If my plaster falls off my ceiling, too bad. I mean, that's something that's just part of whatever he's doing in his mind—he does it.

People look at you as if to say, "My God, are you ever a horrible parent. Can't you control that child? What's wrong with you? Spoiled rotten brat. If he were mine—if he were mine, boy, would I...."

At Amy's birthday party last year, we went to a pizza place and she got scared and upset because of the moving mechanical animals. So I said, "Let me take her out and see if I can calm her down." And she said, "I don't want to go home"—just like I was killing her. I took her out and I said, "Amy, it's all right," but she said, "Get away from me!" She was pulling away from me, and these people walked by saying, "This guy's kidnapping this child." Then a police car came around the front. "Is there a problem?" "No, no, my child is just upset." So I hurried back into the restaurant. Even to this day, whenever we go to that shopping center, Amy says, "Want to go home."

What's punishment? With an autistic kid, sometimes it's hard to tell. We've found a few negative consequences that work. But we use a lot more positive reinforcement.

The discipline we used with Rachel, our other child, was completely inappropriate for Lawrence. We found ourselves using no discipline at all with him. With the help of Lawrence's teachers and a class in behavior modification, we are now trying to impose some limits on his behavior.

Being out in the community with him where people know him can be a really positive experience. They know what to expect and they know what not to expect, and they know how to talk to him—to be very direct and to help.

We thought the need for routine was part of his personality. When he went on his daily walk, he had to take exactly the same route he always followed, cross the street at the same point, stop and look at the same sign, and step on the same stone.

I help him go in the little grocery store down near the day care center. I send him up to the counter to get experience dealing with the salespeople. It's been embarrassing at times, but then, I'm sensitive. That's the energy drain.

He does not learn intuitively at all. I spend a lot of time focusing on things that will be needed later on. I don't know if the skills are age-appropriate or not, but I keep on plugging, keep on trying.

Ben goes to bed at night very easily. Of course, friends have commented that it must have taken an atomic scientist to figure out his routine. It even includes leaving the door open so he can scoot down the hall once before we close his door for the night.

With everything else involved in raising an autistic child, I tend to give the least emphasis to his diet. I figure a lot of normal kids survive on rotten diets and I have only so many hours in a day. There's just no time to force-feed Lawrence every meal.

Even if all goes well and as planned, the anticipatory stress of knowing that something could happen can cause you to avoid social situations rather than participate.

Although we're fairly new at behavior modification, I think it's going to have a positive impact on our lives. We've already seen a change in two behaviors that were really limiting what we could do with our child. Not only that, but when we're using a lot of positive rewards, he seems to pay more attention to what's going on and seems to be learning more.

Routines have become our way of life, even down to the way a napkin gets folded. If the routine gets interrupted for some reason, we pay the price—crying, screaming, you name it. And it usually takes re-doing the chore (the "routine" way) before Brian calms down.

I do not and will not tolerate tantrums from any child, autistic or not. Distraction from whatever caused the tantrum usually seems to help.

Until Lawrence was almost three years old, he woke up every couple of hours all night long. It probably put more stress on our family than anything else. He seems to have grown out of it, though. Now he usually sleeps through the night—thank God.

Behavior modification works best when your child knows that making mistakes is normal and that you still love him when he does.

An awful lot of work goes into teaching him, but there are some good pay-offs. When we can kind of relax.

The tantrums are the hardest thing to take when you're out somewhere and others are around. You really feel like the whole world is criticizing this mother who cannot control her child.

Everything we do with Lawrence—from getting ready for school to playing with his toys—follows an almost unvarying routine. Not only does it make life easier, but it makes it easier for him to learn new skills.

FIVE

Children with Autism and Their Families

MICHAEL D. POWERS, PSY. D.

Finding out that your child has autism may well be the most devastating experience of your life. It is not, however, the end of the world, nor is it the end of your family. True, having a child with autism can be very stressful and can strain families to the limit at times, but there are ways to cope. Your family will face the challenge of coping in its own way, but right from the start you should know that it can be done. Thousands of families have proved that.

Most parents worry about what having a child with autism will do to their families. In particular, they often worry whether their special child will fit into the family. Parents ask, "Will our child's behavior be so abnormal and disruptive that everyday family life will be destroyed? Will her behavior wear me down and ruin her siblings' childhood? Will normal family life come to an end forever?" These are just some of the questions that reflect common concerns of parents of children with autism.

A major part of the worry that you feel is fear of the unknown. But remember, other parents have confronted the same fears and worries. They can tell you that raising a child with autism forced significant changes in their lives that involved hard work and tremendous adjustment. But they can also tell you that they survived—and, what's more, that having a child with autism enriched their lives in unexpected ways.

Being the Parent of a Child with Autism

The single most important thing for a child with autism—more important than good education or proper table manners—is that her family stay together. If you allow your child's autism and her special needs to destroy your family or drive family members away, everyone loses. But the biggest loser by far will be your child with autism. Therefore, in setting your priorities, dividing your time, balancing everyone's needs, and deciding just how much you can take, never allow your child's needs or your devotion to her to jeopardize your family life. Raising a child with autism should not become a choice between her and your family.

Being the parent of a child with autism does require more attention to your own attitudes, hopes, fears, and expectations. How you approach family life will have a profound effect on your child with autism, your other children, your marriage, and, of course, yourself.

Feeling Good about Yourself as a Parent

There are no two ways about it: having a child with autism can be a tremendous blow to the self-confidence and self-esteem of parents. Even parents who have already raised children without autism lose confidence in their ability to be parents of a child with autism. What causes this sudden self-doubt? First and foremost is the mystery that is autism itself. Parents are faced with totally unfamiliar behavior and unique demands. They are simply unprepared for *this* type of parenting, however capable they had felt before as "ordinary" parents. Second, along with autism usually comes a battalion of well-meaning professionals to advise you on the daily care, education, integration, and medical treatment of your child. In a sense this book is part of that—professionals telling you how to do things you had previously considered instinctive. Having professionals inject so much thought and planning into every aspect of raising a child can undermine the self-confidence of any parent. Third, you lack information about what autism is like and what to expect. If your child with autism is your first, you may not have even had the chance to gain confidence from previous successes as a parent.

If you have other children, take some time to consider your successes. Remember that you are a good, loving parent who is both capable and caring. Having a child with autism changes your life, but it does not render you inept. Other parents can tell you that the same skills that help with "normal" children apply in raising a child with autism. Some parents actually decide to have additional children to help reassure themselves that they *can* have "normal" children. Parents who were planning to have more children should not let having a child with autism change their plans—except possibly if their child has Fragile-X syndrome. (See Chapter 1.)

One terrific method to bolster your parental self-confidence is to tally all the many things you do yourself for the care, education, and health of your child with autism without either thinking about it or getting paid for it. Every day you are your child's doctor, nurse, therapist, educator, and advocate, as well as her parent. You know more about her than anyone else. But because you are not labelled a "professional" you don't get credit. Make sure you give yourself that credit. You really are an expert (or fast on your way to becoming one), and you are clearly not helpless without professional help. Demand a working relationship in which your involvement, ideas, and concerns are respected. Some parents go one step further: They take on some of the jobs of professionals, either because professional services are not available in their area or because they are too expensive.

Actually, the more you learn about your child's disorder, the more your confidence will grow. In the beginning, few parents are prepared for the "scenes" that can happen when their child with autism is momentarily out of control. Most parents of children with autism come from family environments that are more tranquil than their own, and are just not prepared to deal with outrageous behavior at first. In fact, the unusual behavior and tantrums of children with autism probably do more than anything else to undermine a parent's feeling of competence. As you learn how to tolerate some of your child's more extreme behavior *and* how to stop it, however, you will find your self-confidence rebounding on its own.

Besides feeling incompetent, some parents also feel that they are constantly scrutinized as a parent. They feel that they cannot be seen getting annoyed, frustrated, or mad at their child with autism. After all, she is helpless to prevent her behavior. In addition, they feel that their friends and family do not understand just how trying a child with autism can be every day. For example, people who do not have to live with a child with autism may not understand why a parent may lose his or her temper over a seemingly small event, such as the child spinning the squeaky wheel of a toy, bouncing a ball, repeating herself, or dropping food on the floor. If these behaviors happened only occasionally—roughly the frequency a friend may witness them—they *would* be tolerable. But parents of children with autism must tolerate behaviors like these every day, sometimes every minute. Friends or professionals who don't live in your shoes shouldn't judge you when you've had it with your child with autism. You should not judge them, either. The feeling that nobody understands what you are going through does, however, make parents feel isolated. This is only one of the many reasons why sharing experiences with other parents of children with autism is so important to your emotional equilibrium.

Family Life

First You Are a Family

Families of children with autism and families of children without a handicap are more alike than different. And parents of children with autism and parents of children without a handicap are more alike than different. Having a child with autism changes your life, but does not change you. You are still the same person you were before your child was diagnosed.

All parents experience some feelings of guilt, incompetence, frustration, and tension. All brothers and sisters are jealous, angry, and embarrassed many times over the course of their childhoods. From time to time, most grandparents disagree with their children about the best way to raise their grandchildren. And almost every married couple has occasional (and not so occasional) arguments. We wouldn't be human if we didn't experience these emotions, and we wouldn't be human if we didn't express them. Having a child with autism does not change these basic facts of family life.

Feelings, conflicts, and problems are usually intensified by the demands of being a parent, sibling, grandparent, aunt, or uncle of a child with autism, but they are still normal responses that are felt by most people. Remember, even if you did not have a child with autism, you would still have these occasional problems.

This is not to say that having a child with autism doesn't change your family—in some families, the change is profound. Every single family member is affected in some way, but so is the family as a unit. For example, remember how it was before your child with autism was born. The family probably had a set of "rules" (usually assumed or informally stated) that everyone tried to follow. These rules could be as simple as: "Daddy takes care of the car and Mommy plans the meals." They could be more complex rules like: "Mommy decides I have been good today and can watch television. Daddy thinks my grades are too low to go out for Little League." By and large, the rules were understood and everybody obeyed them—at least usually. This made family life predictable, organized, and secure. If sudden changes came up—if, for instance, your younger brother moved in with you—family members tried to readjust and cope. Sometimes these adjustments were successful and sometimes they were not. Nevertheless, your family tried to cope together.

After your child with autism was born, all the stresses and changes you had previously grappled with paled in comparison to how you felt. Your ability to manage your time, or to be the kind of parent you knew you were capable of being was drastically altered. Your family had to revise its "rules" in order to cope with the extraordinary demands of your child with autism.

Whether you call it coping or adapting, you have probably already changed your lifestyle to accommodate the new demands and stresses caused by having a child with autism in the family. For example, you may have stopped going to restaurants as a family, or have changed your grocery shopping habits because your child can last only fifteen minutes.

Whatever your feelings about these changes may be, don't blame your *child* for causing them. Blame the *autism*. It is an unfortunate fact that your child has autism. But this fact is not one she would have chosen for herself or her family.

How Families Adapt through Time

There is no absolute "right" way to integrate your child with autism into your family. Most families work hard to secure the future independence of their child with autism through education and training at home and in school. They also try to maintain the mental and physical well-being of all members of the family. You can strive for this balance, too.

Just because your family faces unusual stress does not mean that the common sense approaches to family life no longer apply. Indeed, because the stress of having a child with autism can shake even the strongest family's foundation, it is especially important for you to ground your family life on solid values. This means that love, respect, communication, and hard work—all the elements that help other families run smoothly—are also the keys to your own family's survival.

Chapter 2 discussed dealing with the emotional impact of your child's diagnosis and with the immediate changes autism may cause. After the initial adjustment—after some of the shock wears off—most families settle into a stable routine. Responsibilities are understood. Each family member's involvement with the child with autism is established. And time commitments are set. For example, you have decided who has the responsibility for supervising your child Saturday mornings, or who will take her for her haircut.

Because all families grow and change over time, however, these commitments and responsibilities must also change. What worked before—the division of work, sibling responsibilities, or discipline techniques—may cease to work. As old, comfortable methods of coping become less effective, the family must find new ways to adapt. In the life cycle of the family of a child with autism, there are several important transition points where change usually occurs. Negotiating these transitions successfully requires flexibility and hard work from each member of your family.

Early Years: From Diagnosis to School Age

Moving from the initial shock of their child's diagnosis to coming to grips with the implications of her disability is often the first transitional crisis families face. Suddenly, you have to find special therapeutic and educational services, as well as physicians, dentists, and babysitters who understand and can work with your child. In addition, you have to change your own schedules or other commitments in order to devote more time to your child. For instance, you or your spouse may have to change jobs or quit working completely; one or both of you may have to postpone plans for further education.

Even when a change appears to affect only one family member, it affects everyone. Sometimes the effects are minor, as when a stone thrown into a lake creates ripples that are barely discernable on the far shore. For example, some families decide to bring a "helper" along on family vacations to assist with supervising their child. The cost involved may alter the range of possible vacation spots, but not whether vacations occur. Other times the effects of change are more dramatic. They may cause one or more family members additional stress and even precipitate a crisis, as when a parent becomes depressed over the diagnosis and withdraws from family members.

Because autistic behaviors often are more severe when your child is between the ages of two and four, your family's coping abilities may be stretched to the limits during these early years. Fortunately, however, a variety of strategies can help your family weather this stormy developmental period. You can actively seek out information about autism and learn as much as possible about ways to help your child. You can explore services available for children with autism in your community, and seek advice from professionals. And you can enlist the support and understanding of other parents of children with autism who have already gone through what you are going through now.

School Years (3-12)

When your child with autism enters school, your family must shift gears once again to accommodate her special needs. Family members need to adjust their schedules to create a predictable structure and routine for your child's day, and must also teach important daily living skills at home. For example, it will no longer be appropriate for a parent or older sibling to completely dress your child with autism. To do so would work against her future independence. Teaching her to dress herself and resisting the urge to help out and make it easier will be just one important adaptation during this phase. Independent toileting and remaining with the family on outings are two additional skills your child will need to learn.

Early in this transitional period, you may experience added anxiety if you are not certain that your child has received the best educational placement possible. Once you have found an appropriate school, however, you will probably feel more optimistic about your child's progress. Just having their child out of the house for some time each day helps parents tremendously. Working with teachers gives parents new ideas and techniques for handling their child when she is at home. And especially if parent training services are available, you will likely have more energy to work with her. Chapter 7 discusses these and other aspects of your child's educational program in detail.

During these middle childhood years, parents become more and more aware that their child's needs are unrelenting. These needs—for supervision, toileting, and eating properly, to name but a few—demand enormous amounts of time from parents. Unfortunately, there are only twenty-four hours in a day, and the time you devote to your child's special needs is automatically subtracted from the time you have for other activities. Leisure activities and time alone are often the first to be sacrificed. Some families obtain respite care assistance when they realize that the balance has tipped too far in their child's direction.

Parents with primary caretaking responsibilities frequently feel lonely and unable to relate to parents of children without handicaps. They may feel trapped, helpless, or overwhelmed. In such cases, if the other spouse can relieve some of the burdens of child care, provide companionship, and share the process of integrating the child into the community, the primary care-giving parent's feelings of isolation can be reduced. This is a perfect time to call on the support and help of your extended family as well.

One final hazard that families need to guard against during these school years is stagnation. In a well-functioning family, members mature and take on new and different responsibilities. When there is a child with autism in the family, however, the change process may be brought to a screeching halt, because you may be reluctant to change management strategies as your child matures. When this happens, adaptation ceases and there is little role flexibility—that is, family members may become unable or unwilling to switch individual responsibilities for their child. For example, one parent may always end up with the responsibility for morning supervision (dressing and toileting).

Given the extraordinary demands that having a child with autism places on a family, the loss of flexibility and opportunities to grow can be crippling. Fortunately, it doesn't have to be this way. As long as you are aware of the possibility of stagnation and alert to its dangers, you can talk about what to look out for and how to avoid it. If you notice yourself becoming unnecessarily short-tempered with your spouse or children, or that you are avoiding certain responsibilities, discuss these concerns with your spouse or family members. Try to arrive *first* at a clear definition of the problem, and *then* a solution.

Adolescence

By the time your special child is thirteen, you will be an expert on autism. You will also be older, and perhaps a bit less energetic in dealing with your child. This is understandable. During their child's adolescent years, many parents begin to shift focus and start to consider the long-term future. Issues such as vocational training, financial security, and independent living arrangements for your child may occupy more of your thinking. Often, parents channel their energies into establishing or securing these things.

Even as they concentrate on the future, however, parents must continue to cope with crises in the present. They must, for instance, confront more directly the differences between their child with autism and her peers. While other young people are hurtling toward adulthood, the adolescent with autism usually remains indifferent to social events, career plans, or the struggle for independence. The parents of a 16-year-old daughter with autism may watch with sadness while her peers begin dating and forming those early relationships that often are the foundations for marriage and children. Just talking out your feelings is the first step in coming to terms with these recurrent reminders.

At this stage, parents of a child with autism must also deal with differences between their own marriage and those of others. For example, while other husbands and wives have the chance to reconnect as couples when their teenagers leave home, the parents of a child with autism may be denied that opportunity by their child's continued dependence on them. Even the solution to this crisis—consideration of community-based living options—may precipitate its own crisis. For example, you may find that there are no suitable living options near your home and that you must consider options in other, more distant communities.

The main task of the family of an adolescent with autism is to foster the adolescent's independence in every way possible. Chapter 10 discusses this in greater detail. In addition, the family must come to terms with issues of separation, and parents must begin to redefine their own roles as parents of grown children. With careful financial planning, vocational preparation of their child, and the selection of an appropriate community living setting, most families are able to negotiate this phase of the life cycle successfully.

What Helps

The preceding sections have described how families with children with autism grow and adapt over time. But how do you handle the thousand and one minor crises that daily plague the family of a child with autism? How does a family cope with the stress of raising a child with special needs day in and day out without falling apart under the strain? Coping formulas vary, but in general, three ingredients are essential to success: positive parental attitudes, communication, and support.

Parents' Attitudes

Parents are the key to how well a family adjusts to having a child with autism. Children, other family members, and friends all follow the parents' cues. Because the way you act toward your child sets the pattern for the whole family right from the start, you must take care to treat her with love and acceptance, to set high, but reasonable goals for her, and to encourage her individuality and independence in every way possible.

Love and Acceptance. Autism is a very difficult condition for parents to deal with because of the way it affects their child. The diagnosis usually comes as a shock, and parents often grieve for some time. It is important to remember, though, that your child is not any less a person now that she has a label. She is still a child—your child. And provided you accept her as she is, she can still be just as much a part of your family as anyone else.

Accepting your child does not mean that you should ignore her autism; rather, you need to love her the way she is and see through her autism to glimpse the child underneath. Although this can often be quite a challenge, it is essential to enabling your family to adjust and cope.

All parents of children with disabilities feel some sense of loss for both that "perfect" child they could have had and for themselves. It *is* sad to think how autism will limit your child's potential. But for your child's and your family's sakes you must accept her autism as a fact of her life and of yours. All that you will accomplish by denying your child's condition will be to place a wall between you and her. In contrast, if you accept your child's autism and are comfortable with her, she can learn to fit into your family and your lifestyle. The goal is always to nurture your family; accepting your child and her autism is the first step.

A necessary step in accepting your child is to evaluate carefully just how many of her problems—and yours—are directly attributable to autism. Parents sometimes attribute *all* problem behavior to autism, whereas in reality autism is responsible for only *some*. For example, when a child refuses to eat dinner or hits her sister, it is easy for the parent of a child with autism to blame this misconduct on autism. Yet parents whose children do not have autism will tell you that these things happen in their families, too. In addition, children who do not have autism may be uninquisitive or socially aloof—characteristics associated with autism. Therefore, although autism does make your life more difficult, it is not the cause of all the problems you may experience with your child.

Acceptance should *never* be confused with resignation or capitulation. Accepting your child does not mean surrendering your child to all of autism's potential effects. Many parents are able to transform their anger at their child's autism into a determination which helps fuel a fierce desire not to let autism win every time. If you channel this determination properly, you can use it to protect your child's interests and to push her to achieve her potential. In addition, you can sometimes convert determination into the energy needed in confronting uncaring professionals or callous neighbors.

Expectations. Just like other children, children with autism are born with a wide variety of physical and intellectual abilities. True, autism will limit your child's abilities, but it is impossible to predict any child's full potential at an early age. In fact, to set limits now on what you think your child will be able to accomplish may actually prevent her from reaching her maximum potential. This is because the expectations that both you and other family members have can affect your child's achievements.

Since you are likely to spend more time with your child than anyone else is, it is essential that you project an optimistic attitude about your child's ability to master new skills. For example, if you always dress or undress your child or help her too much with dressing, she may never learn to dress herself. If your other children stop trying to play with her because you give them the impression that your child with autism will always be in her own little world, she may never learn how to act with her peers. In both cases, your child may fail because you have unwittingly not given her the chance to succeed.

Of course, expecting too much can sometimes be as frustrating as expecting too little. Just because you work hard to *teach* your child with autism basic life skills does not always mean she will *learn* them. But not trying ensures that she won't. It is far better to *expect* your child to learn—no matter how slowly—than it is to deprive her of the opportunity to try.

Do not form your expectations in a vacuum. Talk to doctors, teachers, therapists, and other parents of children with autism. It takes information and exposure to set realistic expectations. More importantly, try not to look too far into the future. Focus on the next skill; set short-term goals. After all, every small success your child enjoys today paves the way for a successful tomorrow.

Just as important as setting realistic expectations for your child is setting realistic expectations for yourself. Parents sometimes fall into the trap of feeling that their child with autism needs—and, therefore, deserves—every free moment of their day. They feel that without their constant work, their child with autism will not learn and that an hour not spent teaching a new skill is an hour wasted. The guilt that accompanies this belief is dangerous. You can't possibly do everything that *might* benefit your child with autism. No parent can. And feeling guilty about not using every spare moment doesn't help your child either. Strive for balance. Accept *your* limitations: do not feel guilty if you are not able to turn every event or free moment into teaching opportunities. For example, parents often feel that every mealtime is a potential clinic for teaching independent feeding skills. But if they are occasionally not up to the messes and tantrums that can result, parents should not feel they are failing their child. Sometimes just getting through mealtime is all any parent can manage.

Independence. It is natural to feel that your child is particularly vulnerable because she has autism. It is a natural reaction to feel sorry for your child and to want to protect her. But if you allow your child to remain too dependent on you for too long, she will eventually come to dominate your whole family's life. For the sake of your child's future as well as for your family's, you need to encourage her to function as independently as possible.

As Chapter 7 explains, one of the first steps to independence is to enroll your child in an educational program specifically geared to her special needs. Just as important, though, is the atmosphere you create at home. You and your family should *expect* your child to learn self-help skills like dressing and feeding herself. You should not rush to help her before you have given her the chance to try something on her own, and you should reward her when she asserts her independence in appropriate ways. For example, you should praise your child lavishly if she picks up her shoe and hands it to you when you are dressing her, but not if she gets out of bed in the middle of the night. The first is an appropriate display of independence, while the second is not.

What should you aim for in working toward independence? One suggestion is to work for skills that make it possible to take your child with autism out with you in public. The skills necessary to take your child to the store, a restaurant, or other public place—following simple directions, avoiding inappropriate behavior, and not throwing tantrums—are important in freeing a family from being trapped at home by their child.

Communication

Although parents can often ease their family's adjustment to the child with autism by working to maintain positive attitudes, open and honest communication is also essential. Remember, raising a child with autism is a new experience for everyone involved. Not only is it important for family members to exchange information about what works and what doesn't work, but it is also important that they share their feelings about having a child with special needs in the family.

You should encourage everyone in your family to vent his or her emotions and to listen without judging to what others have to say. Set an atmosphere of acceptance and allow family members to express negative feelings such as hate, anger, fear, worry, and guilt, as well as positive ones. If you share and acknowledge these feelings, you can often work through them together.

Occasionally, family members—especially children—feel so guilty about the anger and frustration the child with autism arouses in them that they suppress their emotions completely. If this happens, reassure them that it is normal to feel as they do, but that it is also healthy to express themselves. Especially with your children, try taking the lead by explaining that *you* are mad or frustrated at times; honesty on your part will create a climate for honest communication from all of your children.

You can urge your children (or arrange for them) to meet with other siblings of special-needs children to work through their feelings. Organizations in your community may sponsor a sibling group, or you can form your own informal group with children of members of your parent support group.

Whatever you do, do not ever accept silence from family members merely because you are afraid they may voice the same negative feelings you are experiencing. Nothing you can do can prevent these feelings, and, left to fester, they may breed serious long-term problems. Sharing emotions with members of your immediate and extended family is the first and most important step in nurturing the supportive environment your family needs in order to grow and thrive.

Support

You will also want to reach out to other parents of children with autism for support. As mentioned earlier, there are few experiences that can make you feel quite so alone as having a child with autism. The isolation can be overt—for example, when friends and family don't visit as often—or it can be subtle—for example, when parents feel that friends and family can't understand what life with a child with autism is really like. In any case, nothing can shatter the isolation quite like talking to parents who have already been there. Not only can you draw strength and inspiration from other families' stories, but you can also gain a great deal of practical information on coping and on the special-needs resources in your community. And you may even find a friend for life.

For help in locating a parent support group, call the local affiliate of the Autism Society of America listed in the Resource Guide in the back of this book. They can direct you to a variety of publications about autism and to the resources and people in your area who can help you. In addition, the Resource Guide lists other organizations you can contact for information about parent groups.

Your child's teacher and professionals such as the psychologist and social worker described in Chapter 1 can also be a tremendous source of support. Because their advice is based on the collective experience of many children and families, they can help you confront and resolve your questions and worries, and also suggest ways for you to cope with your feelings. Nothing works better to relieve worry about a problem with your child with autism than solving that problem. Often just knowing there is someone you can count on to help solve problems can calm your anxiety.

Even with the support of family, friends, and professionals, there still may be times when communication fails and the stress of raising a child with autism completely overwhelms you. If this happens, you should not hesitate to turn to a psychologist or other mental health professional for help. A counselor will be able to reassure you that your feelings are not only real, but justified, and can also provide you with some of the coping skills you need to regain your emotional balance.

What Hurts

Some of the ways that families of children with autism try to adapt do more harm than good. Almost invariably, these ways are "errors of the heart"; the result of good and loving, if misguided, intentions. The three common traps that parents of children with autism should beware of are overinvolvement, overprotectiveness, and rejection.

Overinvolvement

Sometimes one parent gets so wrapped up in the child's need for extra supervision and attention that he spends almost all his waking hours trying to care for, stimulate, and teach the child. Ironically, this overinvolvement may result in a relationship that actually encourages dependence, not independence. The parent may become so skilled at anticipating the child's every need that the child has no incentive to learn appropriate communication skills or good behavior. For example, recognizing that a tantrum after awakening from a nap is a request for juice, and then always providing the juice when the tantrum occurs, will never help your child learn a more appropriate way to request juice.

Not only is overinvolvement self-defeating, but it may also threaten your marital relationship or make your other children feel neglected. After all, when one parent becomes consumed with the needs of a single family member, little time or energy may be left over for his spouse, other children, or himself. Occasionally, neglected family members may direct pent-up anger and resentment at the overinvolved parent or at the child with autism, who is seen as the cause of parental overinvolvement. If you think you may be neglecting your spouse or other children, check it out with them. Establish an open line of communication so that you—and they—have permission to discuss potential overinvolvement. If their complaints persist, it may be that you are not achieving the proper balance, and that professional assistance may help you regain it.

Overprotectiveness

It is a natural impulse for parents to want to shield their child from potential harm. Sometimes, though, parents can go overboard. They may come to view their child with autism as too sick or too disabled to do anything for herself, and may rush to satisfy her every whim.

Even though this overprotectiveness is usually motivated by concern and affection, the results can be disastrous. The child with autism may develop into a little tyrant who rules the family with an iron fist, throwing a tantrum at every limit or demand placed upon her. In addition, the overprotected child with autism often makes her parents feel very inept whenever they ask her to do something and she fails to comply.

If you feel your child is in danger of developing into a little tyrant, now would be a good time to talk to other parents who have "been through it all" and made it to the other side without a little tyrant. They may have tried-and-true suggestions, or can perhaps recommend a professional who was especially helpful to them.

Rejection

Most parents find autistic behaviors like self-stimulation and self-injury very upsetting to watch. To cope with the distress this behavior causes them, some parents may pull away emotionally and physically from their child, ignoring both the child's problems *and* special needs. In its most extreme form, this detachment becomes outright rejection. Ultimately, this hurts both the parents and the child by interfering with the development of the parents' sense of competency and self-esteem. Professional assistance to help the parents regain control of the situation is often very helpful.

Keeping Perspective

Having a child with autism does not magically transform you into "Supermom" or "Superdad," with boundless energy, miraculous teaching abilities, or infinite patience. In addition to all you face with your child with autism, you still have to earn a living, eat, sleep, take care of your other kids, and clean the house. Like everyone else, you have good days and bad days. Many parents of children with autism, however, lament that the world no longer sees them as the mortals they really are, but regards them as somehow gifted. This can set up a very high standard that can haunt parents with guilt. Helen Featherstone, in her fine book, *A Difference in the Family: Life with a Disabled Child*, perhaps states this paradox best:

> Suppose I, an ordinary person, am walking alone beside an icy isolated river and see someone drowning. I have two options: I can jump in and try to save him (risking death myself), or I can agonize on the shore. In the first case I am a hero; in the second a coward. There is no way I can remain what I was before—an ordinary person. As the mother of a profoundly retarded child, I felt I was in the same position: I had to look like a hero or a coward, even though actually

I was still an ordinary person.*

Even though being the parent of a child with autism may require superhuman effort at times, you are still the same person you were before. Set your own goals, standards, and rules. Never forget that what matters is what you think of yourself, not what other people may think.

Brothers and Sisters of Children with Autism

"As close as brothers." "Sisters under the skin." Expressions like these reflect the special bonds of love and loyalty that inextricably draw siblings together in the best of relationships. When your children were small, you may have cherished the hope that they would develop one of these relationships, or, at the very least, that they would become fast friends. Now that your child has been diagnosed with autism, however, you may worry more about the negative effects she may have on her siblings' lives.

Your child's autism will definitely affect the way she relates to her brothers and sisters and the way they relate to her. Do not assume, however, that all these ways will be bad. Far from it. Having a sibling with autism is stressful and enriching, exasperating and fun, distressing and rewarding. In other words, it is not that different from being the brother or sister of any other child. This section reviews the effects—both good and bad—that children with autism have on their siblings, and focuses on what you, the parent, can do to encourage healthy relationships.

Children's Feelings

As soon as they begin to take an interest in the world around them, your other children will have thoughts and feelings about their special sibling. At first, they will notice only that their brother or sister takes longer to learn basic skills like talking, playing with toys, and toileting. Gradually, however, they will begin to under-

---

* Helen Featherstone, *A Difference in the Family: Life with a Disabled Child* (New York: Basic Books, 1980), pp. 83–84.

stand that their brother or sister is handicapped. What follows is a summary of the thoughts and emotions typically experienced by siblings of children with autism.

Preschool Years. Young children are very perceptive, so you can expect them to pick up on your anxiety about your child with autism. They may recognize developmental differences and try to help teach skills, but they will not be able to understand what autism is. They may ask questions. They may also resent the time you spend in home-teaching or early intervention programs with their sibling with autism. In response to this resentment, the nondisabled sibling may regress in order to gain your attention, or to convince you that they, too, are developmentally immature and deserving of special treats or toys. Sometimes young siblings begin to talk less maturely or to bed-wet even though they have been toilet trained for months. Preschoolers tend not to discuss openly their feelings about having a brother or sister with autism. Because they have not yet learned to be judgmental, however, they will accept your child with autism as she is. Best of all, they will likely fall in love with their sibling.

School Years. Somewhere between the ages of three and six, your children will probably begin to wonder what is "wrong" with their special sibling. They may worry about catching autism, or wonder whether there is something the matter with them, too. In addition, they may feel guilty about any negative thoughts they have toward their sibling. For example, the envy they feel about the extra time you spend with your child with autism can arouse feelings of guilt. Sometimes children attempt to make up for their sibling's problems by trying to be especially well-behaved. They may become excessively helpful and obedient beyond limits that are good for them, for your family, or for the child with autism. Other children may respond by deliberately misbehaving as a way to draw your attention to themselves and away from their sibling.

For most of their elementary school years, your other children will have conflicting emotions about their special brother or sister. One moment they may feel good about being needed by their sibling with autism, and the next moment they may think she is a pest. When other children tease their sibling, they may defend her, and then again, they may not. They may resent having to do chores that their brother or sister is unable to do, or complain that you are unfairly babying your child with autism.

Adolescence. More than anything, most teenagers want to conform—to fit in with the right crowd. They become acutely aware of even minor differences between themselves and others. As a result, your teenaged children may be embarrassed by their brother or sister with autism when friends and dates come to the house. Although they still love their special sibling and want to help care for her, they may be torn by a natural desire for freedom and independence. They may resent all responsibilities imposed on them, not just responsibilities for their sibling with autism. In addition, they may begin to worry about their sibling's future, and what effect it may have on their own.

Dealing with Your Children's Emotions

Obviously, being the sibling of a child with autism can be just as stressful as being her parent. By and large, your other children will try to follow your lead in coping with this stress, but their adjustment may be complicated by conflicting emotions. They may feel ambivalent, for instance, about helping a sibling who is so disruptive and takes up so much precious parent time. They may at times feel unloved, rejected, embarrassed, or neglected, but attempt to hide their feelings or act them out in inappropriate ways. This means that before you can help your children deal with their emotions, you must first decipher what they are feeling. To do this effectively takes patience, observation, and listening.

Information. Parents do not have a monopoly on fear of the unknown. Brothers and sisters of children with autism also worry about the ways in which having a sibling with autism may affect them and their family. They may wonder whether they will always have to walk their sibling to school, for example, or worry that they may somehow cause her autism to continue or to get worse. As they grow older, they may begin to worry about having a child with autism of their own, or about caring for their special sibling in the future.

The best way for you to anticipate and deal with such concerns is to provide your children with as much information about autism as they can absorb. Try to be as honest with your children as possible, but be sure that you present the information in a way that respects their ages and cognitive development. For example, don't tell your five-year-old son that his sister has a problem with social interactions. Tell him instead that his sister doesn't know how to play and has trouble learning. Timing is important, too. A lot of information all at once can overwhelm your child. Try to recognize those times when just a little information now will plant a seed for more detailed information later. And whatever your children's ages, be prepared to correct the erroneous information they will undoubtedly pick up from classmates and adults.

Since these coping problems are so common among siblings of children with autism, what can you do about them? Rune Simeonsson and Donald Bailey, Jr., both child psychologists at the University of North Carolina, suggest that parents and professionals can support and foster growth across three areas of psychological adjustment with siblings of children with handicaps:

1. Help your other children recognize and accept that their sibling's development is, and will be, uneven. Despite growing tall and strong, she may still be unable to communicate like others her age.
2. Help your children resolve any personal comparisons they are making with their sibling who has autism, and help them see and accept the differences between all of the children in the family.
3. Help your children recognize their competence with their sibling with autism. When siblings recognize that they are not controlled by the whims of someone they may not understand, and further understand that they can make a positive difference in their brother's or sister's life, then their real and perceived sense of competence is enhanced.

Balance. Always remember that your child with autism is only *part* of your family, not the center of it. Even though your other children may not demand the emotional and physical resources their special sibling does, they still have needs that should not be ignored.

It can be quite a juggling act, but it is important that you balance the many demands on your time so that all your children get their share of parental attention and have their fair share of responsibility. Otherwise, siblings may become extremely jealous of the time you spend with your child with autism and resent her ability to obtain special treats for doing things they are expected to do automatically.

In addition to dividing your attention equitably, you need to impose a fair balance of household responsibilities. Children will not long tolerate being the servant of a sibling with autism without developing resentment. *Everyone* in the family should have to pull some weight; each according to his or her abilities. The key is to have expectations—to make your child with autism help in *some* way. It is almost more important for your children to feel you have expectations than it is for your child with autism to do a great deal.

An important part of balancing family responsibilities is to avoid turning one or more of your nondisabled children into a "parental child" by giving him or her too much responsibility. On the one hand, you should encourage brothers and sisters to take an active part in their special sibling's educational and therapeutic programs—many parents find that doing so actually strengthens the bonds between their children. On the other hand, take care that responsibilities do not interfere with the emotional growth and development of the nondisabled sibling. For example, when a sixteen-year-old sister does not socialize with friends because she feels her mother depends on her to help with her brother with autism, it is not a healthy situation. Even if children seem ready to take on parental roles, they will resent being asked to grow up too quickly.

Balancing goes one step further: It is common advice—advice even given in this book—to celebrate the small victories of your child with autism. And this is good advice; parents of children with autism need to focus on small gains. You should remember, however, that your other children deserve the same treatment. They too have small victories of their own, and need to be noticed. Don't take their development, growth, education, or other achievements for granted. Celebrate *everyone's* victories—accomplishments are accomplishments regardless of whose they are.

Organization. It is all very well to stress the need for balance in your life, but how can you possibly cope with the seemingly endless demands on your attention? After all, there is only so much of you and only so many hours in the day. For many parents, the key lies in organizing their time. Having a child with autism can make this rather complicated, but it is worth the effort.

Of course, even the best-laid plans can be disrupted. Children do not conveniently schedule their crises. They scrape their knees, have nightmares, and fight with one another without advance notice, and when they do, they need your immediate, undivided attention. Barring unforeseen circumstances, however, there are many ways to manage your time so that your family runs more smoothly. Here are some ideas:

- Keep track of how much time you spend with each child. Try to spend some time alone with each child and your spouse.
- To prevent your other children from feeling neglected, try to schedule the periods that must be spent exclusively with your child with autism for times when siblings are not around.
- Encourage group play among all your children when they are at home.
- Keep your children busy. Schedule play times, chores, and outings.
- Enlist the help of others. Organize car pools and play groups and trade babysitting chores with other parents.

Individuality. One of the constant threads running through this book is that you should treat your child with autism as an individual. The same holds true for your other children. They need lives outside of their family. If their identity is not to be limited just to being the brother or sister of a child with autism, they need friends, social acceptance, and non-family responsibilities. Encourage them to try out many roles—athlete, artist, musician, astronomer—wherever their interests and talents lie. When children feel good about themselves as individuals, they are more likely to feel good about being part of a family with a special member and to support both you and their sibling with autism.

Specialness. Besides encouraging your other children to be individuals, you should also try to give them a sense of their own specialness. Help them to understand that having a special sibling also makes them special—in the positive sense of the word. Point out ways they make an important difference in their sibling's life, for instance, or ways they help keep the family running smoothly. Praise their compassion, their coping abilities, and the extra responsibilities they take on. In short, let your children know that they are needed by you and their special sibling, and that their contributions are appreciated.

At the same time you are praising your other children's specialness, you need to recognize that, just like you, they may from time to time yearn to be just ordinary. Being the sibling of a child with autism sometimes brings with it unwanted distinction outside the family and a lack of attention in the family. Helen Featherstone writes:

> Listening to normal brothers and sisters talk about family life, I am struck by a paradox about disability. In the world outside the family, in school and in the neighborhood, children long to fit in, to resemble everyone else. In these contexts...a sibling's disability stigmatizes them as different. Inside the family, however, each child wants to be special. Each needs assurance that he occupies a unique place in the family circle. Here disability confers a certain advantage, a passport to special attention, recognition, and privileges. In consequence, many able-bodied brothers and sisters remember a childhood tinged by jealousy and resentment.*

* Featherstone, p. 47.

There is no foolproof advice for overcoming this dilemma. Common sense, however, dictates that parents give their nonhandicapped children the chance to be special when they want that and the chance to be just like everyone else when they need that.

Dealing with Problems

No matter how carefully you follow the suggestions in the preceding pages, having a child with autism in the family will inevitably create problems for your special child's brothers and sisters. Other children may wound them with teasing or cruel remarks about their sibling, and adults, too, may sometimes confuse them with insensitive comments. As peer acceptance and social interaction become more important to your children, they are likely to be increasingly embarrassed by their sibling. Furthermore, at some point in their lives, your children are bound to resent the added responsibilities that go with having a sibling with autism, and they may fervently wish that their family were not "different."

Although your first instinct may be to try to heal your children's emotional pain yourself—to set things right by telling off everyone who makes your children feel bad about having a special sibling—you should fight the urge to rescue. Instead, teach your children to cope with their feelings themselves. Acknowledge your children's hurt and confusion, but also let them know that you have confidence in them and their ability to handle those hurts. Share with them hurtful experiences you have had, and explain how you responded. And by all means, make sure your children understand that the autism is to blame for their sibling's behavior, not the sibling herself. Not only is it healthier for your children to turn their anger and resentment away from their sibling and toward her autism, but it can also help to reduce their feelings of guilt.

Remember, no parent can solve every problem for his or her children. Even attempting to do so can often do more harm than good. Just as you can adversely affect the development of your child with autism by trying to do too much for her, so, too, can you prevent your other children from learning to cope on their own. Generally, if you keep the lines of communication open and reassure and support your children with information and understanding, they will develop their own effective methods of coping—and without losing their love for their sibling or the friendship of their peers.

If your children have a great deal of trouble adjusting to their special sibling, you may want to consider counseling for them. Talking to an objective, caring professional can be just as helpful for children as it is for adults. Do not deny your children this help because you think that all problems need to be solved within the family. They don't. To seek help for your children is not an admission of failure, but an expression of love and concern. Sometimes giving your children room to adjust with the help of a counselor can accomplish what you cannot.

Your Child with Autism and Your Marriage

Every marriage is unique; every relationship, a highly original blend of shared and divergent values, interests, and experiences. Regardless of each spouse's individual strengths and weaknesses, though, having a child with autism tends to create certain predictable problems in most marriages. All couples, for example, find that coping with their special child's needs reduces the time they have to devote to one another. Relationships are further complicated by the strong, conflicting emotions each partner must deal with as the parent of a child with autism. And all couples are beset by worries about their child's future and the long-term effects her continued dependency may have on their marriage.

In general, if your relationship with your spouse is strong, your marriage can withstand the added stress that goes with having a child with autism. Some parents even feel that their child has drawn them closer together. Whether having a child with autism will have a positive effect on *your* marriage depends on the support you and your spouse give each other.

As discussed earlier, one of the best ways to support one another is to openly share your feelings about your child with autism. Remember, it is normal for your emotions to run the gamut from love to hate; from hope to despair. In most cases, if you share and acknowledge these feelings, you can sort them out together, or together you can seek someone to help you cope.

If one or both of you falls into the trap of misdirected anger, however, it many be somewhat harder for you to rescue one another emotionally. As Chapter 2 explained, parents often become angry after learning that their child has autism. They may fume at God, the obstetrician, or at the genetic counselor who did not recommend against having another child. They may also be angry at the child for all the expense and sleepless nights she costs the family. It is *absolutely* normal for parents to experience anger and frustration temporarily in resolving their feelings about their child and their new circumstances. But it is when a spouse's anger continues over time and becomes directed at his or her partner that it is most damaging.

Sometimes one parent will blame the other for the child's autism—"If you hadn't drunk so much wine during your pregnancy, this never would have happened"; or, "This is all due to the marijuana you smoked in college." If the accused spouse believes the charges are true, he or she may feel tremendous guilt, while the accusing spouse may withdraw emotionally and leave the guilt-ridden spouse feeling even more angry and alone. In another scenario, a husband or wife may be furious at the child with autism for disrupting career and future plans. Because the husband or wife feels very guilty about being angry at a little child with such a severe handicap, however, he or she turns that anger on his or her spouse. Constructive communication breaks down, and emotional withdrawal follows.

Some couples manage to avoid the pitfall of misdirected anger, but still find themselves drifting apart because the demands of raising a child with autism leave them too exhausted to work on their relationship. As Chapter 2 discussed, the key is not to *find* time for each other, but to *make* time. As mentioned before, everyone in your family suffers if your child with autism destroys your marriage, and the biggest loser would be your child with autism. Staying together, then, should be your highest priority, even if that affects the time you can spend teaching, training, and working with your child with autism.

You may also want to investigate opportunities for respite care in your community. Respite care is skilled child care provided by people trained to work with special-needs children. It can be for a few hours each week, or for a weekend. Some agencies provide care in your home, while others have the child brought to a respite worker's home. Public and private agencies generally provide this service. Check with the local Autism Society chapter or the Association for Retarded Citizens in your area for availability. Sometimes, parents find that a few hours or a weekend alone goes a long way in restoring energy.

Sharing the responsibility for caring and working with your child with autism is a very useful way for couples to cope with the added stress. No spouse should feel that he or she has been consigned to endless daily care. Allow each spouse to have successes inside *and* outside the family. It is important that each spouse retain the image he or she had before your child with autism was born. In some marriages, it is helpful for spouses to attend separate support groups. This allows each to voice concerns and feelings they may hesitate to confide to their spouse.

One final stress that you, like all parents of children with autism, must cope with is your uncertainty about your child's future. Whether you express your concerns or not, you and your spouse probably worry constantly about your child's education, her prospects for employment, and her ability to live independently. Although you will want to find more information about these subjects later, in the meanwhile you must learn to live one day at a time. Concentrate on the small gains your child makes, and rejoice in her personal triumphs. And whatever you do, don't spend so much time thinking about getting your child to her destination that you forget to enjoy the parts of the ride that truly are fun.

Single-Parent Families

Sadly, some marriages fail. Although there may be a number of reasons for marriage failure, a child with autism obviously puts a great deal of stress on any relationship. Sometimes a marriage—already teetering—will topple under the weight of this extra stress. When this happens, one parent is left with the major responsibility for raising the child with autism. Of course, single-parent families with children with autism can also result from a variety of other causes.

A single parent raising a child with autism experiences the same range of reactions and needs that couples do. Coping, however, may be considerably harder, because the single parent must make important decisions alone. You may be able to lessen the burden somewhat by asking someone you trust to serve as your sounding board. You could turn to a close friend, a member of the clergy, your brother or sister (but *not* the siblings of the child with autism), a therapist, or a social service worker. What matters is that you have someone to talk to who will be available on a consistent basis—someone who will offer you support, but who will not be afraid to question your decisions, either. Often just knowing that there is someone with whom you can discuss your concerns can help reduce some of the overwhelming feelings of being on your own with your child every day.

Conclusion

The secrets to adapting to a child with autism are really not secrets at all, but just common sense. Just as in any family, hard work, love, acceptance, communication, and support can all help. If you try to see your child with autism as a child first, and then as a person afflicted with autism, you can go a long way toward normalizing family life. True, your child with autism has special needs and strengths that are probably very different from the needs and strengths of other family members. But she is still an individual, with her own unique contributions to make to your family. With hard work and encouragement, she can become a vital part of your family. And with your loving, educated leadership, your family can become a team.

The realization that a child's autism will not go away is a severe blow for many families. It may seem incredible to you right now, but most families survive. They also work, play, laugh, cry, fight, and grow—just like other families. But for the family with a child with autism, there is much more. Having a child with autism in the family teaches lessons of a higher order, lessons other families may never have the chance to learn: love, commitment, mercy, contentment, sacrifice, and dignity. In short, in my experience working with families, I have found that having a child with autism often ennobles parents and siblings. Clara Claiborne Park, in her outstanding book, *The Siege,* says it well:

> This experience [raising a child with autism] we did not choose, which we would have given anything to avoid, has made us different, has made us better. Through it we have learned the lesson that no one studies willingly, the hard, slow lesson...that one grows by suffering....I write now...that if today I were given the choice to accept the experience, with everything that it entails, or to refuse the bitter largesse, I would have to stretch out my hands—because out of it has come, for all of us, an unimagined life.*

References

So much of what I have learned about families has been learned from the best of teachers: the families of the children with autism in New Jersey and Maryland who have opened their lives to me. I owe them a debt of gratitude. In addition to my own work, I must acknowledge the debt to others whose writings I have incorporated into this chapter:

Featherstone, Helen. *A Difference in the Family: Life with a Disabled Child.* New York: Basic Books, 1980.

Harris, S.L. *Families of the Developmentally Disabled.* Elmsford, NY: Pergamon, 1983.

Park, Clara Claiborne. *The Siege: The First Eight Years of an Autistic Child with an Epilogue, Fifteen Years Later.* New York: Atlantic Monthly Press, 1982.

Parent Statements

You have to be Superman personified.

* Clara Claiborne Park, *The Siege: The First Eight Years of an Autistic Child with an Epilogue, Fifteen Years Later* (New York: Atlantic Monthly Press, 1982), p. 320.

I have to play the strong role. I never have time for self-doubts. I had to convince my husband—which I still haven't done—that this is an appropriate label.

In family dynamics, you want to keep everything even-keeled. It could be a lot worse. My husband could say, "Hey, there's something wrong with this kid," which he has never done. We've always known there was something going on. All we've done is disagree on the label. We agreed to disagree on the label, but we agree that something is wrong.

Having a child with autism makes a strong marriage just slightly weaker. I'm afraid to think what it would do to a weak marriage.

Lawrence has had a positive and negative effect on our marriage. On the positive side, he forced two extremely independent people to lean more on each other. Before we had Lawrence, we both felt we could handle anything life threw our way—even without each other. After Lawrence, we changed our minds in a hurry. On the negative side, raising Lawrence leaves us very little time or energy to devote to each other.

I'm not going to send Tommy to a Cub Scout meeting without one of us being there. I'm chicken to do that—to stick Tommy in a situation where nobody knows him or can cope with him. Maybe I'm thinking of the person who's leading the group of kids—it's not fair to them.

We still hug. We still give kisses and love.

I get real angry here in my living room talking about this, but I don't get real angry out in the world.

Our two daughters have been able to accept him as he is, but his brother has had a very difficult time. We should have had family counseling when we started down this road, but I put up this shield all around us and vowed to take care of everybody. It was a huge mistake.

Our daughter seems to take Lawrence's handicap in stride. So far she's managed to enjoy a normal, active life. And I think it's done her some good to be exposed to Lawrence and to the kids in his school. She's very comfortable around handicapped kids, while most of her peers are frightened of them.

There is no way our family could remain intact if it weren't for my husband's commitment, love, and support. He has fed the boys, gotten up from his much needed rest, changed diapers, given baths, and helped with housework.

Brian's autism has put a strain on our marriage, but it becomes less of a strain when we start to see some improvement.

═❖═

I'm worried that my other daughter, Becky, will think she'll have to take care of Janet. She may feel that pressure. Maybe she'll resent her, I don't know. I'll worry about that later.

It was a relief to finally have something concrete to tell Rachel. We could see she wondered why the mentally retarded kids in Lawrence's early intervention program seemed to enjoy her company, while Lawrence barely knew she was alive.

I don't want to lay the burden of guilt on my daughter of her having to take care of Gary, but I want her to do that. That's real. I want to sensitize her, and for her to be loving and caring. I want her to do it because she wants to, not because she feels guilted into it.

When Janet was out one day and one of the kids pushed her, Janet just kind of stood there, and Becky went up and pushed the other kid. It was like she was saying, "You don't push my sister." So, it's kind of automatic for her. I think they just know, you don't do that, not until they can push back.

I was a teacher of young children by profession and not being able to draw on my skills as I'd done for other children was a terrible blow to my self-worth. I'd unraveled the world of learning for so many children, but my efforts in teaching Donny were, at best, limited. This was a hard pill to swallow.

It's important to have another life with the parents of your other children's friends and with your co-workers, but only the parent of another autistic child truly means, "I understand." Meeting other parents is one of the most important things you can do for your sanity.

When we explained to our daughter that autistic kids often have trouble responding to other people I think it was a relief to her. Sometimes I wonder if she didn't blame herself for their lack of a relationship.

SIX

Your Child's Development

SANDRA L. HARRIS, PH.D.*

Mothers and fathers the world over delight in watching their children grow and learn. After all, sharing in a child's achievements—his first faltering steps and first garbled words—is one of the greatest rewards of parenthood. What makes this complex process of growth and change, called *development,* especially exciting for parents is the knowledge that each new skill their child learns takes him further along the road from dependency to maturity.

In observing their children's development, most parents cannot help comparing their children's achievements with other children's. This is a natural impulse. It is also natural for parents to feel proud and elated when their child progresses faster than normal; fearful and discouraged when he lags behind. As the parent of a child with autism, you may find this process of comparison disheartening indeed.

If your child has just been diagnosed with autism, a little

* Sandra L. Harris is Professor and Chair, Department of Clinical Psychology, Graduate School of Applied and Professional Psychology, Rutgers University. She is also the Director of the Douglass Developmental Disabilities Center for children with autism. Dr. Harris received her Ph.D. from SUNY—Buffalo, and is the author of *Families of the Developmentally Disabled: A Guide to Behavioral Intervention* (Pergamon, 1983) and co-author (with J.S. Handleman) of *Educating the Developmentally Disabled: Meeting the Needs of Children and Families* (College-Hill, 1986).

knowledge about the ways this disorder affects development may calm some of your anxiety. To begin with, it can help you to learn what lies in your child's future and what his special needs will be. And it can help you even more to learn that your child, like every child, *is* going to grow and change in the years ahead, and that you can do a great deal to help him reach his maximum potential.

This chapter provides you with some of the information you will need in order to influence your child's development most effectively. It will introduce you to the basics of human development and help you to understand not only how autism affects your child's development, but also how a good educational program and consistent, loving care can make a critical difference in your child's life.

As you read this chapter, you should bear in mind that autism affects different children in different ways. Some children with autism have average or above average intellectual ability, while others have varying degrees of mental retardation. Some children with autism are profoundly withdrawn, while others are more sociable. And some children with autism have seizures or other physical disabilities, while others do not. As this chapter explains, all of these factors can affect a child's long-term development.

What Is Development?

Before you can put your child's development into perspective, you need a basic understanding of human development in general. Actually, you may already know quite a bit about normal development—it was probably the differences in your child's development that led you to seek help to begin with. For example, if you have older children, you may have realized that your special child was not developing in the same way as the others did; if you did not have other children, you may have seen that your child was different from nieces, nephews, or neighbor children. Perhaps you noticed that your child was not babbling or did not seem to be forming an emotional attachment to you. Then again, you may have seen some odd behaviors like hand flapping, body rocking, or resistance to change in routine. In short, because you had some idea of how children typically develop, you knew that your child was not progressing normally. What you didn't know was why.

As a matter of fact, no one knows exactly why children with autism develop as they do. But we do know that all human development depends largely on biological programming—that is, your child's genetic makeup lays the foundation for the way he grows and acquires skills, or *develops.* Other factors—environmental, psychological, and cultural—also play roles in human development.

Since so many variables are involved, no child's developmental profile is quite the same. For example, one child may say his first words several months earlier than another child, but learn to stand several months later. One child may move step by step through the sitting-crawling-walking sequence, while another may skip the crawling stage completely. In other words, no child progresses at exactly the same rate or in the same sequence as any other.

For the most part, however, children tend to develop from top to bottom. That is, they can suck before they can grasp, and sit before they can stand. A child will be able to use his hands before he can control his legs. Children also become increasingly refined in their movements the more they develop. For example, when a baby is excited, his whole body wiggles with delight, while an older child may simply smile.

The development of all children is usually divided into six areas: 1) gross motor; 2) fine motor; 3) cognition; 4) language; 5) social; and 6) self-help. Some working definitions follow:

Gross Motor. In gross motor development, your child learns to control his body by using his large muscles, including those in his legs, arms, and abdomen. Rolling over, sitting up, crawling, and walking are all basic gross motor skills. More advanced gross motor skills include running and climbing. These skills give your child the tools to explore his world and are the foundation for growth in other areas.

Fine Motor. In fine motor development, your child learns to make precise, detailed movements with smaller muscles, such as those in his fingers and hands. Skills like picking up small objects, using the index finger to poke and probe, and squeezing soft objects are all important fine motor skills. So, too, are control of eye muscles, and facial and tongue movements.

Communication. Communication development is usually divided into two areas: the acquisition of receptive language and the acquisition of expressive language. Receptive language is the ability to understand words and gestures. Expressive language is the ability to use gestures, words, and written symbols to communicate. In most children, the understanding of a word—its receptive use—usually precedes its expressive use, but in children with autism this is not always the case.

Cognition. A good working definition of cognition is the ability to reason and solve problems. In the early stages of your child's cognitive development, he comes to understand that objects do not cease to exist when they are out of sight (the concept of object permanence); grasps the principle of cause and effect; and learns to draw conclusions from direct experience. Mastering these skills enables your child to understand how the world works and how he can manipulate his environment.

Social. Your child's social development affects his ability to interact with people. From birth onward, children learn how to respond appropriately to themselves and others. For example, they learn to take turns, share their toys, form attachments to other people, and assert their independence. These are important skills that help children develop into functioning members of society.

Self-help. In this area of development, your child learns how to take care of himself. He progresses from total dependence on you for his survival to being able to look after himself. Some important self-help skills include dressing, feeding, and toileting.

A seventh area, *sensory ability*, is not usually considered a separate area of development itself, because it is so closely tied to development in other areas. In sensory development, your child acquires the ability to process sensations like touch, sound, light, smell, and movement. These skills are refined as your child grows, and they affect all areas of development.

Because these areas of development are all controlled by genetic and environmental factors, a problem in either a child's genetic makeup or in his environment can disrupt the normal process of development. For example, it is possible to inherit a genetic defect which will lead to differences or problems in physical growth. The person we call "dwarfed" stays physically tiny even as other areas of development proceed normally. In contrast, a person might be born with the genetic potential for normal physical development, but fail to reach full height because of an environmental factor like inadequate nutrition.

Fortunately, environmental factors do not always have a negative effect on development. In fact, when positive environmental factors are deliberately optimized, development can be dramatically enhanced. For example, speech therapy and instruction in sign language can help a child with a severe speech impediment develop communication skills; physical therapy and a rigorous exercise program can help a child with weak muscles gain better control of his movements. Particularly when a child has a developmental disability like autism, *intervention*—direct involvement in development—can make a critical difference.

How Do Children Develop?

In human development, there are no hard-and-fast age limits for the achievement of basic developmental skills such as walking and talking. Children can achieve these skills—called *milestones*—at different rates and in different sequences and still be considered "normal." For example, some "normal" children may sit up much earlier than other "normal" children, or say their first words later. Because children do develop within a fairly broad range, the realization that a child has a developmental disorder may sometimes be delayed. Physicians and parents may expect a child to "outgrow" a problem or may explain away a delay with statements like: "He's a boy and boys are slower to talk," or "He's just lazy because all his older sisters and brothers do things for him." When a physician reassures the parents of a normal child that "He'll outgrow this," he is often right. Unfortunately, this is seldom the case for the child with autism.

To give you a yardstick to measure your child's development against, we will look first at how normal children develop in several key areas. Some typical achievements in the areas of cognitive, communication, social-emotional, and motor development are summarized in Table 1, and discussed in more detail below.

Table 1
Some Normal Developmental Milestones

Age	Social	Communication	Motor
10 Mo.	Waves bye-bye	Says mama, dada +one word	Sits indefinitely
12 Mo.	Cooperates with dressing	2 words	Walks with hand held
18 Mo.	Hugs a doll	10 words	Walks fast Scribbles
24 Mo.	Asks for toilet Puts on simple garments Parallel play	3 word sentences Uses I, me, you Refers to self by name	Walks up & down alone Imitates vertical stroke
36 Mo.	Feeds self Pours from pitcher	Uses plurals Tells sex	Alternates feet on stairs Rides tricycle
48 Mo.	Washes & dries hands & face Plays cooperatively	Names colors	Throws over-hand Copies cross
60 Mo.	Dresses & undresses without help Dresses up in adult clothes	Names coins Describes picture Asks meaning of words Counts 10 objects	Skips Copies triangle

Cognitive Development

The term "cognition" refers to our ability to know or understand our environment. For an infant, this means acquiring information about the most basic aspects of life and about his relationship to the rest of the world. In his first year of life, for instance, a baby learns that objects have weight, size, taste, and feel, and that people look and sound different. Between eighteen and twenty-four months, the young child begins to develop an imagination and can pretend, for example, that a doll is alive. From about two years to seven years, the child becomes adept at thinking in abstract terms and no longer needs to see or touch an object in order to learn about it. The young child also learns to devise his own solutions to problems, but is still limited by an inability to take many different dimensions of a problem into account at once. In later childhood, the "normal" child becomes more skilled at thinking in abstractions, and by adolescence, can manipulate mathematical equations, understand that there may be several different explanations for the same event, and speak in metaphor (e.g., "this room is a pig sty"). All through childhood, cognitive development has a profound effect on development in other areas, but particularly on a child's ability to use language.

Motor Skills

In normal children, the development of gross and fine motor skills goes hand in hand. For example, during the first eight months of life while a baby is learning to use his large muscles in turning over, sitting, and crawling, he is also learning to control his smaller muscles by following movements with his eyes, reaching, and transferring objects from hand to hand. By twenty-four months of age, the fine motor skills of the typical child are so highly developed that he can pick up objects as small as a crumb, and his gross motor skills are so refined that he can walk upstairs with two feet to a step. These motor behaviors continue to grow more complex through early childhood as the child learns to throw, catch, skip, jump rope, and run in a smoothly coordinated fashion. By adolescence the human body has developed into a beautifully coordinated mechanism that moves with speed and grace.

Communication

The development of communication skills parallels the child's growing motor abilities. At twenty-eight weeks, most babies play with vowel sounds ("ah-ah-ah," "uh-uh-uh"); by thirty-two weeks, they have added consonants ("da," "ba," "ma"); and by thirty-six weeks, they will imitate sounds like coughs or tongue clicks and also respond to their names. At forty weeks, the typical baby uses "mama" and "dada" to refer to those very important people in his world, and will probably have another word in his repertoire as well. At a little over a year, most babies say three or four words and demonstrate an even greater receptive (understanding) vocabulary. By eighteen months, they point to objects when requested and have a vocabulary of perhaps ten words.

Over the next six months, the average toddler makes an enormous leap forward in language abilities. He adds about two hundred words to his speaking vocabulary, learns to string two or three words together in simple sentences ("want juice"), and begins to use "what" questions. These skills develop so rapidly that by age three, he talks in three-word sentences, asks "where" and "who" questions, and has a speaking vocabulary of perhaps five hundred words. By six, the child knows fifteen hundred to two thousand words and has mastered very complex sentence forms. As he grows, the youngster becomes fully fluent, while continuing to develop an increasingly sophisticated and technical vocabulary that reflects his individual interests.

Social/Emotional Development

Normally, a baby's emotional and social development follows a fairly predictable pattern. By as early as two months, a baby will smile back if you talk and nod to him, and will follow your movement with his eyes. At sixteen weeks, he recognizes his bottle and smiles when people approach. By eight months, the child is so skilled at recognizing family members that strangers may frighten him. This distress usually disappears by about twelve months of age, to be replaced by another kind of emotional concern—that of separation anxiety. In this phase, the toddler may be reluctant to be without his mother or father, but may be quite content and secure as long as one or both parents is nearby.

During the preschool years, the normal child begins to learn important things about self and feelings. He learns how to distinguish gender (am I a boy or a girl?), how to deal with strong emotions, and how to recognize feelings in other people. As he begins to explore his immediate world and his relationships within it, he may often react with shyness, fearfulness, aggression, or anger. The preschool child plays jointly with other children and may act out the roles of his mother, father, or teacher in pretend play.

After he enters school, the typical child begins to form special friendships. Peer relationships gradually take on more and more significance, while the family begins to decline as a source of influence. By late adolescence, the child is well on the road to emotional and social self-sufficiency.

Development of the Child with Autism

As the parent of a child with autism, you know that your child deviated in troubling ways from the patterns of cognitive, communication, and social/emotional development just described. Your child's *motor* skills, on the other hand, may have developed right on schedule, or just a little slower than normal, unless some kind of physical disability affected his motor development. Indeed, the fact that your child rolled over, sat up, and walked on time may have reassured you that all was well. Perhaps it was not until more complex social and communication skills failed to emerge that your child's growth really began to worry you.

Most parents of children with autism do not begin to be seriously concerned about their child's development until late in the first year. Typically, a child's autistic symptoms increase gradually through the second year, peak between the ages of two and four, and then improve somewhat.

The degree of spontaneous improvement *your* child will make depends on the severity of his symptoms: less impaired children who receive appropriate intervention may experience such a dramatic decrease in abnormal behaviors that they may no longer seem autistic by the time they reach school age; children whose problems are very severe from an early age will probably continue to have more severe problems. In any case, if you have a very young child with autism, you can expect his behavior to change for the better in the next couple of years.

Table 2 summarizes some of the developmental differences and difficulties that autism can cause. You may wish to refer to this table for a brief overview of some of the problems in language, social, and other developmental areas that may arise for your child with autism. The following sections discuss these developmental difficulties in more detail and also offer parents some practical advice about helping their children overcome problem behaviors.

Cognitive Development in Children with Autism

Even among normally developing people, there are wide variations in cognitive or intellectual abilities. Although most of us can be described as "about average," there are some people who are very bright and others whose ability is well below average and who we call "mentally retarded." These cognitive abilities can be measured by IQ tests, as well as by how people cope with daily life.

Most children with autism have intellectual abilities that are well below average. In fact, about 70 percent of these youngsters are mentally retarded, while only 30 percent are of normal to above average ability. Children whose abilities are within the normal range can often master much of the material in a normal school curriculum, but still show the symptoms of autism.

Many parents find the distinction between autism and mental retardation a confusing one. It may be helpful to recall that most children who are mentally retarded will develop language and social skills that are consistent with their intellectual abilities, while the child with autism typically has language and social skills that fall below his or her skills in other areas. A young person with autism who is not mentally retarded may be quite proficient at many basic academic subjects, but still speak in a peculiar fashion and be very limited in his ability to negotiate the emotional world of childhood. And although he may learn to follow a set of rules which govern social interaction, his interactions usually lack the smooth, spontaneous quality which marks most people's relationships.

Table 2
Early Symptoms of Autism (Newborn to 5 Years)

Newborn to 6 Months

- May be "too good"
- May be irritable, easily distressed
- Does not reach to be picked up
- Does not babble
- Lack of social smile
- Lack of eye contact
- Motor development may appear normal

6 Months to 12 Months

- Does not cuddle, may be limp or rigid when held
- Relative indifference toward parents
- Does not play simple social games ("Peek-a-boo," "Bye-bye")
- Does not begin to use words
- Does not seem interested in baby toys
- May be fascinated with own hands
- Uneven or delayed motor development
- May not chew or accept solid foods

2 Years to 3 Years

- Interpersonal interest remains limited; may show some improvement
- Uses other people as "tools"
- Limited eye contact

- May sniff or lick objects
- Does not cuddle, may be limp or rigid when held
- Relative indifference toward parents

4 Years to 5 Years

- If speech develops may be echolalic (Repeats in rote fashion what others say, either immediately or later)
- Odd voice quality (high-pitched or monotone, for example)
- Very upset by changes in routine
- Eye contact still limited, although may show some improvement
- Gradual increase in affection, but still limited
- Tantrums and aggression continue, but may gradually improve
- Self-injury
- Self-stimulation

Regardless of whether your child with autism is among the majority who show some mental retardation, or that smaller percentage who have higher skills, you will want to ensure that your child is exposed to a wide range of opportunities to learn from the environment. Repeated opportunities to celebrate holidays, go to the grocery store, watch children's programs on television, and learn the cause and effect relationships among the many routinely occurring events at home and in the community will help your child collect a fund of knowledge about the world and about how to cope with day-to-day activities. Children with lower intellectual abilities will need more repeated exposure in smaller chunks than the brighter child, but every child with autism can learn over time.

Language Development in Children with Autism

Probably one of the first symptoms of autism you noticed in your child was his failure to begin talking. In fact, studies of children with autism suggest that their language development may be abnormal from as early as two months of age. Babies with autism may not babble at all, may show less variety in their sounds, or may make primarily high-pitched squealing sounds.

Delays in language development are usually readily apparent by twelve months of age. While normal infants generally know "mama," "dada," and one other word by this time, babies with autism will generally not have learned any words, nor can they be coaxed into imitating their parents' nonsense sounds. At two, when normal toddlers are surging ahead in their language development—learning to speak in three-word sentences and constantly carrying on imaginary conversations with themselves—the child with autism may actually lose the use of those few words he has previously acquired.

Between the ages of four and five, the child with autism finally begins to make slow progress in language development. He may learn some words by rote, but will probably have only a limited ability to use them to communicate. At four years of age, only about a quarter of children with autism can use speech meaningfully, and then only to express an immediate need—to ask for a drink of milk, for example. More than half of all children with autism still have no useful speech by this age, while an additional 25 percent are *echolalic*—they can parrot other people's words, but without understanding.

Over time, all children with autism do make gains in language development. Even young people who are so severely impaired that they never develop functional speech acquire at least some skill in understanding language. Other young people with autism may eventually develop near normal speech, and find their ability to communicate hampered only by an odd lack of voice inflection that makes their speech sound somewhat mechanical. Most children with autism fall somewhere between these two extremes.

Regardless of the severity of *your* child's autism, there are ways you can help him develop his language skills to the fullest. These techniques are best learned under the direction of an experienced speech therapist or teacher, and include such strategies as using simple language with your child, insisting that he use the language he has, and providing reinforcing responses to your child's attempts to communicate.

Social Development in Children with Autism

Next to your child's language delays, you probably found his lack of progress in social development most alarming. Although most children with autism (roughly 2 out of 3) do not actually begin to withdraw until around two years of age, parents usually notice other problems in social development long before that. In the first few months, for instance, it may have bothered you that your child would not reach to be picked up as a "normal" child would, or that he never smiled. At one year of age, your child may have stiffened when you held him and seemed completely uninterested in playing typical baby games like waving "bye-bye." Also in contrast to "normal" children, your child probably showed little or no separation anxiety when you left him alone or with strangers.

Despite these early differences in social development, you—like most parents—were still probably caught off guard by the new problems that began to surface around your child's second birthday. When your child began to withdraw from the outside world and engage in self-stimulation behaviors like hand flapping, whirling, or staring, you may have tried to link the change to some major event in your child's life—an illness or the birth of a sibling, perhaps. In fact, there is no reason to believe that these experiences help trigger a child's withdrawal. As explained earlier, autism is caused by biological factors, and certainly not by child-rearing practices.

As with other developmental areas, the amount of progress your child will ultimately make in social development is related to his cognitive abilities. Children who are more intellectually impaired usually show fewer changes, while children who are less impaired make more progress. Be assured, though, that your child *will* make strides in social development.

In most cases, the social behavior of a child with autism takes a turn for the better beginning around the age of four. For instance, a child may continue to engage in self-stimulation and self-injury, but may also begin to show some affection towards family members. And, although he may still become very upset at changes in routine, the frequency and intensity of his tantrums may decrease.

As they enter adolesence, most young people with autism become more flexible in how they respond to their environment and pose fewer management problems, although a small percentage of children with autism show a decline in the development of cognitive abilities. The child whose need for routine limited his or her activities in earlier years may become more able to tolerate some change, while the child who had tantrums when frustrated may have developed the communication skills to diminish the need for this disruptive behavior.

Teenagers with milder forms of autism may develop an interest in other people, but may have trouble approaching them and interacting with them in satisfying ways. For some young people this can be a source of distress as they begin to recognize the gap between themselves and others. Other adolescents and adults with autism who function at a lower intellectual level may remain profoundly withdrawn, but perhaps show more attachment to their family than they did when they were younger. Whatever their cognitive abilities, young people with autism typically remain very limited in their ability to be sensitive to other people's feelings. The subtle cues that would tell us we had offended another person, or that someone was pleased or annoyed with us may not be picked up by the person with autism. As a result, even those people with autism who can hold jobs in the regular work force may need help in managing their relationships with peers and supervisors.

What about other problem areas in social development—aggression, tantrums, and self-injury? Do these change with age? We know that hyperactive behavior and self-stimulation tend to decline as the child gets older, but we are not so sure about self-injury or aggression. Because these behaviors may not decline with age, it is very important that they be thoroughly treated in childhood. After all, aggression that is tolerable in a five-year-old would be unbearable in a twenty-year-old.

In general, it is not as easy to influence the social development of a child with autism as it is to influence his language development, but there are still many ways you can help your child grow.

One of the most useful steps you can take is to ensure that your child is exposed to a range of social experiences. Although your child may not at first seem interested in, or responsive to, other people, it is nonetheless important that you keep trying. Keep the social contact short so that your child does not find the experience too unpleasant, but do not give in to your child's desire to remain alone. Do not rely only on the classroom for providing opportunities for socialization. The experience of learning to be with others needs to extend beyond school to the world outside the classroom.

Other Developmental Problems

Along with social and language problems, children with autism often experience developmental delays in acquiring self-help skills. Learning to use the toilet, for example, is an especially large stumbling block for many children with autism. While most normal children are toilet trained between the ages of two and three, nearly half of all children with autism are still not toilet trained by the age of four. In addition, many children with autism have trouble acquiring good feeding habits. As infants, they may refuse to chew or eat solid foods; later on, they may binge for months at a time on one particular food.

A third problem area for many children with autism is developing normal sleeping patterns. Particularly between the ages of two and three, many children with autism resist going to sleep and wake up frequently during the night. Although it is not unusual for a normal preschooler to climb into his mother's or father's bed when he has been frightened by a nightmare, the child with autism may not be able to sleep alone until well into childhood. Sleep disturbances are covered fully in Chapter 4.

As Chapters 1 and 4 explained, parents can fight these self-help problems with a variety of behavior modification (applied behavior analysis) strategies. Some of these techniques may help your child and some may not; some may help him sometimes and not other times. Do not be surprised if you do not immediately discover a strategy that works, but do not be discouraged, either. It may take a lot of hard work from you and your child, but eventually you *will* see gratifying improvement in your child's self-help skills.

What to Expect for Your Own Child

You undoubtedly have serious concerns about what *your* child's current developmental differences mean for the years ahead. Will he ever start to speak? Will the self-stimulation that is so much a part of his daily routine ever decrease? Will your child's resistance to change ever diminish to the point where your family can lead a more normal life? When will he be toilet trained and sleep in his own bed?

No amount of general information could possibly set your mind at ease about your child's specific problems. Still, the information presented in this chapter about the general development of children with autism should help you make an educated projection of the long-term course of your child's development.

As Chapter 1 discusses, an expert in human development and autism such as a clinical child psychologist, pediatric neurologist, or other specialist can make an even more informed judgement. Since it may be helpful to that expert if you have records of your child's development, you may want to keep track of some of your child's unusual behaviors in a notebook.

Some typical problem behaviors to look for are listed in Table 3. If you copy this list into your notebook, then each time you notice one of these behaviors, you can simply jot down the date you first observed it. For instance, if your child starts refusing to stay in bed when he is two, you should make a note of it under "sleep disorders." You should also record observations about the ways your child's problem behaviors change over time. For example, if your child does a lot of body rocking between the ages of three and four, but then stops the behavior, you should make a note of both the date it starts and the date it stops. If you use special procedures like rewarding quiet sitting or appropriate play to help your child learn self-control of the behavior, put that in your notebook, too.

Table 3
Problem Behaviors

- Eating pattern (for example, only eats a few foods or will not use utensils)
- Sleeping pattern (for example, wakes often at night or has trouble falling asleep)
- Toileting problems
- Self-stimulation (for example, rocks, waves fingers, or flips an object in front of eyes)
- Resistance to change
- Self-injury
- Tantrums
- Withdrawal (is not responsive to other people)
- Aggression (injures other people when frustrated)
- Echolalia (repeats in rote fashion what others say)
- Pronoun reversal (for example, says "you" for "I")
- Jargon in speech (makes up words that may not have obvious meaning to others)

Besides keeping a record of your child's autistic behaviors, you should also get into the habit of describing your child's normal developmental achievements in a notebook. By referring to Table 4, you can make four charts: one each for recording your child's cognitive, communication, social-emotional, and motor development. Then, whenever your child reaches one of the developmental milestones listed in Table 4, write down the date and a few examples of the new skill. For instance, the first time you notice your child using a two-word sentence, note the date, as well as exactly what he says.

Table 4

My Child's Cognitive Skills

Searched for an object that was moved out of sight
Recognized him- or herself in mirror
Counted to six
Drew a picture of a person including a head, body, and arms or legs
Remembered the main facts in a short story
Printed letters or words with small and capital letters
Named the days of the week
Knew multiplication tables
Did long division
Read the newspaper

My Child's Communication Skills

Babbled
Said "Mama" and "Dada"
First words
Put 2 words together
Put 3 words together
Used name to refer to self
Used "I," "Me," "You"
Used plurals
Named colors
Asked questions
Described pictures
Talked about feelings of self and others

My Child's Social-Emotional Skills

Reached to be picked up
Waved "bye-bye"
Cooperated with dressing by inserting arms or legs into clothing
Hugged doll
Pulled off shoes and socks
Parallel play (played near another child on individual task)
Used basic utensils such as spoon and fork
Poured from pitcher

Washed and dried hands and face
Cooperative play (played with another child on single task)
Dressed and undressed without help

My Child's Motor Skills

Sat alone
Crawled
Walked with one hand held
Walked well
Scribbled with crayon
Walked up and down stairs alone
Copied vertical line
Alternated feet on stairs
Rode tricycle
Copied circle
Threw overhand
Copied cross
Skipped
Copied triangle

When you compare your child's achievements with those on the normal developmental chart, do not be surprised if you find that your child is reaching his milestones not only at different ages, but also in a different order from the normal sequence. Some children with autism do things in a different order than other children, while others may simply be slower, but pass through the same general patterns of development. In this respect, children with autism are just like any other children. Since each child has his own individual learning style, strengths, and weaknesses, it is normal for one child to develop differently than any other.

What Can You Do to Help?

First and foremost, you can shower your child with every bit of developmental help you can round up. In some states, children with autism are eligible for publicly funded early infant education through local school districts. In these programs—described in Chapter 7—children receive early infant intervention aimed at maximizing their potential. Since not all states provide education for handicapped children under the age of three, you should check with your local school district or state department of education to determine when your child will be eligible for services.

If public school services are unavailable, you may be able to make use of private teachers and therapists—especially if your medical insurance covers their services. Local organizations, advocacy groups, and other parents of children with autism will also gladly help you locate developmental aid for your child.

Finally, do not underestimate the enormous difference a supportive home environment can make in your child's life. Even though your child's autism is a biological disorder and his developmental progress is tied in some ways to that biology, taking the time now to teach your child self-help, social, and language skills will pay off in dramatic ways later. The more time you spend with your child the better, but even thirty minutes a day devoted to home teaching adds up to thousands of hours across the childhood and adolescence of your child. Work with your child as much as you can, and remember, it is not how *soon* your child learns a particular skill that matters, but how *well* he is eventually able to do it.

Conclusion

There is no one "right way" for children to develop. All children are born with different potentials and grow and learn according to their own unique timetables. Because of the way autism affects your child, however, you can expect that he will develop more slowly than most children and have trouble mastering cognitive, communication, social, and self-help skills. Fortunately, you can help offset some of these developmental delays by providing a good educational program and a supportive home environment for your child. Children with autism *do* acquire self-care skills, master basic academic concepts, develop at least the rudiments of communication, and learn to cooperate in group settings. With your help and encouragement, your child will master these skills that much faster and more thoroughly.

References

The information in this chapter does not come just from my own experience and study, but from the work of a number of dedicated researchers. In the name of clarity I avoided names in the text, but I do want to acknowledge their contributions.

Brodzinsky, D., A. Gormly, and S.R. Ambron. *Lifespan Human Development.* New York: Holt, Rinehart, & Winston, 1987.

Ando, H., and I. Yoshimura. "Effects of Age on Communication Skill Levels and Prevalence of Maladaptive Behaviors in Autistic and Mentally Retarded Children." *Journal of Autism and Developmental Disorders* 9 (1979): 83-93.

Ando, H., I. Yoshimura, and S. Wakabayashi. "Effects of Age on Adaptive Behavior Levels and Academic Skill Levels in Autistic and Mentally Retarded Children." *Journal of Autism and Developmental Disorders* 10 (1980): 173-84.

DeMyer, M.K. *Parents and Children in Autism.* New York: Wiley, 1979.

DeMyer, M.K., S. Barton, W.E. DeMyer, J.A. Norton, J. Allen, and R. Steele. "Prognosis in Autism: A Follow-up Study." *Journal of Autism and Childhood Schizophrenia* 3 (1973): 199-246.

Mesibov, G.B. "Current Perspectives and Issues in Autism and Adolescence." In *Autism in Adolescents and Adults,* edited by E. Schopler and G.B. Mesibov, 37-53. New York: Plenum, 1983.

Ornitz, E.M., D. Guthrie, and A.H. Farley. "The Early Development of Autistic Children." *Journal of Autism and Childhood Schizophrenia* 7 (1977): 207-229.

Parent Statements

We noticed there was something wrong with Ray at two. He wasn't chewing. And we asked the pediatrician, "Why isn't he chewing?" And she said, "Well, he'll chew when he gets ready. Just don't give him anything he can choke on."

At six months he wasn't turning over, and the pediatrician said, "He's a big boy—he'll learn." You take what you're given at this point. I mean, he was our first child; we didn't know any different.

We knew that when Sheila was the same age, she was doing a lot of things faster than Bart was. So, at that point we started putting two and two together, saying, "Well, Bart's not as advanced as she is. Just where do we go from here?"

Lawrence can say about twenty words. He's been saying the same words for about two years, with no addition to his vocabulary. I don't think he'll ever sign, either. His fine motor skills are too poor. I'm hoping he'll develop a few more words and maybe use a speech board.

When your child can't talk as well as the other kids can, you start to feel like you still have a baby while the other parents have a little companion.

She couldn't interact with the children in the neighborhood that well. She was content to stay in the playpen; she was content to be by herself. And when the other children tried to play with her, she just walked away from them as if to say, "I've had enough."

One Christmas a couple of years ago, two neighbor girls came over to play. They kept trying to have a conversation with him, and I started crying, because he was not relating.

Janet says, "Don't talk to strangers," but yet, she does talk to strangers. I don't think they really understand what strangers are. They're trusting and they think everybody's their friend.

My child is the turtle in the game of life, but each milestone he wins—no matter how slowly—helps me to appreciate life that much more.

When he was two, we had a day care mother who had a son a couple months younger than ours who was doing things that Alan wasn't doing. Through this mother we got the idea that something was wrong. Alan was our first child—we had no idea.

You have no idea how excited we become when Brian says a word we thought he didn't know. Of course, then he turns into a parrot and keeps saying it. It may be echolalia, but it's still music to our ears!

By the time he was two, he had lost the five or six words he had previously had. Every time I asked the pediatrician about this, his response was the same: "If he can hear, it doesn't worry me." A few months later, he was diagnosed as having autistic behavior.

Lawrence self-stimulates constantly. Rocking, weird breathing patterns, hand waving, rolling his eyes—he's in constant motion. Out in public, people are always watching him. We try to see the humor in it. He *is* a funny-looking little guy.

He's seven, going on eight—someday he's going to be fifteen, going on sixteen—and if we hadn't done what we've done so far, he might be at the developmental stage of seven going on eight when he's fifteen going on sixteen. There could be a lot of repercussions when he's twenty going on twenty-one.

The "self-stims" do cause some staring when we're in public, but you can't let it get to you. And if you see a movement coming, sometimes you can change it.

I say that growth—slight, a lot, sometimes—would be fun.

He had terrible tantrums at fifteen months of age. If one block fell off a pile, he would throw the whole pile and scream. The pediatrician said that children who have temper tantrums before eighteen months are usually very bright!

I ask that question a lot. I say, "Where should he be?"

The way I deal with the hyperactivity is just to look at him and say, "Oh, well, it must be 'Star Trek' time." As long as he's not hurt, so what?

During the day, Lawrence's hyperactivity isn't too bad. In the evenings, he is so wild he drives me crazy. If he isn't ripping the house to shreds, he's leaping on me. And this is all done with high-volume sound effects. While he's awake I can't even consider watching T.V. or reading a book.

At three and a half, Doug can use some picture communication, but has never said one word. All my friends and relatives tell me of dreams they have where Doug is talking. I've never had such a dream, and when I try to envision him speaking, I really can't.

The social interactions between Scott and the other kids seem to lag behind so much.

Self-help skills have been extremely difficult for Lawrence. He's learned to "help" feed himself, go potty in the toilet, and "help" some with dressing, but he hasn't mastered anything. He's progressed so far and no farther in all of these areas. I keep hoping he'll learn a few skills well enough so that he can do them somewhat independently.

We never had a problem when we went out to dinner; Brian always fed himself—usually with his hands. Now he's mastered utensils, and it's just neater dining.

When she gets in a Brownie group and they gather around in a circle, what they talk about is over her head, because it's abstract. They ask her what she thinks of this and that—like she's a regular six-, seven-, or eight-year-old, and she's just left out in the cold. She can't focus in on what the scout leader is trying to say.

I've found that a great majority of things have to be taught.

We were trying to teach Donny the common answer to the common question, “How are you?” The answer we were looking for was “fine.” It didn’t take long for him to catch on to the idea and to use the response appropriately. Shortly afterwards, while recovering from a virus, Donny overheard my husband and me comment on how the virus had made him look so pale and white. Donny had not totally recovered from the virus when I asked him how he was feeling. He answered, “White.” We were delighted because he had spontaneously learned a word to tell us he was not yet well.

SEVEN

Finding the Right Educational Program

ANDREW L. EGEL, PH.D.*

Introduction

In theory, you may already know that the surest route to a fulfilling, independent future for your child is through the right educational program. In practice, however, you may be at a loss as to how to find the best placement for her. This is understandable because there are a bewildering number and variety of programs available, many with different, even contradictory philosophies.

This chapter is designed to ease your entry into the world of special education. It presents an overview of common placement options in special education programs, and reviews the evaluation and eligibility process. The professionals likely to have roles in your child's education are introduced as well as skills you might expect your child to learn in school. Finally, to help you obtain the best possible educational program for your child, this chapter offers guidance on what to look for in an educational program, what questions to ask, and how to evaluate the information you receive.

---

* Andrew L. Egel, Ph.D., is an Associate Professor in the Department of Special Education at the University of Maryland, College Park. He received his M.A. and Ph.D. from the University of California at Santa Barbara. Dr. Egel has received numerous federal grants designed to develop model educational programs for children with autism. He is co-editor of *Educating and Understanding Autistic Children* (College-Hill, 1982) and author of several chapters and papers on the education of children with autism.

What Is Special Education?

Special education is instruction designed to meet the unique needs of a child with special needs. It is provided by one or more professionals trained in helping children overcome the learning problems associated with their disabilities. Depending on your child's age, these professionals may come to your home, or may work with your child in a variety of other settings, such as public or private school classrooms or hospitals. Services included in a child's special education vary according to the child's needs, and frequently include the so-called "related services" she needs in order to benefit from her educational program. Speech therapy, occupational or physical therapy, social services, and transportation to and from school are just some of the related services a child with autism might receive. Depending on your child's age, your school system may offer you a half-day or a full-day program. Parents of very young children may find that a full-day program is too much for their children to handle. By age two and a half to three, however, many children with autism will benefit most from a full school day of 5–6 hours.

Early Intervention

In the past, special education services were customarily offered only to school-aged children, but now even very young children with handicaps can receive services through early intervention programs. As explained in Chapter 8, some states provide these services for children with disabilities from birth onward. Under the terms of Public Law 99–457, significantly more will begin offering early intervention services over the next several years.

Early intervention programs provide special education for children younger than three. Programs come in many different forms and can include a variety of services and professionals. Their goal, however, is always the same: to minimize the effects of handicaps that can delay development in infants and toddlers. Early intervention specialists use specific therapeutic and educational techniques to help children with disabilities master skills they are having trouble learning; they also teach the parents how to help their child master these skills and maintain them over time.

Children with autism are excellent candidates for early intervention services because they have a range of developmental problems. All can benefit from early and intensive training in communication, cognitive, and social skills, and the sooner most children with autism begin work to overcome behavioral problems such as tantrums and self-injury, the less likely these behaviors are to interfere with future learning.

Types of Early Intervention Programs

Very young children with autism are typically offered one of two types of programs: home-based or school-based. In home-based programs, members of an early intervention team come to your home to work with you and your child. They may all visit together or they may come separately during the week. How many teachers or therapists visit and how often they visit will vary depending on your child's needs and the services available in your area. Home-based services usually are provided up to age two, although some programs provide services until three years of age.

During a visit, the teacher will work with your child, focusing on the different areas of development. Particular emphasis should be given to the areas presenting the greatest difficulty to children with autism: socialization, communication, and cognitive skills. The teacher will try various activities with your child, and may want you to try them, too. He or she may work with your child alone, with you alone, or with you and your child together. At the end of the session you should have a clear idea of what skills were emphasized, what was learned (by you and your child), and how to help your child build upon her progress. The teacher may leave you with suggestions of activities to try with your child until the next session.

Home visits are also a good time to discuss your child's problem behavior. Many children with autism have trouble sleeping through the night; others have frequent temper tantrums. Discussing these problems with your child's teacher will help the teacher focus on the areas of greatest importance to you and your family.

It will also help you learn techniques to manage challenging behaviors at home and in the community.

Home-based services for children with autism age two and older generally cannot adequately meet the child's need for socialization and communication training. Older children require more teaching time and much more intensive programming than is available in a few one-hour visits each week. For these reasons, a school-based program will typically be more appropriate for your child with autism after two years of age.

School-based programs are located in public schools or private facilities. Some programs are "segregated," serving only children with autism, or both children with autism and those with various handicaps. Other programs are "integrated," providing instruction to children with autism in the same classroom attended by non-handicapped children for at least a portion of the day.

School-based programs should be staffed by teachers who have special knowledge about working with children with autism or other severe developmental disabilities. The student to teacher ratio is also very important. A ratio of three children to one staff member is often appropriate, but the ratio should generally be determined by the child's needs. For example, extremely challenging children may initially require a smaller ratio of 1:1 or 2:1, while more self-sufficient children may do better with less supervision (with a ratio such as 6:1). Too much supervision may prevent the more competent child from learning the skills needed to become independent; too little supervision of the more challenging child may mean insufficient opportunities to practice skills, as well as insufficient teacher time to intervene with behaviors such as tantrums, self-stimulation, or self-injury.

Classrooms in school-based programs for children with autism ages two through four usually resemble those for other preschool-age children, with toys, a housekeeping area, and materials to stimulate large and small muscle development. In addition, a variety of toys and materials appealing to the sensory interests of children with autism might be available. The classroom should also contain areas for large group activities (e.g., circle time), small group instruction, and free-play.

Like staff in home-based programs, school-based teachers often involve the parents in their child's education. Frequently, parent education services are provided to teach parents how to help their child use skills or behaviors at home that she has learned in school. For example, parents may be taught to toilet train their child following a program used at school.

Programs for School-Aged Children

Just as there are different types of special education programs for younger children with autism, so too are there different types of special education programs for children five and older. Some programs are provided within the public school system, others by private schools. Public school programs may be located within elementary or secondary schools that also have classes for nondisabled students, or in special centers just for children with special needs (and in some cases, just for children with autism). For both preschool and school-aged children, you may find that some schools provide an educational program throughout the year (twelve months), while others are in session only for the regular school year, typically September through June.

There may also be considerable differences between programs for school-aged children and those for younger children. For example, older students are likely to spend more time in structured activities. Furthermore, many of the curriculum goals may differ because they should be related to the older children's "next environment"—or the next setting to which they will be transitioned (e.g., elementary school to junior high). More teaching will also occur in non-school settings, especially as children reach adolescence.

The type of program that is best for your child will ultimately depend on her needs, but some information about these different program types may help you make your decision. In all cases, the characteristics of appropriate programs described later in this chapter and the Program Checklist in Table 1 will help you sort out the pros and cons of any program you are considering.

Whether a public or private school will be most appropriate for your child often depends on where you live. Some public school systems have made special efforts to create educational programs that meet the specific learning and behavioral needs of children with autism. In other areas of the country, private schools have taken the lead because the public schools have not. In these cases, public and private schools often have agreements that children with autism from a particular town or county will automatically be referred to the private school because it provides a more appropriate educational experience.

Occasionally, parents may find that they cannot properly meet the needs of their child with autism on a day-to-day basis. In these cases, a residential program may be considered. These programs tend to be private and they are more expensive than day programs. However, if the school system determines that the child's behavior in school or at home is preventing her from benefiting from a day program, then the local school system and the state education agency will pay for the residential program that is most appropriate given your child's needs. Sometimes there is no question that the home situation is hurting a child's educational progress, but more often some degree of advocacy and legal assistance is needed before the school district will agree to pay for residential services. Even in the most obvious situations, a great deal of information and documentation must be gathered, and it is critical that you maintain communication with the school and the local education agency. Chapters 8 and 9 will help you understand your legal rights in this kind of situation, as well as how to exercise these rights and other influence to obtain the best services for your child.

Curriculum: What Your Child Is Taught

We know that children with autism have special needs in many developmental areas, particularly in social interactions and communication. Naturally, it is important that your child's educational program address these two critical areas. But your child's curriculum, or teaching program, must cover other areas as well. For young children with autism, these include cognitive skills, self-help skills, gross and fine motor skills, and behavior problems. As your child enters adolescence, the emphasis of instruction may shift to teaching functional living skills in areas such as community (e.g., bus riding), leisure/recreational (e.g., video games, bowling), domestic (e.g., preparing foods, personal hygiene), and vocational (e.g., answering a supervisor's questions, learning specific job skills).

There is no one curriculum for all children with autism. Children with autism, like all children, have strong and weak points when it comes to learning. For example, some children with autism have more trouble learning communication skills than they do learning cognitive skills. In autism, this "discontinuity," or tendency to progress at different rates in different developmental areas, is generally the case, and is one of the reasons that autism is so puzzling. Moreover, there can be uneven performance within a single area. For example, some children with autism have unique, and very highly developed visual perceptual skills and can read almost any word. While this particular cognitive skill may be well above average, the same child may be completely unable to comprehend what she has read.

Because each child with autism *is* unique, your child's curriculum will have to be tailored to her unique needs. In general, however, you should expect that your child will receive instruction in each developmental area in which she has learning needs. Here is a list of skills children with autism may need to be taught. These lists are provided merely as examples. The order in which skills are listed is not necessarily the order in which they would or should be taught to your child. Remember, it should always be clear why your child is learning a particular skill and how this skill fits with some ultimate goal.

Cognitive Skills. Cognitive skills can be thought of as the "building blocks" of learning. They include such basic "thinking" skills as the ability to tell the difference between two objects, as well as such complex skills as abstract reasoning. Many children with autism have problems with the most basic cognitive skills and need to be taught them methodically. Others have both strong and weak skills in this area, so that a graph of their cognitive abilities looks like a series of peaks and valleys. Some early cognitive skills that often require attention are discriminating among different people, objects, and events, and imitating the actions of other people. Additional cognitive skills that your child may be taught in school include:

- matching pictures to objects;
- identifying colors and shapes;
- telling the difference between "big" and "little";
- reading basic and more advanced words, depending on cognitive abilities;
- writing her first and last name.

Social Skills. In determining that your child has autism, the professional making the diagnosis paid special attention to your child's social interactive skills. He probably noted that your child lagged behind in the development of both elementary and complex social skills. An example of an elementary skill is the "social smile" that most nondisabled babies develop by two months of age. A more complex social skill would be understanding what to do when you see that a stranger has inadvertently left his wallet at a store counter. Nondisabled children are able to learn many elementary and complex social skills simply by observing and imitating other people. Most children with autism, in contrast, do not learn social skills this way, and must be taught formally. Some examples of social skills that are taught to children with autism include:

- *engagement*, the ability to remain focused and interactive (responsive to) a person or object;
- greeting others;
- independent play skills;
- waiting turns;
- following directions from a co-worker or supervisor.

Communication. This is the other developmental area that professionals observed very carefully when examining your child.

As Chapter 6 explains, it takes two separate skills to communicate. It takes expressive language—the ability to express yourself through gestures, words, or symbols—and it takes receptive language—the ability to understand what is being communicated to you through gestures, words, or actions. Children with autism often experience problems with either or both of these skills, and receive extensive training from teachers and speech/language pathologists to help them learn to communicate better.

But there is more to communication than just sending or receiving messages; communication is also part of a social interaction. For instance, have you ever felt that your child was communicating something to you, such as a request for juice, but that she just was not "there" with you, and that you could just as well have been some stranger capable of meeting her need? She was communicating with you, but without any social recognition or eye-contact. Professionals identify this type of problem as one of "social communication," and it, too, represents an important area for teaching children with autism.

Here are some examples of communication skills that may be taught to your child:

- basic attending skills (e.g., making eye contact);
- imitating others' words or sounds;
- using objects, action words, or both;
- using one-, two-, or three-word sentences;
- mastering the concepts of *recurrence* ("more"), *negation* ("all done/gone"), and *affirmation* ("yes");
- using an alternative communication system such as sign language or a picture board.

Self-Help Skills. These skills represent those activities of daily living that all people need to participate as fully and independently as possible in their families, communities, and schools. Many nondisabled children learn self-help skills—washing themselves, using the toilet, and eating with a spoon and fork—by watching other children and their parents and then imitating what they have seen. Learning through watching and imitating is very hard for children with autism, so these skills often must be taught systematically. It is sometimes tempting to expect that all children will learn self-help skills on their own, but this is a big mistake if your child has autism. To acquire these important skills, children with autism require consistent teaching—teaching that should take place both at home and in school in the context in which they occur naturally. For example, the best time to teach your child to put on her coat is each time she wants to go outside. Examples of self-help skills that might be taught in school include:

- dressing and undressing;
- using the toilet;
- grooming/personal hygiene;
- care of one's own belongings (e.g., making the bed, washing clothes);
- cooking and meal preparation skills.

Motor Skills. You may have read or been told that children with autism usually have motor abilities that are typical of children of their chronological age. While children with autism generally are far less disabled in this area than in communication or social interactions, some do have trouble with fine or gross motor skills. For example, some children with autism may have problems with fine motor skills such as picking up small objects between the thumb and forefinger or gripping a pencil correctly. Others may have problems with gross motor skills such as walking with a steady gait or riding a tricycle. Examples of motor skills that might be taught in school include:

- riding a tricycle;
- catching and throwing a ball;
- cutting with scissors;
- placing coins in vending machines;
- applying make-up
- shaving

Vocational Skills. As your child gets older, more emphasis should be placed on teaching domestic, leisure/recreational, community, and vocational skills. These skills become particularly important because they are the ones your child needs to ultimately function as independently as possible. Significant attention has been focused recently on preparing individuals with developmental disabilities for the eventual transition to the world of work. In the past, adults with autism rarely were considered as candidates for any "real" job. That is now changing thanks to programs that are demonstrating that, with sufficient support (e.g., a job coach), many individuals with autism can be employed in a variety of jobs. These jobs have included library assistant, food service worker, file clerk, printer, and cable operator.

Preparation for the transition to work must begin long before your child is ready to leave school. Vocational training, if your child is under eighteen years old, should provide her with various work experiences in different types of jobs. The types of jobs should be narrowed as she grows older so that preparation can focus on a particular job placement. Of course, this requires teachers to survey the community to identify types of jobs that are available and the skills most employers require for a particular type of job. Chapter 10 discusses vocational options for young adults with autism in more detail.

Behavioral Problems. By now, you have undoubtedly noticed that your child repeats certain actions such as hand-flapping, throwing tantrums, spinning objects, or lining up toys more often than other children do. Professionals call these behaviors "behavioral excesses." Behavioral excesses can present problems, especially in school, because they may interfere with learning. For example, if your child is more interested in spinning the wheels of an overturned car than in rolling the car back and forth to a classmate, the likelihood that other children will want to play with her decreases. Behavioral excesses can be problems at home, too. Behavioral excesses require attention wherever they interfere with learning or participating fully in the family or community.

"Behavioral deficits" are behaviors your child might be expected to have mastered by a certain age, but has not. These can include playing appropriately with toys, maintaining interest in an activity for more than a few seconds, or using social language ("hi"; "bye").

Each child with autism has her own unique set of behavioral excesses and deficits. These problems should be addressed at school whenever they interfere with learning or participation in community activities.

How Your Child Is Taught

Over the past twenty-five years, much has been learned about how children with autism learn best. We know, for example, that an approach based on *applied behavior analysis*—sometimes called *behavior modification* or *behavior therapy*—is by far the most effective. This method involves systematic study and manipulation of environmental events that precede and follow behaviors in order to replace behavioral deficits and change behavioral excesses with more appropriate behavior. This is combined with systematic and consistent instruction, on-going evaluation of progress, and reinforcement of desired behavior.

A good behavioral teaching program must satisfy several requirements. First, there must be a clear description of the goal to be achieved (exactly what will be learned, or what problem behavior will be decreased). This should include the level or rate of the behavior that will be considered acceptable, and at which point the teacher will say the behavior has been acquired. Second, the teaching procedure must be clear, and the program must list each step to be followed by anyone using it. Third, the rewards to be used to encourage the behavior being taught must be specified, and must be meaningful to your child—that is, they must be something she is willing to work to achieve. Fourth, the effectiveness of the teaching program must be frequently evaluated using a method sometimes called "data collection." By keeping track of your child's response to a teaching program, the teacher can quickly determine whether the program is achieving the desired results, and make changes at once if it is not. Finally, the program should specify how the skill just taught will be transferred to other people and places in the environment. This is called "generalization," and it is an extremely important part of any teaching plan. Without it, your child may learn how to do something very useful in one place—school, for instance—but nowhere else.

The *name* of the teaching approach a program uses is less important than its use of the proper teaching strategies. All teachers who provide educational programs for children with autism should be able to tell you exactly how they teach what they teach, their reasons for using those techniques, and the specific way they evaluate the effectiveness of their teaching. What they do, how they do it, and how they tell whether it works should be open to everyone for review, and should be judged by professionals to reflect the best practices for educating children with autism. If a program is unwilling or unable to meet these standards, then you should look for another program for your child.

Evaluation and Eligibility

Knowing that your child is entitled to early intervention and special education services is just the first step in securing those services. To receive services, your child must first be evaluated, and her need for special education services must be determined.

This evaluation and eligibility process begins with a referral (from you, your pediatrician or another professional, teachers) to the Special Education Division of your local school system. Typically, your child will be assigned a *case manager* who represents the school system's placement committee and is responsible for obtaining all of the information required by the committee in order to recommend appropriate programs. The case manager gathers this information by interviewing you, observing your child, and reviewing reports from previous teachers and support personnel, pediatricians and other doctors, and any other professionals who have worked with you and your child. When additional information is required, the placement committee will request that the appropriate professionals conduct further assessments. As a result, you and your child may see a speech-language pathologist, educational specialist, occupational therapist, physical therapist, or any of the professionals described in Chapter 1 who may have been involved in your child's diagnosis. If your child's needs require it, some of these professionals may continue to work with your child after she begins her early intervention or special education program.

The *speech-language pathologist* (speech therapist) is trained to evaluate how your child communicates using words, gestures, and symbols and also specific speech disorders (e.g., articulation problems, and problems with voice quality, pitch, and loudness). The former is most likely to be assessed in children diagnosed with autism. The speech therapist will also work directly with your child *and* your child's teacher. It is especially important for the speech therapist to consult with the early intervention or special education staff. In so doing, the therapist can ensure that the teaching staff is using the same techniques to build communication skills throughout the day.

To assess your child's communication abilities, the speech-language pathologist usually will observe your child interacting with others. The evaluation may include an assessment of your child's ability to: 1) understand language (e.g., identify objects upon request, follow directions, answer questions); 2) initiate communication using words, gestures, and/or symbols (e.g., getting someone's attention and making a request, identifying objects and actions in the environment); and 3) use of communication in interacting with others (e.g., playing a game, turn-taking, requesting and sharing information).

Your child might also require evaluation by an *occupational therapist* (OT) or a *physical therapist* (PT). An OT specializes in assessing and improving the development of fine motor skills such as holding a pencil or tying shoelaces and the relationship between motor input and output. OTs can also be helpful if your child has problems with feeding and eating because they are trained to provide treatment for problems with *oral-motor control*—the use of muscles in and around the face. Often the OT will work with the speech language pathologist, especially if your child has difficulty with feeding and eating skills. An OT may use standardized tests as well as direct observation to evaluate your child for problems with movement and perception. A physical therapist will assess your child for problems involving gross motor skills such as mobility (e.g., walking), posture (sitting), and balance.

Finally, to develop an overall picture of your child's educational needs, an *educational specialist* may examine your child. The educational specialist (sometimes called an educational diagnostician or child development specialist) will determine your child's abilities in a number of areas using information gathered from you, standardized tests, observation, and direct interaction with your child. Areas the educational specialist may assess include communication skills; readiness for educational instruction (e.g., the ability to sit still, make eye contact, and follow directions); pre-academic and academic skills in language, math, and reading; play skills; and self-help skills such as washing, dressing, and clothing selection. After placement, recommendations developed by the educational specialist will be included in the special education teacher's curriculum for your child.

Once your child's evaluations have all been completed, the school placement committee (sometimes called the Child Study Team) must hold an eligibility hearing to decide whether your child should receive special educational services. Throughout this process, you, as parents, have certain important rights. These are outlined in Chapter 8. Of all the rights you have, the most important one is the right to appeal almost any decision—including eligibility—that you feel is incorrect.

Assuming that your child is found to be eligible for special education services, the next phase of the process is to determine placement. The same team that determined eligibility will probably also recommend placement options to you. Some teams may recommend several programs for you to visit; others may have only one choice to offer. Certain parts of the country are more sparsely populated than others, have fewer children with autism, and fewer programs to serve them. Nevertheless, it is the responsibility of the public school system to provide an appropriate program (public or private) for your child even if your child is the only one with autism in the school system. Your child cannot be put into an inappropriate program because she is the only one with this condition, or because no teacher trained in working with children with autism is available, or because your child lives too far from the school. If your child has been declared eligible, then she must be provided an appropriate educational program.

We have learned over the years that programs for students with autism must have certain characteristics if they are to be successful. As a parent, such information will be helpful in identifying the right program for your child. The following section explains how to gather information about potential programs and then check this information against the characteristics of an appropriate program.

Gathering Information

Your school district's special education placement office should provide you with a list of the programs being considered for your child. If at all possible, try to visit all of these placement options before the formal placement meeting is held.

You can obtain the information you need to make a fully informed decision about a specific program from several sources. The principal, for example, is important to meet because she can provide you with information such as:

1. The philosophy of the program—for example, how does the program promote integration with nondisabled peers? Try to determine if there is a philosophy and whether you agree with it.
2. The availability of an extended-year program.
3. Current staff-to-student ratio, and, equally important, whether that ratio is likely to change in the near future.
4. The availability of services such as speech and language therapy, occupational therapy, and physical therapy.

Weigh each of these issues carefully. For example, a student–teacher ratio of 2:1 might be excellent for your child; however, the classroom might not be appropriate if the ratio has the potential for increasing.

Another important source of information is the speech and language therapist. You need to know how language services are provided to other students in the class. In the past (and to some extent currently) students were typically removed from the classroom in order to work with the speech-language pathologist. This practice has serious drawbacks because it does not promote the transfer of language skills to settings outside of the speech/language room. A child with autism is more likely to transfer skills learned at school to the home and community if the therapist conducts training as part of an ongoing instructional activity in the classroom (as opposed to "pull-out" services). For this method to be effective, the therapist must work with teachers to ensure that all instructional programs are designed to increase a child's language.

As important as it is to talk to the educators involved in the program, you should spend the majority of your time observing actual classroom activities. Before visiting, call the school office and ask for the classroom schedule so that you can decide on the most informative time to observe. Try to see as many different activities as possible in order to determine whether the teacher and the assistants are consistent in the way that they react to students' attempts at communication, their responses to instructions, and their acting-out behavior such as tantrums. Ideally, spend some time observing during the morning and afternoon hours so you can develop an understanding of what your child's day would include. This is important because many classrooms schedule more intense teaching time for morning, and concentrate on activities such as art, music, and physical education during the afternoon. Parents who have limited time to observe could perhaps schedule more than one visit at different time periods.

Characteristics of an Appropriate Program

Educators, researchers, and advocates have thoroughly debated the features of appropriate classrooms for children with autism and other handicaps, and have reached a general consensus from an educational standpoint. Legally, however, these features may not be required in determining whether a program is "appropriate." This is because the United States Supreme Court has established that an "appropriate" education is one that is "reasonably calculated to provide meaningful educational benefits." It does not have to maximize educational potential, opportunities, or benefits.

Given the Supreme Court's ruling, it is still our view that the characteristics listed below *are* essential components of educational programs for children and adolescents with autism. Knowing these features will be one of your primary resources as you begin the evaluation process. The order in which they are discussed does not reflect the importance of one over another. Ideally, parents would find a program or many programs that contain all of the features described below. Unfortunately, the ideal is rarely available; therefore, parents should seriously consider programs that have a majority of the ingredients discussed while continuing to advocate for the ideal.

1. Functional Activities. One of your major goals in evaluating programs should be to determine whether the skills taught and the materials used are *functional.* That is, the skills emphasized should be those the students need in order to function as normally as possible in the real world. Furthermore, they should be skills that are appropriate for the students' ages. For example, learning to play with three-piece puzzles may be a functional leisure skill for a child in preschool, but would not be for a student in junior high. You should expect to see more emphasis on community-based instruction and other functional living skills (e.g., street crossing, bus riding, shopping, cooking) the older the students are.

In general, you can determine whether skills are functional by asking yourself three questions:

1. Does it appear that the skills being taught are immediately useful to the students?
2. Are the materials used likely to be found in the students' everyday environment?
3. Will learning a particular skill decrease the probability that someone else will have to do it for her in the future?

Affirmative answers to these questions are critical, if the skills your child acquires are to be used in situations outside the classroom. Suppose, for example, you observe a ten-year-old girl with autism learning coin identification using play money. Although the skill may be functional, the play money would be considered nonfunctional because the child would not use it outside of the teaching session. As a result, it is very unlikely that she will be able to select the correct coins when asked to get two quarters from a pocket full of change in order to buy a soda. Teaching the same student to identify geometric shapes on a form board would be considered nonfunctional because the skill is not immediately useful or likely to be required in the real world.

Whether or not a skill is taught in a functional manner can also be determined by observing the sequence in which it is taught. For example, it is functional to teach tooth brushing following a snack or lunch, zipping and unzipping as students are putting on or taking off their jackets, or clothes folding after getting the clothes out of the dryer. Some students will need additional practice outside the natural sequence, but you should try to determine through observation and discussion with the teacher whether natural sequences are emphasized.

2. Chronological Age Appropriateness. As you observe the program, notice whether it is based on the concept of age appropriateness. This means that curricula and materials used within a classroom should suit the students' chronological, rather than developmental, ages. Age appropriateness may be less of an issue with preschool-aged (or younger) children because the gap between chronological age and developmental level may not be as pronounced as it is likely to become later. For example, having a morning circle and singing nursery rhymes may be chronologically age appropriate as well as appropriate to the developmental level of a three-year-old, but teaching the same skill to a high school student would be inappropriate regardless of the child's developmental level. Similarly, you should notice whether the physical environment of the classroom is designed with age appropriateness in mind: posters of the Care Bears and Muppets are expected in classrooms for preschool and some primary-age children, but are not appropriate in junior and senior high classrooms.

The importance of age appropriateness cannot be overemphasized, especially considering how hard it can be to get children with autism to use skills outside of the classroom. If the materials used and the skills taught are not age appropriate, there is even less chance they will be useful to students outside of the classroom. For example, interactions typical of high school students might include sharing video games, going to dances, or just "hanging out" and talking or listening to music. If students with autism are to fit in with other students, their teacher must provide instruction in skills that are appropriate to the age group and setting. Teaching them leisure skills more appropriate to their developmental level would essentially shut them out of their peer group.

3. Punishment. The use of punishment has historically concerned parents of children with special needs. By definition, punishment refers to a process in which the consequence for a behavior reduces the probability that the behavior will occur in the future. In the classroom, this might be accomplished by removing a child from a group for a specific period of time following a particular behavior ("time out"); by admonishing a student for a particular behavior (verbal reprimand); or by requiring a child to practice repeatedly the correct form of a behavior following a specific, inappropriate behavior ("overcorrection").

Among educators, there has been considerable controversy over whether or not to use punishment to curb behaviors that interfere with learning—especially those procedures referred to as "aversives" which are considered extreme forms of punishment. The controversy has been fueled by reports that some programs routinely use aversive procedures. As a result, parent organizations such as the Autism Society of America (ASA) have adopted resolutions regarding the use of punishment. ASA's policy, as summarized by Sue Pratt, the current President, is based on the belief that everyone is entitled to the "highest quality of life possible and [to] be treated at all times with the same dignity and respect accorded to everyone else." (Pratt, p. 2) She points out that ASA's resolution does not prohibit the use of any procedures; instead, it suggests that positive programming be used as an alternative to punishment procedures. "Positive programming" has been used to describe procedures that are designed to reduce severe behavior problems through the use of strategies based on reinforcement (e.g., rewards for refraining from behaviors or for engaging in appropriate, alternative behaviors). ASA feels that this type of programming should be the norm.

Because of the controversy, you may encounter professionals who believe that punishment is never justified, professionals who believe punishment is a necessary component of every program, and professionals who stick to a more middle ground. Where your child is concerned, be sure to obtain sufficient information from your observations and discussions with classroom staff to determine if punishment procedures are used, and if so, whether you think they are appropriate. When interviewing teachers or principals, ask whether the school has guidelines governing the use of punishment procedures. These guidelines should help you determine the answers to the following questions:

1. Under what conditions will punishment procedures be considered?
2. Who is involved in making the decision (e.g, parents, teachers, principal, psychologist)?
3. Who will monitor/evaluate the administration and effectiveness of punishment? Parents, classroom staff, and the principal should at least be involved.
4. How often will this evaluation occur (no less frequently than every three days) and what data will be used to support the continued use of punishment?
5. Are parents required to provide informed consent before punishment is used? If not, you should question the appropriateness of the program very seriously.

If you see a punishment procedure used in the classroom, you should ask whether previous attempts have been made to reduce the behavior using nonpunitive methods. The teaching staff should be committed to teaching alternative, appropriate behaviors before using punishment procedures. For example, it would be more desirable to teach students to get attention by raising their hands rather than to punish tantrums that serve the same purpose. Some exemplary programs for children with autism may use punishment under certain conditions; however, they will always concurrently teach another skill to replace the behavior to be reduced, and will also be able to provide you with satisfactory answers to the above questions.

4. Data-based Instruction. You have probably experienced the variability of your child's behavior. One day your child completes a task; another day she appears not to understand what is being asked. The same type of problems occur in the classroom, and the only way teachers can judge student progress accurately is to record and chart each student's performance consistently. Data collection that occurs prior to and throughout an instructional program enables a teacher to identify a student's entry skill level, monitor the effectiveness of a teaching program, and, if necessary, modify the course of instruction.

You will discover that many programs assess students' progress only at the beginning, middle, and end of the year using standardized tests. Because so much time passes between assessments, it is difficult for teachers to determine how well—or if—a student is progressing and whether changes might be needed in the educational program. They are more likely to plan effective programs if they record how a student actually does throughout the course of instruction.

Ask the staff how often data are collected, charted, and reviewed, and also observe whether any data collection occurs during your visit. Teachers may report that data collection as described above does not occur because it is too time-consuming, interferes with actual instruction, and is unnecessary in determining a student's level of performance. However, there are many ways that teachers can reduce the burden of data collection (e.g., use timers, counters, and stopwatches to help them count or to signal the time to observe; schedule data collection for three times per week rather than every day) and still obtain information that is substantially more valuable than that provided by tests given at six- and twelve-month intervals. Finally, in most situations, teachers of children with autism and other severe handicaps cannot judge student performance accurately unless they collect data regularly.

5. Instruction in Nonschool Environments. As you gather information about programs, you should ask for a copy of the weekly schedule to determine how much instruction takes place outside the classroom (e.g., in grocery stores, homes, libraries). This information is important because until recently, children with autism were taught almost exclusively in the classroom. Instruction in the community was accomplished through "educational" field trips. Unfortunately, children with autism are not likely to learn skills by being exposed to the community only once or twice a week.

Over the past ten years, many professionals have argued that children with autism need frequent and systematic teaching outside of school in order to learn how to respond appropriately to the wide range of cues and consequences in the real world. For example, students taught to shop in supermarkets are more likely to learn how to respond to cues found in markets—placement of aisle headings or location of cashiers—than are students taught only in the classroom. In addition, instruction outside of school increases the probability of students learning important skills such as street crossing that are not needed in a classroom.

Although community-based instruction will become more important as your child gets older, all programs should provide some instruction outside of the classroom. For example, young children can be taught age-appropriate skills such as accompanying their parents to stores and libraries without engaging in severe tantrums or other disruptive behavior. Older children might learn skills such as locating and selecting items in a supermarket, checking out library books, and riding a bus. You should look for instructional goals that reflect this type of teaching strategy and, for older children, a classroom schedule that permits frequent trips in the community.

6. Social Integration. As discussed earlier, educational programs for children with autism have only recently moved into public schools serving nonhandicapped children. Although some parents may be concerned about how their child will be treated by nonhandicapped children and staff in an integrated school, these placements provide many advantages not available when children with autism attend segregated schools. The primary advantage is that nonhandicapped peers are more likely to encourage any attempts at social behavior that children with autism may make. Conversely, because segregated classrooms typically serve other handicapped children with equally poor social skills, it is doubtful that peers will respond appropriately to social behaviors such as greetings, sharing, and interactive play. As a result, children with autism are not likely to maintain their social behavior. In addition to allowing more opportunities for social interaction, integration enables nonhandicapped students to gain a better understanding of children with autism or other handicaps. Finally, as several programs for preschool children have shown, integration can help children with autism develop social interaction, cognitive, and communication skills.

As you visit programs, you may be exposed to two different methods of integration, depending on the age of your child. At the preschool level, integrated programs usually provide instruction to children with autism and nonhandicapped children in the same classroom, with the nonhandicapped children receiving training in how to interact with, and be a tutor for, the children with autism. For older students, integration involves locating classrooms in regular public schools, and providing systematic instruction with nonhandicapped children in a variety of settings such as physical education, lunch, recess, and after-school activities. In both cases, parents should check carefully to ensure that the program does not just provide opportunities for children with autism to have contact with nonhandicapped students without also teaching them the skills they need to interact with their peers. There is clear evidence that nearness or physical integration alone does not promote interaction between children with autism and nonhandicapped children. Locating the classroom near the students' chronological age-appropriate peers, and devising a classroom schedule that allows students with autism to be at student gathering places at appropriate times will make it easier for staff to provide systematic instruction. How well a classroom provides for structured integration and the support that it receives in the school are critical tests of the appropriateness of a program.

7. Extended-Year Programming. As this chapter has emphasized, one of the most important features of an appropriate program is classroom instruction that continues beyond the traditional nine- or ten-month school year. If your child does not receive instruction during the summer, it will be very difficult to ensure that she maintains the skills she has learned in the past school year. In addition, valuable teaching time will be spent in the fall reteaching those skills lost over the vacation. Therefore, if at all possible, you should insist on a year-round program for your child.

8. Parent Involvement. The opportunity for parents and other family members to become actively involved in the education of their children is an important part of all appropriate educational programs. This has been shown to be especially true for parents of children with autism, and should be recognized by the staff in any classroom you visit. Teachers should realize that you know your child best because you spend significantly more time with her, and that you can make classroom instruction easier by continuing to work at home on skills taught in school. In other words, the parent-professional relationship must be a two-way street: you can learn various teaching strategies from the classroom staff, while they can learn about you and your family and how your child interacts with the environment. Never forget that you and your child have very specific rights under the law and you must be prepared to ensure that they are not abused.

Parents should also have the chance to be involved in other ways. For example, programs should provide parents with the opportunity to receive training in teaching new skills, practicing skills previously acquired, and controlling disruptive behavior in home and community situations. Furthermore, parent training programs should be flexible enough to serve both parents who want intensive training and those who just want assistance teaching a specific skill, such as learning not to handle food in a grocery store. An appropriate program will offer parents the type of systematic training that best serves the needs of their family.

There are other ways for you to determine the extent to which a program encourages family participation. For example, programs that include a system for daily—or weekly at the very least—contact with parents (e.g., through school–home notes) and have a flexible visitation policy promote parent involvement. In contrast, a classroom policy that restricts contact unreasonably may indicate a program that discourages such involvement.

Conclusion

The guidelines discussed above are based on a review of recommendations provided by professionals over the past ten years. In many places, these guidelines have been incorporated into programs for children with autism. The New Jersey Council of Organizations and Schools for Autistic Children and Adults, (COSAC), for example, has developed an excellent summary of educational program requirements for children, adolescents, and adults with autism. These evaluation guidelines are reproduced at the end of the chapter with their permission.

Although programs that satisfy all or most of these requirements exist, finding an appropriate placement for your child is never an easy task. Being an informed parent, however, is the first step toward ensuring that you are an active and knowledgeable participant in the placement process. As you review various programs, remember that it is important that you keep the ideal classroom in mind—one that incorporates all of the features discussed above. The ideal classroom may be difficult to find, but it is well worth your effort to keep looking. In the end, a program that includes a majority of these characteristics is more likely to effectively address the needs of your child and of your family.

Education Program Evaluation Guidelines

- **Early diagnosis and appropriate intervention** are vital to the development of individuals with autism;

- **Highly structured, skill-oriented teaching and treatment programs** (programs which simultaneously address skill deficits and problem behaviors by utilizing both skill building and behavior reduction techniques throughout the day), based upon the principles of applied behavior analysis are the most effective in improving the skills and behavior of individuals with autism;

- **Programs must be tailored to the specific needs of the individual** and delivered in a comprehensive, consistent, systematic, and coordinated manner. Since many children and adults with autism have deficits in many skill areas, providing comprehensive instruction is necessary;

- **Programs should be data-based.** Behaviors should be operationally defined. Teaching and treatment procedures should be outlined. The occurrence of behavior should be recorded before (baseline), during, and after (follow-up) the implementation of teaching and treatment procedures. A summary (i.e., graphs, charts) of data should be provided. Data-based programs permit objective evaluation of the effects of the intervention. On the basis of these data, programs should be revised as needed to assure continued progress;

- **Programs should use individualized motivational systems** (i.e., primary systems [food], token systems, behavior contracts, etc.) and appropriate reinforcement schedules (i.e., continuous, fixed ration, etc.). Motivational systems are based upon the learning principle that individuals tend to repeat or increase behaviors which are followed by positive consequences;

- **Teaching areas should be structured, organized, and distraction-free environments which incorporate intensive one-to-one and small group sessions. Schedules of routines and activities should proceed smoothly and reliably within and across days. Time spent "waiting" should be kept to a**

minimum. Classrooms should be equipped with one-way mirrors for observation. For those individuals ready for transition to other settings, larger group sessions ("normal") classrooms should be provided;

- **To provide the consistency necessary for generalization** and maintenance of skills and appropriate behavior:

  — Programs should be offered on a **full-day, year-round basis** from preschool through adulthood;

  — **Individuals should be taught in multiple settings**, by multiple therapists using a variety of stimuli;

  — **A comprehensive home programming/parent training program** should be provided to foster coordination of day and evening programming. Parents should be provided with support groups and extensive in-home behavior management training, which also gives parents a method of coping with many of the child's behavior problems;

- All personnel involved with individuals with autism should be extensively, specifically **trained and continuously evaluated.** On-going skill-based staff training and evaluation are necessary to help ensure staff excellence.

References

Bates, P., A. Renzaglis, and P. Wehman. "Characteristics of an Appropriate Education for Severely and Profoundly Handicapped Students." *Education and Training of the Mentally Retarded* 16 (1981): 142-49.

Donnellan, A. "An Educational Perspective of Autism: Implications for Curriculum Development and Personnel Development. In *Critical Issues in Educating Autistic Children and Youth*, edited by B. Wilcox and A. Thompson, 53-88. Washington, D.C.: U.S. Department of Education, Office of Special Education, 1980.

Egel, A.L., and Gradel, K. "Social Integration of Autistic Children: Evaluations and Recommendations." *The Behavior Therapist*, 11 (1988): 7–11..

Gaylord-Ross, R., and V. Pitts-Conway. "Social Behavior Development in Integrated Secondary Autistic Programs." In *Public School Integration of Severely Handicapped Students: Rational Issues and Progressive Alternatives*, edited by N. Certo, N. Haring, & R. York, 197-219. Baltimore: Paul H. Brookes Publishing Co., 1984.

Hoyson, M., B. Jamieson, and P.S. Strain. "Individualized Group Instruction of Normally Developing and Autistic-like Children: A Description and Evaluation of the LEAP Curriculum Model." *Journal of the Division for Early Childhood* 8 (1984): 157-72.
Koegel, R.L., A. Rincover, and A.L. Egel. *Educating and Understanding Autistic Children*. San Diego: College-Hill, 1982.
LaVigna, G.W., and A. Donnellan. *Alternatives to Punishment: Solving Behavior Problems with Non-Aversive Strategies*. New York: Irvington Publishers, 1986.
Pratt, Sue. "Resolution Discussed and Concerns Stated" [Editorial]. *Advocate*, 20, no. 4 (1988): 2.
Sasso, G.M., R.L. Simpson, and C.G. Novak. "Procedures for Facilitating Integration of Autistic Children in Public School Settings." *Analysis and Intervention in Developmental Disabilities* 5 (1985): 233-46.
Schopler, E. "Editorial: Treatment Abuse and Its Reduction." *Journal of Autism and Developmental Disabilities* 16 (1986): 99-103.
Snell, M., and N. Grigg. "Instructional Assessment and Curriculum Development." In *Systematic Instruction of Persons with Severe Handicaps*, edited by M. Snell, 64-109. Columbus, OH: Merrill Publishing Co., 1987.
Strain, P.S., M. Hoyson, and B. Jamieson. "Classroom Deportment and Social Outcomes for Normally Developing and Autistic-like Children in an Integrated Preschool." *Journal of the Division for Early Childhood* 10 (1986): 105-15.
Wilcox, B., and G.T. Bellamy. *Designing High School Programs for Severely Handicapped Students*. Baltimore: Paul H. Brookes Publishing Co., 1982.

Parent Statements

Early intervention was our lifesaver. I just wish Brian's program and his diagnosis had happened earlier.

Even in Special Education, the term *autistic* turns people off.

Early intervention was a very negative experience for me. At the time, we didn't know Lawrence had autism. I was surrounded by little Down syndrome babies smiling and learning how to throw balls and stack blocks while Lawrence wouldn't even look at the toys. I'd always ask myself, "Why are these kids learning and making progress while Lawrence is doing absolutely nothing?" No one mentioned autism to me.

You can't afford to alienate anybody. You have to be nice to the administrators, you have to be nice to the classroom teacher—you have to learn to be a politician.

The speech pathologist suggested taking him to Child Find, which we did, and he was diagnosed as language impaired. They put him in the Early Beginnings Program—by that time he was almost three.

All our friends now are in Special Education. All we do is in Special Education.

Initially, a component of Donny's school program required my active participation at home. Being an active participant in Donny's play and behavior management helped restore my self-worth.

Lawrence has never been in a twelve-month program. One year he went to summer school; the next year he didn't. He'll never miss summer school again.

Every time I see that someone is not doing what they should be doing, or not working for him, I get furious. After all, everyone says we should all be working together.

He went into a residential school at age 9. I wish we had enrolled him sooner—for his sake as well as ours. I always felt so guilty thinking about him being away, but I never considered anybody else's life in our home. Now we can relax somewhat and live a "normal" life when he's at school.

My frustration is they're not helping him as I think they should be—to become that best welder, or that best mail carrier, that best lawn mower. I want him to develop to his potential!

When I first heard about full-day school and long bus rides for a two-year-old, I cried. But he loved it right from the beginning. And once he started school, he progressed so quickly!

I feel like saying to the teachers, "We're supposed to work together, so let's work together. You've got him eight hours a day; we've got him the rest. He's ours, and you might like him, but we love him." I don't find the support that I need, but I think that I need a lot of support.

The way he reads is incredible. He'll read anything, and he is getting so he understands a lot of what he's reading. And his math skills are almost up to his age.

If anyone offered a twelve-month program, I'd jump at it. Lawrence needs a continuous program. And I think I need it more than he does.

He comes home from school fairly often and it's not so hard to take anymore. We go back to our old way of living temporarily. But he's

always glad to go back to school. He does so much better with the twenty-four-hour structure, which certainly doesn't exist at home.

Amy's trying to read. She can write her letters, more or less, A through M. She's done some math. She can count objects and then match the number that she counted—circle the right answer. But, again, the interaction with other children—her staying on task—that's one concern her teacher has right now. She can't stay on task that long.

I was adversarial with Laura's educational system all the way through, but I had lots of questions that I couldn't get answers to.

"We teach during the day—part of our job is not to educate parents, it's only to educate kids. Find that someplace else," was the message I was getting from teachers. "You're taking too much of my time. I don't have time to do that."

Mainstreaming is a good idea—and eventually, we want that for Lawrence. Unfortunately, in the programs we've seen, when they start mainstreaming, the teacher-student ratio starts to climb and the programs seem to become less intensive.

I felt like I didn't have the right to ask the educators to spend the time because they work so hard and are so underpaid—all that kind of attitude thing.

There are a few teachers out there who are masterpieces, who will give that extra mile. Sometimes they give an extra 500 miles—There are some real champs out there who will spend the time.

They shouldn't try to do all of the testing at one time, because children get frustrated just like parents—taking a test for two or three hours straight. After the first half hour or forty-five minutes, the child gets frustrated, and he just doesn't want to be there anymore. I really think if they're going to put him through a battery of tests, they should break it up, even if it has to be over a week's time. Don't try to cram everything into two or three days, because that's really not enough time and you can't get the child to perform his best.

Four hours testing for a three-year-old? Cut me some slack. Now, maybe they've done seven million kids and they know after forty-five minutes exactly what to write down. They just finish out the test. I hope that's not true. But when you get bitter—you know, some of us might be—you tend to react to those sort of things.

Donny tried two early intervention programs, but neither one did him much good. The teachers tried very hard, but Donny just didn't seem to sit and attend. His behavior interfered with whatever the staff tried to do. They were not equipped to deal with a child like Donny. He cried and tantrummed a lot and barely made any gains. He just didn't seem to fit in with the other kids.

No *one* program has the "miracle cure," and you may have to do some shopping around before you find the program that serves your child best.

EIGHT

Legal Rights and Hurdles

JAMES E. KAPLAN AND RALPH J. MOORE, JR.*

Introduction

Because your child has autism, you know that he has very special needs. You may not know, however, that he also has many rights. These rights, which include the right to a free appropriate public education, are provided by federal, state, and local laws. They can be essential in helping your child reach his potential by opening the door to education, training, and special services. Understanding how these laws can ensure that your child receives all the services he needs is crucial for you as the parent of a child with autism.

There are no federal laws that deal specifically with autism. Rather, the rights of children with autism are provided for in the laws and regulations for people with handicaps generally. In other words, the same laws that protect all children with disabilities can also protect your child. To effectively exercise your rights and fully protect your child, you should understand those laws.

---

* Ralph J. Moore, Jr., and James E. Kaplan are partners in the Washington, D.C., law firm of Shea & Gardner, and are active in the area of the legal rights of handicapped children. They are the co-authors of "Legal Rights and Hurdles: Being a Good Advocate for Your Child" in *Babies with Down Syndrome: A New Parents Guide* (Woodbine House, 1986) and "Legal Rights and Hurdles" in *Children with Epilepsy: A Parents Guide* (Woodbine House, 1986). Mr. Moore is the author of *Handbook on Estate Planning for Families of Developmentally Disabled Persons in Maryland, the District of Columbia, and Virginia* (MD DD Council, 3rd edition, 1989).

Because autism usually causes serious lasting disabilities, parents will have additional concern about the future—especially about how to care for their child when they, the parents, are no longer alive. This chapter reviews some of the extremely important legal issues parents must face to protect their child's future. Finally, we summarize briefly the disability benefits generally available from federal and state governments after your child is grown.

It would be impossible to discuss the law of every state or locality. Instead, we provide an overview of the most important legal concepts you need to know. For information about the law in your area, contact the Autism Society of America (ASA) or your local or state ASA affiliate.

You should understand that this chapter is designed to provide accurate and authoritative information about the legal aspects of raising a child with autism. The authors and the publisher, however, are not acting as lawyers and are not rendering legal, accounting, or other professional advice. If you need legal or other advice, you should consult a competent professional.

Your Child's Right to an Education

Perhaps nothing has done so much to improve the educational opportunities for children with autism as The Education for All Handicapped Children Act of 1975, better known as Public Law 94–142 or the EAHCA. This comprehensive law has created vastly improved educational opportunities for almost all exceptional children across the country. Administered by the Department of Education and by each state, the law works on a carrot-and-stick basis.

Under Public Law 94–142, the federal government provides funds for the education of children with handicaps to each state that has a special education program that meets a variety of federal standards. To qualify for the federal funds, a state must demonstrate, through a detailed plan submitted for federal approval, that it has a policy assuring all children with handicaps a "free appropriate public education." What this means is that states accepting federal funds under Public Law 94–142 must provide both approved educational services and a variety of procedural rights to children with handicaps and their parents. The lure of federal funds has been attractive enough to induce all of the states to create special education plans that can truly help children with autism.

The EAHCA establishes the *minimum* requirements in special education programs for states wishing to receive federal funds. The federal requirements *do not require* states to adopt an ideal educational program or a program that parents feel is "the best." Because states have leeway under Public Law 94–142, there are differences from state to state in the programs or services available. The minimum "appropriate" program required by federal law may not be the best or optimum program for your child with autism.

States *can* create special education programs that are better than those required by Public Law 94–142, and some have. For children with autism this is very important. Parents, organizations, and advocacy groups continually push their states to go beyond the federal requirements and provide the highest quality special education possible as early as possible. Parents should check with their local school district to find out exactly what services are available to their child.

What Public Law 94–142 Provides

The EAHCA contains many important provisions that can directly affect your child. It is worth knowing what the law says and how it works. This section reviews the important provisions of Public Law 94–142.

Coverage. There is no question that children with autism are covered by Public Law 94–142. The 1990 amendments to the law specifically list autism as a covered condition. Mental retardation, learning disabilities, and serious emotional disturbances are also covered conditions. A diagnosis of autism should be enough to establish that the EAHCA applies to your child.

When Coverage under Public Law 94–142 Begins. Generally speaking, Public Law 94–142 requires that states provide special education to children with handicaps between the ages of six and eighteen. States may provide services to children between birth and age six and between ages eighteen and twenty-one, even though the EAHCA does not necessarily require it. Parents need to check with the state where they reside to determine exactly when publicly funded services are available.

Congress recently amended Public Law 94–142 to provide for educational services at earlier ages. Beginning in 1991, states will be required to provide services to all children with handicaps from the age of three. In addition, Congress has established a program of grants to support states that offer services to children from birth.

Currently, there is wide variation among the states as to when they start providing services. A few provide services from birth onward; some provide services at age two; most, however provide services between the ages of three and five. Unfortunately, a few states do not offer services until age six. With the amendment of Public Law 94–142, however, every state will, by 1991, start services at age three, if not earlier.

There are many different programs available to children with handicaps in every state. In addition to Public Law 94–142, states or local school districts may provide early intervention services or other educational programs. There is also a federal law making grants available to local school districts for infant and toddler programs. *Even if your state does not start services under Public Law 94–142 until quite late, there may be programs available to your child now.* Check with your state department of education, your local autism group, the ASA, and other parents. The Resource Guide at the end of the book contains listings of national and state agencies, organizations, and programs. Call them to find out exactly when services under Public Law 94–142 begin and what other services are available to your child now.

Length of Services. Currently under Public Law 94–142, states must provide more than the traditional 180–day school year when the unique needs of a child indicate that year-round instruction is a necessary part of a "free appropriate public education." In many states, the decision to offer summer instruction depends on whether the child will regress substantially without summer services. If so, the services must be provided at public expense.

Because children with autism typically regress without year-round services, your child should be eligible for continuous instruction, and you should not hesitate to ask for it.

Identification and Evaluation. Because the EAHCA applies only to children with handicaps, your child must be evaluated before he is eligible for special education. Public Law 94–142 requires each state to develop testing and evaluation procedures designed to identify and evaluate the needs and abilities of each child before he is placed into a special education program. All areas of development must be tested: health, vision, hearing, social and emotional status, general intelligence, academic performance, communication ability, and motor skills. On these and other issues, the evaluation procedure is required to take into account the parents' input. That means that parents—who understand their child's developmental needs best—should take an active role in the evaluation. Parents should gather as much information as they can to establish what special education services their child needs.

"Free Appropriate Public Education." At the heart of Public Law 94–142 is the requirement that children with handicaps receive a free appropriate public education. The law defines this to mean "special education and related services." In turn, "special education" means specially designed instruction tailored to meet the unique needs of the child with handicaps, including classroom instruction, physical education, home instruction, and—if necessary—instruction in private schools, hospitals, or institutions. A twenty-four-hour residential placement may well be appropriate to meet the unique needs of children with autism.

"Related services" are defined as transportation and other developmental, corrective, and supportive services necessary to enable the child to benefit from special education. Services provided by a trained occupational therapist, physical therapist, speech therapist, psychologist, social worker, school nurse, aide, or any other qualified person may be required under Public Law 94–142. Some services, however, are specifically excluded. Most important among these exclusions are strictly medical services that must be provided by a licensed physician or hospital.

As mentioned above, the EAHCA does not prescribe a specific educational program, but rather sets a minimum standard for the states to follow. In this way states have considerable leeway in designing special education programs. Let's examine more precisely what "free appropriate public education" means.

"Free" means that, regardless of the parents' ability to pay, every part of a child's special education program must be provided at public expense. This is true if the child is placed in a program in a public school or, if a suitable public program is not available, in a private school or residential setting. As mentioned above, if a private school or residential placement is necessary to provide an appropriate educational program—not merely the parents' preference—then the school district must place the child in the private school and pay the tuition. In many areas, private schools have programs that are better suited to the needs of children with autism. Remember, the EAHCA does not provide for tuition payment for educational services *not* approved by the school district or other governing agency (unless, as explained elsewhere in this chapter, parents are able to overturn the decision of their school district). Parents who place their child in an unapproved program face having to bear the full cost of tuition themselves.

It often is difficult for parents to understand that the "free appropriate public education" mandated by the EAHCA does not secure for their child either the best education that money can buy or even an educational opportunity equal to that given to nonhandicapped children. The law is more modest; it only requires that children with handicaps be given access to specialized educational services individually designed to benefit the child. A few years ago, the United States Supreme Court decided that a "free appropriate public education" need not be designed to enable a child with handicaps to maximize his potential or to develop self-sufficiency. Instead, the basic floor of educational opportunity may be satisfied by a variety of instructional and related services, the extent of which is determined on a child-by-child basis. The law in this area is still evolving.

It is up to parents to secure the most appropriate placement and services for their child. Under the EAHCA, parents and educators are supposed to work together to design the individualized education program for each child. But to convince a school district to make the best placement for the child, parents must demonstrate to school officials not only that the school district's preferred placement might not be appropriate, but that the parents' preferred placement *is* appropriate. Hopefully in the end there is agreement on the appropriate placement. If not, there are procedures for resolving disputes that we discuss later in the chapter.

"Least Restrictive Environment." Public Law 94–142 requires that children with handicaps must "to the maximum extent appropriate" be educated in the *least restrictive environment* with children who are *not* handicapped. Under Public Law 94–142, there is therefore a strong preference for mainstreaming children with handicaps, including children with autism.

In practice, the law requires that children with handicaps be integrated into their community's regular schools, if possible. For some this means a combination of special classes, along with physical education, assemblies, and other classes taken with the rest of the school. Special services and extra teaching material can be used to provide the extra educational input special children need. The law was intended to end the historical practice of isolating children with handicaps.

The EAHCA also recognizes that regular classrooms may not be suitable for the education of some children with handicaps. In these cases, the law allows for placement in separate classes, separate public schools, private schools, or even residential settings if this kind of placement is required to meet the individual educational needs of the child. For children for whom placement within the community's public schools is not appropriate, the law still requires that they be placed in the least restrictive educational environment suitable to their individual needs.

"Individualized Education Program." Public Law 94–142 recognizes that each child with handicaps is unique. As a result, the law requires that special education programs be tailored to the individual needs of each child. Based on your child's evaluation, a program specifically designed to address his developmental problems will be devised. This is called an "individualized education program" or, more commonly, an "IEP."

The IEP is a written report that describes:

1. the child's present level of development;
2. both the short-term and annual goals of the special education program;
3. the specific educational services that the child will receive;
4. the date services will start and their expected duration;
5. standards for determining whether the goals of the educational program are being met; and
6. the extent to which the child will be able to participate in regular educational programs.

A child's IEP is usually developed during a series of meetings among the parents, teachers, and representatives of the school district. Even the child himself may be present. School districts are required to establish committees to make these placement and program decisions. These committees, sometimes called "Admission, Review, and Dismissal" committees, decide what services your child will receive in addition to deciding where he will receive them.

The effort to write an IEP is ideally a cooperative one, with parents, teachers, and school officials conferring on what goals are appropriate and how best to achieve them. Preliminary drafts of the IEP are reviewed and revised until what hopefully is a mutually acceptable program is developed.

IEPs should be very detailed. Although initially this may seem intimidating, detailed IEPs enable parents to closely monitor the education their child receives and to make sure their child is actually receiving the services prescribed. In addition, the law requires that IEPs be reviewed and revised at least once a year (or more often if necessary) to ensure the child's educational program continues to meet his changing needs.

Designing a suitable IEP requires direct parent involvement. You cannot always depend on teachers or school officials to recognize your child's unique needs as you do. To obtain the full range of services, you may need to demonstrate that withholding these services would result in an education that would *not* be "appropriate." For example, if parents feel a private school program is best for their child, they must demonstrate that placement in the public school program would not be appropriate for their child's special needs.

Because a child with autism has special needs, it is essential that his IEP be written with care to meet those needs. Unless parents request specific services, they may be overlooked. Make sure school officials recognize the unique needs of your child—the needs that make him different from other children with handicaps.

How can parents prepare for the IEP process? First, survey available educational programs, including public, private, federal, state, county, and municipal programs. Observe classes and see for yourself which program is best suited to your child. Local school districts and local organizations can provide you with information about programs in your community. Second, collect a complete set of developmental evaluations—get your own if you doubt the accuracy of the school district's evaluation. Third and most important, decide for yourself what program and services are best for your child, then request that placement.

To support placement in a particular type of program, parents should collect "evidence" about their child's special needs. Parents should support their position that a particular type of placement is appropriate by presenting letters from doctors, psychologists, therapists (physical, speech, or occupational), teachers, developmental experts, and other professionals. In addition, you may want members of the interdisciplinary team that diagnosed your child to present their information. This evidence may help persuade a school district that it would not be appropriate to deny your child the requested placement. Other suggestions to help parents through the IEP process are:

1. Don't go to IEP meetings alone—bring others for support, such as spouses, doctors, teachers, and friends;
2. Keep close track of what everyone involved in your child's case is doing; and

3. *Get everything in writing.* Children with unique developmental challenges need parents to be assertive advocates during their IEP process.

Resolution of Disputes under Public Law 94–142

It is usually best to resolve disputes with your school district over your child's educational program *during* the IEP process, before hard positions have been formed. Although Public Law 94–142 establishes dispute resolution procedures that are designed to be fair to parents, it is easier and far less costly to avoid disputes by coming to some agreement during the IEP process. Accordingly, you should first of all try to accomplish your objectives by persuasion. If there is a dispute that simply cannot be resolved with the school district, however, this section discusses how Public Law 94–142 and other laws can be used to resolve that dispute.

In order to protect the rights of children with handicaps and their parents, Public Law 94–142 establishes a variety of safeguards. For instance, prior written notice is always required for any change made in your child's identification, evaluation, or educational placement. A school district is prohibited from making unilateral decisions or from deceiving parents. School officials must state in writing what they want to do, when, and why.

Beyond the requirement of written notice, the EAHCA allows parents to file a formal complaint locally about *any matter* "relating to the identification, evaluation, or educational placement of the child, or the provision of free appropriate public education to such child." What this means is that parents can make a complaint about virtually any problem they may have with any part of their child's educational program if they have been unable to resolve that problem with school officials. This is a very broad right of appeal, one that parents have successfully used in the past to correct serious problems in their children's educational programs.

The process of challenging a school district's decisions about your child's education can be started simply by sending a letter of complaint. This letter, which should explain the nature of the dispute and your desired outcome, is sent to the school district. For information about starting appeals, you can contact your school district, advocacy groups, and other parents.

The first step in the appeal process is usually an "impartial due process hearing" held before a hearing examiner. This hearing, usually held on the local level, is the parents' first opportunity to explain their complaint before an impartial person who is required to listen to both sides, and then to render a decision. At the hearing, parents are entitled to be represented by an attorney or lay advocate; they can present evidence; and they can examine, cross-examine, and compel the attendance of witnesses. The child has a right to be present at the hearing as well. At the end of the hearing, parents have a right to receive a written record of the hearing, of the written findings, and of the hearing examiner's conclusions.

Just as with the IEP process, parents need to present facts that show that the school district's decisions about a child's educational program are wrong. To overturn the school district's decision, parents must show that the disputed placement or program does not provide their child with the "free appropriate public education" that is required by the EAHCA. Evidence in the form of letters, testimony, and expert evaluations is usually essential to a successful appeal.

Parents or school districts may appeal the decision of a hearing examiner. The appeal usually goes to the state's educational agency. This state agency is required to make an independent decision upon its review of the record of the due process hearing and of any additional evidence presented. The state agency then issues its own decision.

The right to appeal does not stop there. Parents or school officials can appeal beyond the state level by bringing a lawsuit under the EAHCA and other laws in a state or federal court. In this kind of legal action, the court must determine whether there is a preponderance of the evidence (that is, whether it is more likely than not) that the school district's placement is proper for that child. In reaching its decision, the court must give weight to the expertise of the school officials responsible for providing the child's education, but parents can and should also present their own expert evidence.

During all administrative and judicial proceedings, Public Law 94–142 requires that your child remain in his current educational placement, unless you and the local or state agencies agree to a move. Parents who unilaterally place their child in a different program risk having to bear the full cost of that program. If, however, the school district is found to have erred, it may be required to reimburse parents for the expenses of the changed placement. Accordingly, you should make a change of program only after carefully considering the potential cost of that decision.

As with any legal dispute, each phase—complaint, hearings, appeals, and court cases—can be expensive, time-consuming, and emotionally draining. As mentioned earlier, it is wise for you to try to resolve problems without filing a formal complaint or bringing suit. For example, you should consult with other parents who have filed complaints and should talk to sympathetic school officials. When informal means fail to resolve a problem, however, formal channels should be pursued. Your child's best interests must come first. The EAHCA grants important rights that parents need not be bashful about exercising.

Regarding expenses, parents who ultimately win their dispute with a school district may recover attorneys' fees thanks to a recent amendment to Public Law 94–142. In the past, parents had to pay their own attorneys' fees even when they won their challenge. The law was changed to allow courts, at their discretion, to award attorneys' fees to prevailing parents in cases either pending or initiated after July 3, 1984. Even if you prevail at the local or state level (without bringing a lawsuit), you likely are entitled to recover attorneys' fees, although this issue is currently under consideration in the federal courts. A word of caution, however: a court can limit or refuse attorneys' fees if you reject an offer of settlement from the school district, and then do not obtain a better outcome.

The EAHCA is a powerful tool in the hands of parents. It can be used to provide unparalleled educational opportunities to children with autism. Using it effectively, however, requires an understanding of how it works. The Reading List at the end of this book includes several good guidebooks to Public Law 94–142 and the special education system. With knowledge of this vital law, parents will be far better able to help their child realize his potential.

Federal Antidiscrimination Laws

Section 504 of the Rehabilitation Act of 1973 prohibits discrimination against "otherwise qualified" handicapped persons and increases their opportunities to participate in and benefit from federally funded programs. A handicapped individual is anyone having a physical or mental impairment that substantially interferes with "caring for one's self, performing manual tasks, walking, seeing, hearing, speaking, breathing, learning, and working." The United States Supreme Court has determined that an "otherwise qualified" handicapped individual is one who is "able to meet all of a program's requirements in spite of his handicap." Programs or activities receiving federal funding must make reasonable accommodation to permit the participation by otherwise qualified handicapped persons.

A recent amendment to Public Law 94–142 frequently makes it possible for parents to pursue a claim against their local school district under both the EAHCA and the Rehabilitation Act. Parents should, however, pursue all claims and appeals at the administrative level *before* suing under either law. The Rehabilitation Act also comes into play to assert rights beyond secondary school or rights unrelated to education. Prevailing parties may recover attorneys' fees under the Rehabilitation Act.

As of this writing, the Senate has passed the Americans with Disabilities Act (ADA), which would expand the ban on discrimination against handicapped persons well beyond federally funded programs. The ADA would prohibit discrimination against otherwise qualified handicapped persons in private employment, public services and transportation, places of public accommodation (such as restaurants, hotels, banks, grocery stores, and shopping centers), and telephone services. It is expected that these expanded rights and protections will become law by the end of 1989.

Educational Programs and Services When Your Child is an Adult

Most children with autism will not be independent as adults. Some will have varying needs for special services depending on how autism affects them. Most, because of the impact of their autism, will need support and supervision in employment and daily living. This support and supervision can be provided through employment and residential programs. In addition, in some areas there are strong movements toward noninstitutional community residential services and supported employment programs. Regrettably, if these kinds of programs are unavailable, parents are left on their own to provide the necessary support and supervision for as long as possible.

Programs vary from state to state and from community to community. As a result of state and federal budget cuts, these programs typically have long waiting lists and generally are underfunded. After your child reaches age eighteen, his right to a public education may end in many states, even though his needs may continue. Currently, the sad truth is that under Public Law 94–142 thousands of children receive education and training that equip them to live as independently and productively as possible, only to be sent home when they complete school with nowhere to go and nothing to do.

Now is the time to work to change this sad reality. As waiting lists grow, your child may be deprived of needed services. Charitable funds are limited and most families do not have the resources to pay the full cost of group homes and employment programs. The only other remedy is public funding. Just as parents banded together in the 1970s to demand enactment of the EAHCA, parents must band together now to persuade local, state, and federal officials to take the steps necessary to allow disabled people to live in dignity. This nation can afford to do this, and can't afford not to.

Parents of handicapped *children* should not leave this job to parents of handicapped *adults,* for children become adults—all too soon. Chapter 9 explains how to become an advocate for your child and for the rights of people with autism.

Under the federal Developmentally Disabled Assistance and Bill of Rights Act, states which meet the law's requirements can receive grants for a variety of programs. Important among them is a protection and advocacy (P&A) system. A P&A system works to protect and advocate for the civil and legal rights of people with developmental disabilities. Because people who are disabled by autism may not be in a position to protect their own rights or speak out for themselves, it is important that each state's P&A system offer adequate protection.

Vocational Training Programs

There is one educational program supported by federal funding that is available to adults with autism who need it. Operating much like Public Law 94–142, several federal laws make funds available to support vocational training and rehabilitation. Again, states that want federal funds must submit plans for approval. Federal law provides that all people who have a mental disability that constitutes a "substantial handicap to employment" and who can be expected to benefit from vocational services are eligible. Unlike the EAHCA, however, these laws do not grant people with handicaps enforceable rights and procedures.

In the past, most people with autism were considered too severely affected to benefit from vocational training services because they likely could not achieve the law's goal of full-time or part-time employment. Recent amendments to the law require services and training to people with severe handicaps (such as autism) even if all they will achieve is "supported employment." This term means employment in a setting which includes ongoing services necessary to allow an individual to perform work.

The state Departments of Vocational Rehabilitation are sometimes called "DVR" or "Voc Rehab." People who apply for Voc Rehab services are evaluated and an "Individualized Written Rehabilitation Plan," similar to an IEP, is developed. Under these programs, adults with autism can continue to receive vocational education after they reach age twenty-one. Parents should contact their state vocational rehabilitation department, the ASA, or the local ASA affiliate for specific information on services available to their child with autism. Despite shrinking federal and state budgets, some states and communities offer their own programs, such as group homes, supported employment programs, and life-skills classes. Contact other parents and organizations for information about programs available in your area.

Planning for Your Child's Future

The possibility that your child may be dependent all of his life can be overwhelming. To meet your child's future needs, you need information in areas you may never have thought about before and you must find inner resources you may not believe exist. In most families, parents remain primarily responsible for ensuring their child's well-being. Consequently, questions that deeply trouble parents include: "What will happen to my child when I die? Who will look after him? How will his financial needs be met?"

Some parents of children with autism delay dealing with these issues, coping instead with the immediate demands of the present. Others begin to address the future. They add to their insurance, begin (alone or with grandparents) to set aside funds for their child, and share with family and friends their concerns about their child's future needs. Whatever the course, parents need to understand in advance some serious problems that affect planning for a disabled child's future. Failure to avoid these pitfalls can have dire future consequences for your child and for other family members.

There are three important issues that families of children with autism need to consider in planning for the future. These are:

1. the potential for cost-of-care liability;
2. the complex rules governing eligibility for government benefits; and
3. the child's ability to handle his own affairs.

Of course, there are many other matters that may be different for parents of special children. For example, insurance needs may be affected, and the important choice of trustees and guardians is more difficult. But these types of concerns face most parents in one form or another. Cost-of-care liability, government benefits, and the inability to manage one's own affairs, however, present issues that are unique to the parents of children with handicaps.

Cost-of-Care Liability

When a state provides residential services to a person with handicaps, it usually requires that person to pay for them if he has the funds to do so. Called "cost-of-care liability," this requirement allows states to tap the handicapped person's own funds to pay for the services the state provides. States can reach funds owned outright by a person with handicaps and even funds set aside in some trusts. A few states go farther. Some impose liability on parents for the care of an adult with handicaps; and some impose liability for other services in addition to residential care. This is an area parents need to look into early and carefully.

Parents should understand that payments required to be made to satisfy cost-of-care liability do *not* benefit the person with handicaps. Ordinarily they add nothing to the care and services the individual receives. Instead, the money is added to the general funds of the state to pay for roads, schools, public officials' salaries, and so on.

It is natural for parents to want to pass their material resources on to their children by will or gift. The unfortunate effect of allowing a child with autism to inherit a portion of your estate, however, may be the same as naming the state in your will—something most people would not do voluntarily, any more than they would voluntarily pay more taxes than the law requires. Similarly, setting aside funds in your child's name, in a support trust, or in a Uniform Gifts to Minors Act (UGMA) account may be the same as giving the state money—money that could better be used to meet the future needs of your child.

What, then, can parents do? The answer depends on circumstances and the law of your state. Here are three basic strategies parents use:

First, strange as it may seem, in some cases the best solution may be to disinherit a child with autism, leaving funds instead to siblings in the hope that they will use these funds for their disabled sibling's benefit, even though they will be under *no* legal obligation to do so. The absence of a legal obligation is crucial. It protects the funds from cost-of-care claims. The state will simply have no basis for claiming that the person with handicaps owns the funds. This strategy, however, runs the risk that the funds will not be used for your child with autism if the siblings: 1) choose not to use them that way; 2) suffer financial reversals or domestic problems of their own, exposing the funds to creditors or spouses; or 3) die without making arrangements that safeguard the funds.

A second method, in states where the law is favorable, is to leave funds intended for the benefit of your child with autism in what is called a "discretionary" trust. This kind of trust is created to supplement, rather than replace, state benefits. The trustee of such a trust (the person in charge of the trust assets) has the power to use or not use the trust funds for any particular purpose as long as it benefits the beneficiary—the child with handicaps. In many states, these discretionary trusts are not subject to cost-of-care claims because the trust does not impose any legal obligation on the trustee to spend funds for care and support. In contrast, "support" trusts *require* the trustee to use the funds for the care and support of the child and can be subjected to state cost-of-care claims. Discretionary trusts can be created under your will or during your lifetime, but, as with all legal documents, must be carefully written. In some states, to protect the trust against cost-of-care claims, it is necessary to add provisions stating clearly that it is to be used to supplement rather than replace publicly funded services and benefits.

A third method to avoid cost-of-care claims is to create a trust, either under your will or during your lifetime, that describes the kind of allowable expenditures to be made for your child with autism in a way that excludes care in state-funded programs. Like discretionary trusts, these trusts—sometimes called "luxury" trusts—are intended to supplement, rather than take the place of, state benefits. The state cannot reach these funds because the trust forbids spending any funds on care in state institutions.

In using these estate planning techniques, parents should consult a qualified attorney who is experienced in estate planning for parents of children with handicaps. Because each state's laws differ and because each family has unique circumstances, individualized estate planning is essential.

Eligibility for Government Benefits

There are a wide variety of federal, state, and local programs for people with handicaps. Each of these programs provides different services and each has its own complex eligibility requirements. What parents and grandparents do now to provide financially for their child with autism can have important effects on that child's eligibility for government assistance in the future.

There are four major federally-funded programs that can help people with autism. First, "Supplemental Security Income" (SSI), a public assistance program, and "Social Security Disability Insurance" (SSDI), a disability insurance program, can both be applicable to people with autism. Both are designed to provide a monthly income to qualified disabled persons.

To qualify as "disabled" for either of these programs, the applicant's autism must be so disabling that he cannot engage in "substantial gainful activity." This means that he cannot perform any job, whether or not a suitable job can be found for him. The Social Security Administration regulations prescribe a set of tests for making this determination. Under those regulations, autism meets the test of severity when one of the following four tests is satisfied:

1. the applicant's autism is so severe that the use of standardized intelligence tests is precluded; or
2. the applicant's "verbal, performance, or full scale IQ" on a standardized test is 59 or lower; or
3. the applicant's "verbal, performance, or full scale IQ" on a standardized test is under 70 and he has a physical or other mental impairment imposing additional and significant work-related limitation of functions; or

4. his score on a standardized test is between 60 and 69 or he has gross deficits of social and communicative skills and he has two of the following: 1) marked restriction of activities of daily living; 2) marked difficulties in maintaining social functioning; 3) deficiencies of concentration, persistence, or pace resulting in frequent failure to complete tasks in a timely manner; or 4) repeated episodes of deterioration or decompensation in work-like settings which cause the individual to withdraw or to experience exacerbation of signs and symptoms.

The eligibility requirements, however, do not end there. Eligibility for SSI is based on financial need, and thus an applicant's resources and other income can disqualify him from receiving SSI. On the other hand, eligibility for SSDI is not based on financial need. It is based on the disabled person's own work record prior to disability or on a retired or deceased parent's Social Security coverage in the case of persons disabled before age eighteen. What your child owns in his own name and what income he is entitled to receive under a trust can prevent him from receiving SSI benefits, but not SSDI benefits. Disabled surviving children of deceased federal employees and military personnel may also be entitled to monthly survivor's benefits under the retirement systems for these people.

Medicare and Medicaid are also potentially important to people with autism, but each has its own eligibility requirements. Medicaid provides medical assistance to persons who are eligible for SSI and to other people with incomes deemed insufficient to pay for medical care. Because eligibility is based on financial need, placing assets in the name of a child with autism or providing that child with income through a trust can disqualify the child. Medicare, however, is not based on financial need. Instead, people entitled to receive benefits under Social Security are entitled to Medicare coverage.

It is important for parents to become familiar with the rules governing SSI, SSDI, Medicaid, and Medicare. It is even more important to avoid an unwitting mistake that could disqualify your child from receiving these benefits. If your child may be disabled as an adult, do not set aside funds in your child's own name, create a support trust, or establish a custodial account under the Uniform Gifts to Minors Act UGMA (discussed below). Follow the type of strategies outlined above. You will need competent professional assistance, of course, because these are quite technical matters.

Competence to Manage Financial Affairs

Even if your child with autism may never need state-funded residential care or government benefits, it is likely he will need to have his financial affairs managed throughout his life. Care must be exercised in deciding how to make assets available for your child. There are a wide variety of trusts that can allow someone else to control the ways in which money is spent after you die. Of course, the choice of the best arrangements depends on many different circumstances, such as your child's capacity to manage assets, his relationship with his siblings, and your financial status. Each family's situation is different. A knowledgeable attorney can review the various alternatives and help you pick the one best suited to your family.

Need for Guardians

Parents frequently ask whether they should appoint themselves or others as guardians for a child with autism when the child becomes an adult. The appointment of a guardian costs money and may result in the curtailment of your child's civil rights—the right to marry, to have a checking account, to vote, and so on. Therefore, a guardian should be appointed only if and when needed. If one is not needed during the parents' lifetimes, it usually is sufficient for the parents to name guardians in their wills.

A guardian will be needed if your child inherits or acquires property that he lacks the capacity to manage. Also, a guardian may need to be appointed because a medical or service provider refuses to serve your child without authorization by a guardian. Occasionally it is necessary to have a guardian appointed in order to gain access to important records. Unless there is a specific need that can be solved by the appointment of a guardian, however, a guardianship should not be established simply because your child is disabled.

Life Insurance

Parents of children with autism should review the adequacy of their life insurance coverage. The most important use of life insurance is to meet financial needs that would arise if the insured person dies. Many people who support dependents with their wages or salaries are underinsured. This problem is aggravated by wasting hard-earned dollars on insurance that does not provide the amount and kind of protection that could and should be purchased. It is therefore essential for any person with dependents—certainly for the parents of a child with autism—to understand basic facts about insurance.

The first question to consider is: Who should be insured? Life insurance deals with the financial risks of death. The principal financial risk of death in most families is the danger that the death of the breadwinner or breadwinners will deprive dependents of their support. Therefore, life insurance coverage should be considered primarily for the parent or parents on whose earning power the children depend, rather than on the lives of children or dependents.

The second question is whether your insurance is adequate to meet the financial needs that will arise if you die. You should carefully evaluate whether your insurance coverage is adequate. To help you, *Life Insurance*, a book published in 1988 by Consumers Union, gives a step-by-step method of calculating the amount of insurance you need.

The next question is: What kind of insurance policy should you buy? Insurance policies are of two basic types: term insurance, which provides "pure" insurance without any significant build-up of cash value or reserves, and other types (called "whole life," "universal life," and "variable life"), which, in addition to providing insurance, include a savings or investment factor. The latter kinds of policies are really a combined package of insurance and investment. The different types of insurance are described in more detail in the Consumers Union book, *Life Insurance*. Whether you buy term insurance and keep your savings and investment program separate, or whether you buy one of the other kinds of policies that combines them, you should make sure that the insurance part of your program is adequate to meet financial needs if you die. A sound financial plan will meet these needs and will deal with savings and retirement objectives in a way that does not sacrifice adequate insurance coverage.

Finally, it is essential to coordinate your life insurance with the rest of your estate plan. This is done by designating the beneficiary—choosing who is to receive any insurance proceeds when you die. The beneficiary designation should be reviewed when you make your will. Frequently it is desirable to designate a trustee in your will, or in a separate revocable life insurance trust, as the recipient of insurance proceeds that you want to make available for the support of your child with autism after you die.

Estate Planning for Parents of Children with Autism

More than most parents, the parents of a child with autism need to attend to estate planning. Because of cost-of-care liability, government benefits, and competency concerns, it is vital that you make plans. Parents need to name the people who will care for their special child when they die. They need to review their insurance to be sure it is adequate to meet their child's special needs. They need to make sure their retirement plans will help meet their child's needs as an adult. They need to inform grandparents of cost-of-care liability, government benefits, and competency problems to make sure the grandparents do not inadvertently waste resources that could otherwise benefit their grandchild's future. Most of all, they need to make a will so that their hopes and plans are realized and the disastrous consequences of dying without a will are avoided.

Proper estate planning differs for each family. Every will needs to be tailored to individual needs. There are no formula wills, especially for parents of a child with autism. There are, however, some common mistakes to avoid. Here is a list:

No Will. If parents die without first making wills, the law generally requires that each child in the family share equally in the parents' estate. The result is that your child with autism will inherit property in his own name. His inheritance may become subject to cost-of-care claims and could jeopardize eligibility for government benefits. These and other problems can be avoided with a properly drafted will. Parents should never allow the state to determine how their property will be divided upon their deaths. Planning can make you feel uneasy, but it is too important to ignore.

A Will Leaving Property Outright to the Child with Autism. Like having no will at all, a will that leaves property to a child with autism in his own name may subject the inheritance to cost-of-care liability and may risk disqualifying him from government benefits. Parents of children with autism do not just need any will, they need a will that meets their special needs.

A Will Creating a Support Trust for the Child with Autism. A will that creates a support trust presents much the same problem as a will that leaves property outright to the child with autism. The funds in these trusts may be subject to cost-of-care claims and jeopardize government benefits. Have a will drafted that avoids this problem.

Insurance and Retirement Plans Naming the Child with Autism as a Beneficiary. Many parents own life insurance policies or maintain retirement plans that name a child with autism as a beneficiary or contingent beneficiary, either alone or in common with siblings. The result: funds may go outright to your child with autism, creating cost-of-care liability and government benefits eligibility problems. Parents should designate the funds to go to someone else or to go into a properly drawn trust.

Insurance on the Life of the Child with Autism. Some well-meaning parents and grandparents waste money insuring the life of their handicapped child. This money could be far better used to insure the *parents'* lives. The purpose of life insurance is to protect against the *financial* risks of the death of the insured. If a wage-earning parent dies, the family is deprived of his or her earnings. If a homemaker dies, it may be necessary to hire sitters or household help. In contrast, the death of a child does not have these consequences; typically it creates no financial risk that is appropriate for insurance. As a result, life insurance for your child with autism helps no one except the insurance agent.

Use of Joint Tenancy in Lieu of Wills. Spouses sometimes avoid making wills by placing all their property in joint tenancies with right of survivorship. In joint tenancies, property is owned equally by each spouse; when one spouse dies, the survivor automatically becomes the sole owner. Parents try to use joint tenancies instead of wills, relying on the surviving spouse to properly take care of all estate planning matters. This plan, however, fails completely if both parents die in the same disaster, if the surviving spouse becomes incapacitated, or if the surviving spouse neglects to make a proper will. The result is the same as if neither spouse made any will at all—the child with autism shares equally in the parents' estates. This may expose the assets to cost-of-care liability and give rise to problems with government benefits. Therefore, even when all property is held by spouses in joint tenancy, it is necessary that both spouses make wills.

Establishing UGMA Accounts for the Child with Autism. Over and over again well-meaning parents and grandparents of children with handicaps set up accounts under the Uniform Gift to Minors Act (UGMA). When the child reaches age eighteen or twenty-one, the account becomes the property of the child, and may therefore be subject to cost-of-care liability. Perhaps more important, most disabled persons first become eligible for SSI and Medicaid at age 18, but the UGMA funds will have to be spent before financial eligibility can be established. Parents should *never* set up UGMA accounts for their child with autism, nor should they open other bank accounts in the child's name.

Failing to Advise Grandparents and Relatives of the Need for Special Arrangements. Just as the parents of a child with autism need properly drafted wills or trusts, so do grandparents and other relatives who may leave (or give) property to the child. If these people are not aware of the special concerns—cost-of-care liability, government benefits, and competency—their plans may go awry and their generosity wasted. Make sure anyone planning gifts to your child with autism understands what is at stake.

Children and adults with autism are entitled to lead full and rewarding lives. To do so, they need proper financial support. Planning for the future *now* is the best way to assure they will have that support when they need it. Doing otherwise can tragically shortchange their future.

Conclusion

Parenthood brings responsibilities for all parents. Extra responsibilities confront parents of a child with autism. You need to know and assert your child's rights to guarantee that he will receive the education and government benefits to which he is entitled. Understanding the pitfalls for the future and planning to avoid them helps parents to meet the special responsibilities. Being a good advocate for your child requires more than knowledge; you must also be determined to use that knowledge effectively and, when necessary, forcefully.

References

Burgdorf, R., and P. Spicer. *The Legal Rights of Handicapped Persons.* Baltimore: Paul H. Brookes Publishing Co., 1980 & Supp. 1983.

Herr, S., S. Arons, and R. Wallace, Jr. *Legal Rights and Mental-Health Care.* Lexington, MA: D.C. Heath & Co., 1983.

Herr, S. *Rights and Advocacy for Retarded People.* Lexington, MA: D.C. Heath & Company, 1983.

Rothstein, L. *Rights of Physically Handicapped Persons.* New York: McGraw-Hill, 1984 & Supp. 1986.

"Children with Special Needs." Parts 1, 2. *Law and Contemporary Problems* 48 (Winter, Spring 1985).

Parent Statements

You never get to talk to the school administrators, so you just get a lawyer. And the lawyer knows what to say. So, it costs you $500, because it usually doesn't go to a hearing, because the lawyer knows what the law really is and what they have to do.

When we called the attorney, she wasn't really very receptive. Her attitude was, "Well, try and get it on your own and save your money," and that kind of thing.

I think what's hardest for me to understand about the law (Public Law 94-142) is that "appropriate" doesn't necessarily mean "best"—at least not to the schools, it doesn't.

We've been taking estate planning really seriously because we feel that it shouldn't be up to our other children to provide for Carl later on. I mean, if they want to, fine, but we're not going to make them feel as if they have to.

When it comes to understanding the ins and outs of Public Law 94-142, there's nothing like having another parent who's already dealt with the system explain everything to you.

We've been through one due-process hearing—when Lawrence was denied speech therapy. We won, but they worded the decision in such a way that when it came time to begin speech therapy the school was able to get around it by having the therapist look over the teacher's shoulder but not work with Lawrence directly. When I threatened to go through due process again, they relented and Lawrence began to get direct services.

By the time we were finished with the due-process procedures, I was tired of a school system that I felt was unresponsive to severely handicapped youngsters. We moved to a county we knew had more options for autistic children, and so far we've been happy here.

When I first started working with the school, I thought nobody there would be able to recognize an appropriate program for Bobby if it fell on them—but I was wrong. For the most part, the school's been very receptive to my suggestions. You can't ever rest, though. You've got to be constantly monitoring your child's progress.

My only advice is that you plan the best you can. You sit down with a good lawyer and draw up a will. You try to decide who will best look out for your child's needs and his well-being. You pick a good back-up for that person and then you stop worrying about the "what if's": what if this person you've left in charge has an accident and is sued; what if this person you've left in charge is widowed and remarries and he runs off with the money?

You plan the absolute best you can, you cover every track you can think of, you pray it will be okay, and then you stop agonizing about it because there's nothing else you can do.

Lawrence's IEPs always look like small books. His teacher and therapists have their goals and I have mine.

I always make sure everything in the IEP is written out in as much detail as possible, especially how the teacher is attempting to teach each skill. My child learns differently from other children, and if someone uses an inappropriate method of teaching, it can do more harm than good.

NINE

Becoming an Advocate

BERNICE FRIEDLANDER*

Introduction

Do not be intimidated by the title of this chapter. Contrary to what you may have heard, you do not need a law degree to be an advocate for your child or to understand the principles behind advocacy. Some advocates *are* lawyers, but many more are teachers, mental health and medical personnel, or concerned parents and citizens like you. Some advocacy does take place in the courtroom, but much more takes place in schools, hospitals, or the home. Advocacy is accomplished through sworn testimony, but also through letter-writing campaigns and phone calls.

What, then, is advocacy? Simply put, to advocate means to plead someone's cause. In the special-needs arena, this usually involves working to change how society views children with disabilities, and working to obtain needed services and benefits for them.

This chapter provides an overview of some of the ways advocacy has been used in the past to help children with autism and other special needs. It describes how individuals and organizations

---

* Bernice Friedlander was the public information and legislative affairs consultant in the national office of the Autism Society of America. Ms. Friedlander holds a master's degree in public administration from Harvard University. Presently, she is the senior Public Affairs Specialist with the Women's Bureau, Office of the Secretary, U.S. Department of Labor, Washington, D.C.

can work to achieve educational, legislative, and other reforms, and leads you step by step through the advocacy process. Most importantly, this chapter explains how you, the parent, can get involved in advocating for your child in order to ensure that her future is as fulfilling as possible.

The Need for Advocacy

As Chapter 8 explained, a variety of state and federal laws are intended to guarantee your child important rights—in education, employment, and access to health care, for example. Of primary importance to children with autism and their families is the Education for All Handicapped Children Act (EAHCA) of 1975, also known as Public Law 94–142.

Public Law 94–142 exists in part because thousands of parents of children with autism and other disabilities fought for the right of their children to be educated in the public school system. In fact, it is probably safe to say that parent advocates have played critical roles in the passage of all recent legislation benefiting children with special needs. The reason for this is simple: since elected officials seldom have time to keep up with every issue affecting the handicapped, they rely on experts to tell them what legislation is needed by children with autism or other disabilities.

In many instances, the "experts" who can best convince officials of the need for improved services are parents like you who have firsthand experience in raising children with special needs. Parents can not only persuade officials to propose new legislation, but they can also play major roles in clinching the support needed to pass a particular law. For instance, when a bill is being debated before a crucial vote, members of Congress frequently read from letters of support they have received from parents.

Besides using their expertise to help get new legislation passed, parents can also practice other, less formal kinds of advocacy—most importantly, on behalf of their own children. Because children with autism usually have communication problems and cannot speak out for their own rights, you may find yourself using this brand of advocacy often. This does not mean that you should expect to see your child's rights trampled at every turn, but, rather that there may be times when someone else's ignorance of your child's unique needs prompts a decision that is not in your child's best interests.

As an example, you may feel that your child is not receiving the special services you think she needs. In this case, even though Public Law 94–142 specifies that parents and educators are supposed to work together to develop each child's Individualized Education Program (IEP), it is up to you to convince the educators that your child needs additional services to help her realize her potential. School officials are often simply unaware of the special needs of children with autism, so *you* must ensure that your child's IEP will meet those needs. For instance, delayed speech requires therapy involving various language stimulation techniques, but unless you advocate that your child be given this therapy, she may not receive it.

Advocacy in Action

The principle behind advocacy is simple: the squeaky wheel gets the grease. If you have valid concerns about the treatment your child is, or is not receiving, you *will* get results, provided you attract the right people's attention. Sometimes you can resolve the problem on your own. Particularly in cases where you feel that a specific situation is adversely affecting only your child, a phone call to an elected official or a well-worded letter to the editor of the local newspaper may work wonders. Other times, the best strategy may be to band together with other parents to advocate for change. It is usually especially important to work with a group when attempting to get changes made that will benefit all children with autism or all handicapped children.

In recent years, both individuals and groups have enjoyed considerable success in advocating for children with autism. In the account below, Lillian Tommasone, the co-author of Chapter 2, describes how she and her husband obtained needed educational services for their child:

"Our personal involvement in advocacy began at a PTA meeting. We heard that a Pennsylvania court had ruled that a twelve-month education program was sometimes necessary to meet the special needs of an exceptional child. According to the court, a ten-month program did not always adequately fulfill the child's right to a "free and appropriate education," as provided in Public Law 94–142. In such cases, an extended school year could help maintain a child's appropriate skills and behaviors, and, more significantly, help prevent him from losing those skills.

"We had mixed feelings about the twelve-month program. Although we were thrilled about our toddler's steady gains and proud of his hard-won struggles to master simple tasks, somehow we felt sorrowful and cheated. It didn't seem fair to send Mike to school during the summer. But as we saw the consequences of regression, we decided it would be a good idea to replace our usual summer activities with added instruction for Mike.

"At once, we set out to get Mike into an extended program. Being novice advocates, we thought a simple verbal request to the Supervisor of Child Study in our local school district would be sufficient. The supervisor, however, told us that our request was unconventional and not in keeping with current Board of Education policy. At first we were shocked and angry, but we learned that he was absolutely correct: there was no local or state provision for extended school programs. The board was not required by law to provide one. On the other hand, there was no law that said it couldn't be done, either, if the board should choose to do so.

"In the beginning, we felt powerless and frightened at the thought of questioning or making recommendations to the authorities. Then we realized that what we needed to do was to show the board that the extended school year was necessary, easy-to-implement, and cost-efficient—in short, the best solution for everyone involved. To do this, we needed more information, preparation, and a systematic plan.

"We began to learn all we could about autism and the law. We attended workshops and seminars on advocacy to familiarize ourselves with the procedures for obtaining services. We contacted the state protection and advocacy office and asked questions about things we didn't understand. We spoke with "seasoned parents," who told us about some of the pitfalls in dealing with the Child Study Team (CST). We attended local Board of Education meetings to identify key players sensitive to children with special needs and requested documentation of Mike's special needs from his teachers and school administrators. Finally, we kept a diary of the regression that took place on days Mike was not in school.

"Bolstered by the confidence that our thorough preparation had given us, we now began to advocate in earnest. We wrote letters to the CST, the Superintendent of Schools, and Board members documenting Mike's needs and requesting funding for an extended school year. We arranged for a conference to explore together the possibilities of securing services. We also continued to attend Board of Education meetings, where we expressed our concerns and explained that surrounding states were offering twelve-month services.

"By contacting local and state legislators—especially those on the Appropriations and Education Committees—we developed a feeling for what was going on. Several legislators hinted that a mandate concerning the provision was on the horizon. The need, however, hadn't been demonstrated in our state and a bill had yet to be written on the subject.

"Then we learned through the Education Committee that grant monies were available to communities who wanted to participate in the development of innovative approaches to special education.

"Our research, planning, and persistence were beginning to pay off! We contacted the CST and told them about the exciting new opportunities to obtain funding. Surely the Board wanted to be a model for other communities to emulate, we said. Then, striking while the iron was still hot, we offered to make trade-offs. If the School Board would pay tuition for Mike's summer schooling, we promised that we would provide transportation. We also suggested that we could all sit down together at the end of the first summer and evaluate whether or not the program was helping Mike.

"When the Board agreed to our proposals, we were ecstatic. True to our word, we kept the Board informed about the program and Mike's progress. A show of good faith, a cooperative partnership, and Mike's continued development were instrumental in his receiving both tuition and transportation the following summer.

"Our story is not a dramatic one. By gathering needed information, developing a systematic plan, and being both assertive and persistent, we succeeded in building a working partnership with "those on the other side of the fence."

"By following a few simple steps, you too can become an effective advocate:

1. Become informed—Read, read, read.
2. Explore all avenues—don't leave any source unturned—parents, legislators, educators.
3. Be patient, yet persistent; it pays off.
4. Identify the key players—those sensitive to special needs.
5. Stay objective. Being emotional can be disastrous—it clouds objectivity and diplomacy.
6. Save copies of correspondence and make notes of phone calls to keep the memory fresh.
7. Make compromises and develop partnerships. Remember, a slice of the pie is better than none.
8. Share your experiences with other parents.
9. Say "thank you" to those who helped.
10. Believe in yourself.

"One final piece of advice: in working to help your child today, remember that advocacy does not just involve children. Some of the most important advocacy work for parents is longer term. For example, there is much to advocate for in vocational training, supported employment, residential living options for adults, and availability of other programs. All of these are, and will continue to be, subjects of advocacy by concerned parents. Being an advocate for your child is good training for being an advocate in the future.

"There is a lot you can do as an individual. We know! We did it ourselves. But sometimes the job can be done better, faster, and more completely by an organization. That is why the Autism Society of America (ASA) can be so important to all of us."

The Autism Society of America

One of the ASA's primary missions is to serve as an advocate for people with autism. The ASA often can be more effective than a single parent, or even a small group of parents. ASA speaks as the voice of *all* people concerned with the special needs of people with autism. It has the resources to monitor legislation, to reach the media, and to keep large numbers of people informed about what is going on. Most importantly, it can intercede when governmental programs and legislation are not adequately serving the needs of people with autism. The following is a good example of how the ASA works:

On May 28, 1986, the ASA was shocked to learn that the Department of Health and Human Services had just announced that people with autism would no longer be eligible for Medicaid-financed residential services. The ASA's shock quickly turned to outrage when it learned the process the U.S. Health Care Finance Administration (HCFA) had used to approve this change in the regulations. Rather than submitting the proposed change to public comment, as is required by law, the HCFA had made its decision solely on the basis of one comment from one individual. Worse still, the comment—which was to the effect that autism was a mental illness and should never had been covered by the regulation to begin with—was totally inaccurate.

When the ASA found out about this bureaucratic blunder, the effective date for the change in regulation was less than a month away. Immediately, the ASA sprang into action and developed a two-pronged strategy: 1) It would try to convince HCFA of its error in depriving people with autism of a much-needed service and to get the HCFA to retract the harmful change of regulation; and 2) It would challenge the regulation in court on the grounds that the HCFA had violated the legal requirements of proper public notice by not publishing the change before issuing the final regulation.

Strategy 1 was accomplished by issuing action alerts to ASA members and activists nationwide, urging them to write HCFA and stress the wrongness of HCFA's action, the number of people who would be affected, and the serious need these people had for residential services. At the same time, ASA held meetings with HCFA officials to explain the consequences of their proposed action and to ask them to correct it. Meanwhile, strategy 2 was addressed by a letter from ASA's attorney to HCFA citing the violated federal codes and procedures.

After about six months, HCFA agreed to send out a letter of clarification to the Medicaid field offices, specifying that people with autism were still eligible for residential services. While this was a substantial victory, the ASA continued to press HCFA to publish a retraction or technical correction notice in the *Federal Register* (where federal government agencies publish their regulations) to publicly amend its error so that this mistake does not come back to haunt this or other programs. The Society also began discussions with Members of Congress to introduce corrective legislation that would unequivocally state that people with autism are eligible for Intermediate Care Facilities services and that autism not be included under the category of "mental illness."

As you can see, advocacy organizations like the Autism Society of America can accomplish a great deal on the national level. But they can't do it without input and support from parents and other concerned individuals. Unless parents keep the ASA informed, the ASA can't possibly keep track of all the local issues that affect children with autism. And the Society can't influence public policy without proof—in the form of letters, telegrams, and phone calls—that thousands of citizens support its positions.

The Autism Society of America concentrates its advocacy on national issues. Matters of concern to parents like you on the local and state levels can more effectively be addressed through local ASA chapters and other parent and advocacy groups. The next sections are designed to provide a step-by-step guide for you and your parents' groups to help you become effective advocates.

At the Legislative Level

Know Your Issue

In recent decades, parents and other citizen-advocates have played crucial roles in obtaining federal, state, and local legislation benefiting millions of Americans with disabilities. There is still a herculean amount of work to be done, however—not only to improve existing laws, but also to secure the passage of new ones. Many parents believe, for example, that the minimum standards set by the Education for All Handicapped Children Act (Public Law 94–142) should be higher than they are at present. And there is little dispute about the crying need for public funding of group homes and employment programs for adolescents and adults with special needs.

As the parent of a child with autism, you will undoubtedly want to keep abreast of all pending or proposed legislation that may affect the welfare of your child. One of the simplest ways for you to find out about important issues is to write to the ASA national office and ask that your name be added to the ASA ALERT list. Once you have registered, you will automatically be notified of any legislative developments affecting children with autism (just as members were alerted when the HCFA threatened to disallow Medicaid-financed residential services for people with autism).

A subscription to ASA NEWS, a news service of the national office, can also keep you up-to-date on new regulations regarding the handicapped and on ASA's legislative positions, and provide you with information about recent publications and resources of interest to ASA members. In addition, you may find it helpful to read ASA's *Legislative Update,* available from the national office, which periodically publishes the status of all pending measures of importance to the special-needs community. Finally, other parents, community newspapers, and radio and television stations can be valuable sources of information about both local and national issues affecting children with autism.

Of course, every issue you read or hear about is not going to rouse you to action. Eventually, though, an issue may strike close enough to home that you may decide to make a foray into advocacy.

At this point, you need to do some homework. Now is the time to get all the facts straight, marshal rational, irrefutable arguments, and make sure that you understand the issue inside and out. After all, if you are going to sway a public official's opinion, your command of the issues will have to be as good as his or hers, if not better.

The following information is written to address legislative matters before United States Congressmen and Senators. However, these suggestions are equally applicable when you are devising a strategy for lobbying or advocating before state legislators, county government officials, city council members, or any other elected representative.

Position Paper

In the process of getting to know your issue, you may find it useful to develop a position paper detailing exactly where you stand. These are some points to include:

1. Know the formal name of the bill, act, or public law that is affected by the legislation you support and be able to refer to it properly. For example: Who are the sponsors of the measure in the Senate and House? Which Committee(s) was the measure referred to for consideration? Which Subcommittee(s) are charged with considering the bill within each Committee?
2. Categorically refute all major arguments being used against the measure you are supporting. Frequently, objections will involve cost or "local rights." When no cost or low cost is involved, this is something you will want to state clearly and often in all of your communications with public officials.
3. Work important buzz words like "children's rights," "parents' rights," "the right to a free and appropriate education," or "in order to bring justice to our children" into your arguments. Issues involving the preservation of basic rights, justice, and the welfare of children often cut across partisan and ideological lines and can be supported by most legislators.

4. List or refer to organizations, special interest groups, coalitions, and influential members of your community that support your point of view.
5. Cite newspaper or magazine editorials that agree with your stand.

Although putting your position in writing may seem like so much unnecessary busywork at first, it actually serves several useful purposes. To begin with, it forces you to look objectively at issues that may arouse your deepest emotions. In addition, the process of writing down your thoughts can help you pinpoint any logical inconsistencies in your own arguments, as well as in those of your opponents. And, more importantly, detailing your stand in writing will help you feel confident about your grasp of the issue.

Know Your Elected Official

Once you have a good grasp of the issue, the next step is to gather information about your elected official. Your interest here is to learn enough about the official's background to help you determine the angle to use in asking for his or her support. For example, if the official has small children, you may want to appeal to him or her as a father or mother. If your elected official made campaign promises about increased funding for special education and then failed to deliver, you may want to remind him or her of that fact. In general, your background investigation should cover the following:

Personal Profile. This includes family background, education, occupation, and social, community, and religious affiliations. You can usually obtain a formal biography by requesting it from your Congressman or Senator. Your local newspaper office can also provide much of this information.

Political Profile. This includes current and past political offices held, party affiliation and participation, special interest group constituencies such as school boards, educators, and medical societies, and names of key advisors and staff aides. You should also make an analysis of votes cast by the legislator on issues relevant to ASA and of his or her campaign promises.

Base of Political Support. From whom did your legislator receive his or her greatest financial and voting support? It is important to determine who the elected official owes both financially and politically. This information can make it easier for activists to contact people sympathetic to their position when a crucial vote is at stake.

A complete list of all contributors of $250 or more to any candidate for federal office is available from the Federal Election Commission, Records Office, 1325 K St., N.W., Washington, D.C. 20463. You may also phone (toll free, 800–424–9530) to request a free printout of contributors to any Congressional or Senatorial candidate. Be sure your request includes the candidate's name, political affiliation, election year, and office sought. This information is available without charge from the FEC.

Contact Your Elected Officials

After you have gathered the pertinent background information about the issue and the elected official, it is time to contact the elected official and let him or her know where you stand and what you want.

If you are like many first-time advocates, you may begin to get cold feet when you reach this stage of the advocacy process. You may worry that you are not "important" enough to disturb your Senator or Congressman or that he or she will not be interested in what you have to say. Nothing could be further from the truth.

To begin with, Senators and Congressmen do not make laws in a vacuum. They want to hear from constituents who would be affected by pending legislation. Since a third of the Senate and all members of the House of Representatives are up for re-election every two years, elected officials are always anxious to please the voters back home. So when you contact your Senator or Congressman, you are not imposing at all, but actually doing him or her a service.

Article 1 of the U.S. Constitution guarantees every American the right "...to petition the government for a redress of grievances." This is what you are doing when you seek to meet with any elected official. Remember, any elected official who refuses to meet with you or respond to you is endangering his political future. It is in his or her own best interest to listen to your point of view. To obtain his or her support, you will have to emphasize the merits of the issue and your personal interest in seeing it favorably resolved. You should indicate that you intend to pursue this matter until it is favorably resolved.

What follows is a description of how you can contact your elected officials through writing, visiting, or telephoning. But remember, your message should be clear and you must remember to follow through after each stage of the contact.

Write Your Elected Officials

Believe it or not, one of the most effective ways to contact your elected officials is to write them a letter. This is because each letter received on a particular issue is presumed to represent twenty to thirty other people who did not write. Therefore, when a Congressional or Senatorial office receives ten or fifteen letters on one subject, you can be sure the topic will get the attention of a senior staff member.

Many Congressmen personally review their mail each day. Most Senators find this impossible since they receive mail from an entire state, but legislative assistants keep counts of the mail received on each subject and bring these reports to the Senator's attention when specific legislation is pending for his or her vote.

Both Congressional and Senatorial offices put a high priority on answering letters from constituents. Congressmen usually respond within a week; Senators, within three weeks.

Here are some guidelines to keep in mind when writing to elected officials:

1. Know the issue and state your position clearly and concisely. One-page letters are preferable, but it is sometimes difficult to handle a complex topic in such a brief form.
2. Write legibly in your own handwriting or typewrite, and be sure to sign the letter in your own handwriting. Always identify yourself as the parent of a child with autism.
3. Limit your remarks to one or two issues per letter.

4. Refer to pertinent legislation by the proper bill or public law number and/or title.
5. If possible, include materials such as recent editorials or articles supporting your position. If you cannot actually include an article, make reference to it. Articles from local newspapers are especially effective because the official will know that many people back home have probably seen the article too.

Occasionally, you and your group may want to conduct an extensive letter-writing campaign in a relatively short period of time—for example, right before a bill is to be debated in Committee or Subcommittee, or just prior to final consideration of a bill in either house of Congress. Often, the quickest, most efficient way to handle these situations is to hold a letter-writing party.

To get the party started, invite ASA members and supporters to an informal gathering at someone's home. Ask your guests to bring personal or business stationery. Instruct everyone to write their messages in their own words, taking care to state clearly what your group supports as well as the proper titles and numbers of the bills involved. Because individually written messages are usually most effective, you should avoid preprinted messages unless time is of the essence. If you feel you must use preprinted letters or cards, however, make sure everyone signs clearly and includes his or her return address.

By the end of the letter-writing party, all letters and cards should be completed, stamped, and ready for delivery to the mail box or post office. Unless time dictates immediate delivery, stagger the mailing over several days so that the letters are not all received at once.

As an alternative to writing letters, you may want to consider sending Public Opinion Messages. POMs are sent via Western Union and are delivered within two hours. They can contain up to twenty words, excluding your name and address. The flat rate is $4.45. Multiple signatures beyond the first twenty words are charged at the rate of $2.00 per twenty words. Western Union can charge the cost to your telephone bill or a major credit card, or you may prepay at any Western Union office.

Remember: Send a copy of all letters, wires, or other messages you send to your elected officials to the ASA national office, to the attention of the Legislative Officer. This will enable the national office to follow up with the Member(s) you contacted and remind them that ASA is monitoring their votes and will report on their actions to the membership.

Visit Your Elected Officials

As a parent advocate, you can accomplish a great deal through visits with your elected representatives or their legislative aides. You can get a clear idea of your representative's legislative priorities and educate him or her about the special needs of children with autism. You can also get immediate feedback about your concerns.

In planning your visits to Congressional offices, be sure to call or write requesting an appointment at least two weeks in advance. If you are unable to plan that far ahead, call as soon as you know when you will be in Washington, D.C. Congressmen and Senators maintain offices at home in their districts, and if you find it easier to visit a local office, your appointment can be arranged for a time when the Congressman or Senator is in your area.

You may wish to visit alone or with a small delegation. If you assemble a delegation, try to include a cross section of the community, including politically influential citizens who support your views and someone who may have been politically supportive of the Congressman or Senator in the past.

An important part of your visit is the presentation of an issues packet to the legislator. The issues packet should include:

1. A cover letter urging support of specific legislation.
2. Copies of editorials or similar written endorsements.
3. One to three pieces of factual background information about the bill you are supporting.
4. A fact sheet about autism. This can be obtained from the national ASA office.

5. A list of organizations, interest groups, national figures, and local leaders who support your position.

You should present a second copy of the same issues packet to the legislative assistant who handles disability issues.

You will probably have only a limited amount of time to speak with your legislator, so you will want to make every word count. During your meeting, try to accomplish the following:

1. Summarize the contents of the issues packet so your legislator can understand exactly what you want him or her to do about specific proposals that are being brought before his or her committee or house of Congress.
2. Listen to explanations by the legislator or his aide about his philosophy or past record on similar issues. Listen also for any reservations he may express about the legislation.
3. Where appropriate, try to correct any misconceptions or misunderstandings the legislator or aide may have about pending legislation or about autism in general.
4. Do not hesitate to use your personal experience to explain the everyday problems faced by children with autism and their families.
5. Give the legislator some idea of the larger group of voters you or the delegation represent. (How many members are in your ASA chapter? How large is the support group which favors your bill back home?)
6. Make sure you meet the assistant who handles disability issues because he or she will be the key contact person for you in months to come. Let him or her know that you or your chapter would be happy to keep the office informed about new developments and any new information about the specific measure and autism in general.

Remember: Staff members can be valuable resources, as many elected officials rely on them both for their political judgment and their knowledge of issues. If you ever find yourself in disagreement with a staff person, be diplomatic. NEVER threaten to go over the staff person's head. You always retain the right to contact the Member directly when he or she is back in the home district or state. Avoid stepping on anyone's toes, because that could cut you off from further meaningful contact with the office and thus hurt your efforts to educate and win the lawmaker over to your side. No one is going to see everything your way. Just keep the information flowing and keep your cool.

It is a good idea to stay in touch with officials and staff throughout the year, especially on the district office level. This way you can develop a working relationship and keep your legislator up to date on your issues. If time is a problem, you can spread the responsibility for such contacts among several people in your chapter. For example, each person could serve as the official liaison to a particular official for a complete legislative session (one year).

Reaching the Media

Press Releases

Press releases should announce an event or happening that will be of some use to the general community (regular meeting, guest speaker, major event, celebrity fund-raiser), provide background information on a particular issue, or make a declaration of support or challenge on an issue (such as a chapter's decision on aversive therapy or the zoning for a group home).

A press release should be written as concisely as possible with the most important information appearing in the first paragraph and the rest of the information included in descending order of importance. And of course, do not forget the five "W's" of journalism: who, what, where, when, and why. It is not a press release without that information.

Be sure to include your contact person's name along with a daytime and evening telephone number so your local newspaper or news organization can contact you for further information.

If you are trying to interest a news organization in covering a meeting or event, be sure you leave enough time (about a week) from the time you send or deliver the release and the event itself. About three days before the event, call each news organization and speak to the editor or assignment editor and ask if he or she intends to send a reporter to cover the happening. If the editor does not, ask if you can furnish a report on the event. Some weekly newspapers will accept your own account of the meeting because they cannot cover every event but would like to feature your group.

Local radio stations will sometimes offer you the opportunity to do a "feed." They will record you on tape for 15 to 60 seconds, during which time you describe your event or your opinion on the issue at hand, and they will include this in their regular news coverage.

Do not be afraid to ask editors or assignment editors about the kind of "news" they want to cover. That is the only way you will learn to meet their needs and use them to publicize the important advocacy you are doing.

Letters to the Editor

Writing letters to the editor can be a most effective and inexpensive way to educate the public about your issue, as well as about the special needs of children with autism. Long after reporters or newscasters have lost interest in a story, you can keep the issue in the public's consciousness through letters to the editor. To increase your chances of having a letter published, follow these guidelines:

1. Limit letters to about 150 words and strive for tightly composed sentences.
2. Use specific examples in order to make specific points.
3. Address only one major issue in your letter.
4. Use accurate and up-to-date information.
5. Always include your signature, address, and telephone number. Some newspapers will call you first before they print your letter to verify that you wrote the letter and to inform you that your letter will be printed.

If your group wishes to conduct a letters-to-the-editor campaign because of a great deal of disagreement with a stand adopted by a paper or a television or radio station, you may wish to stagger your mailings so that only a few letters are sent each week. Keep copies of all letters sent for follow-up possibilities. Be sure also to send your elected officials appropriate clippings of letters to the editor whenever you write to them about the issue.

In your search for forums in which to air your views, do not overlook general magazines or the more specialized journals for medical, social science, and legal professionals. Many periodicals publish letters to the editor or invite guest editorials on issues of interest to their subscribers. Publishing letters in these periodicals can sometimes be the quickest way of reaching the people with the most clout.

Conclusion

Advocacy can be a powerful tool in the hands of a skilled parent advocate. You can use it to chisel away at ignorance about autism, to cut through bureaucratic red tape, and to hammer together a better future for children with autism. You can advocate singly or in a group; at home or in a public setting; on local or on national issues.

It is to your advantage—and to your child's advantage—for you to learn how to effectively practice all types of advocacy. Remember, as the expert on your child and her special needs, you are in the best, most knowledgeable position to explain her problems to people who can help. And if *you* don't speak up on your child's behalf, who will?

Parent Statements

Nobody is an advocate for your kid but yourself. You see potential when nobody else sees potential and you see problems when nobody else sees problems.

═❖═

I have a real need to become involved and not just let it happen or turn it over to "professionals."

I work in a bureaucracy. I see bureaucracy every day, and I know what it's like to be where the bureaucrats are. I used to be too empathetic to their problems, but I've stopped a lot of that. To hell with their budget. That's their problem. We need more services.

Exposure, time, and practice have taught me how to advocate effectively for my children so that I now have much greater control in educational decision-making.

I always make it a point to meet informally with everyone involved in Lawrence's education *before* any problems or questions arise. This includes teachers, therapists, principals, the people at the area office, and anyone who might be involved in Lawrence's future education. I believe we've avoided an awful lot of conflict that way.

In my opinion, it's not just the squeaky wheel that gets the oil—it's also the most familiar one.

I believe in power. Money is power. Politics is power. You get yourself in a position to come from power. Don't expect to get anything out of sympathy or moral issue or moral right. It's a business, like anything else. I mean, they call it a bureaucracy, and it is. That means everybody is asking this group that's supposed to take care of everybody what they want them to do. Work on a power base.

You *must* be ready to fight for services for your child if that's what it takes. We have taken our concerns to the school superintendent when we had to—and all of a sudden, doors opened.

Because of certain books and movies, a lot of public attention seems to be focused on autism right now. I think we should capitalize on that interest before it fades. We need to push for more services *now*.

If the Governor were my cousin, we wouldn't be having this problem. It's that simple.

My best advice: GET INVOLVED. The best thing you can do for yourself is become friends with other people who have children who also spit two hundred times in an hour. They understand you and where you're coming from.

My sister has been especially helpful in my efforts at advocacy. She has given me her insights and comments and typed hundreds of letters and papers.

This year, for the first time in my life, I picked up the phone and called my representatives' and senator's offices to oppose an unjust bill being considered that would affect Lawrence as an adult. It's too early to say whether all the parents who called and wrote will make a difference. But it felt good to take some sort of action, no matter how small. And maybe it *will* make a difference.

Autistic kids usually can't tell you what they need, and people without everyday contact with autism don't understand your frustration. Step on toes if you must, but don't sit back and assume it will work out.

TEN

The Years Ahead: Adults with Autism

DAVID L. HOLMES, ED.D.*

Introduction

Someday your child will grow up. He will become an adult with autism. Right now, while you are concentrating on getting the best possible care for him as a child, this fact may seem irrelevant. But don't forget, the "best possible care" for your child also involves planning toward the best possible future. Understanding what life is presently like for adults with autism, as well as what it *should* be like, is crucial to your child's future. Without this knowledge, you cannot help the "should be" become "is."

Some parents of young children with autism find coping with the present so overwhelming that they just don't feel up to planning for the future. This is understandable. Other parents begin worrying about the future early on, and find that planning helps them cope with their anxieties. Whatever your method of coping, you can use the information in this chapter as a guide when you are ready to plan your child's future.

---

* Dr. David L. Holmes has a master's degree in special education from Rutgers University and a doctorate in educational psychology from Rutgers University. He is the President and Executive Director of the Eden Family of Programs, which serves children and adults with autism in the Princeton, New Jersey area. Dr. Holmes is President of the National Association of Private Schools for Exceptional Children and Chairman of the Board of The Center for Non-Profit Corporations.

This chapter reviews the four issues parents worry about most when thinking about the future: 1) nurturing independence in their child; 2) choosing a place to live for their child; 3) finding employment and training for their child; and 4) coping with the changes the future may bring. In discussing these concerns, this chapter introduces you to what the future of your child *might* be like: it presents a combination of what life is like today for adults with autism and what life *can* and should be like in the future. Remember, as earlier chapters have emphasized, the future for children with autism is constantly changing. It is up to you and parents like you to make your child's future a good one by advocating for better services.

Who Are Adults with Autism?

Until recently, children with autism never grew up to be called adults with autism. Instead, they were called schizophrenic or mentally retarded, and were usually institutionalized. Why weren't adults with autism called "autistic"? Until recently, there were no residential, training, or employment services for adults with autism, so the only way they could receive services was to be labelled something else. And once labelled, the easiest thing to do was to shut them away in institutions.

Now more services are available for adults with autism, including group homes and other alternative living arrangements and a variety of employment and training opportunities. This development of services for adults with autism is still in its infancy, with some states providing a great number of adult services, and many other states offering no services at all.

As a result of increased services, we have finally begun to see adults with autism for who they are. They are people who usually require intensive, continuing training in order to lead fulfilling lives. And like children with autism, most of them need structure, supervision, and guidance in much of what they do.

No one can say exactly what your child's life will be like when he is an adult. We do know that it will depend somewhat on your child's capacity for learning and achieving—on his intelligence, health, work skills, behavior, and level of functioning. But because society's treatment of children with autism has recently improved so much, we just do not know what effect this improved treatment will have on them as adults. Most likely, though, they will have more skills than in the past. For example, adults with autism who receive intensive communication therapy as children are usually far ahead of those raised in institutions. Likewise, stereotyped behavior often diminishes in young adults who continue to receive treatment and therapy.

Children with autism usually carry with them into adulthood the same behavior, preferences, and demands they have had throughout life. This can be both good and bad. The bad news is that undesirable behavior does not end with adulthood. Many adults with autism, for example, retain their need for sameness and continue to throw temper tantrums. But the good news is that adults with autism do not usually acquire new behavior problems, nor do they lose the progress they have already made in controlling their behavior and in meeting their own needs.

As far as we know, adults with autism should have normal life spans given appropriate services. They do not usually develop new medical problems, such as seizures, that they did not have as children or adolescents. In addition, medication used in childhood to control behavior can often be weaned away in adulthood. Finding quality medical care, however, can be a problem. Some pediatricians are willing to continue treating children with autism when they become adults. More commonly, pediatricians will suggest that an internist or family practitioner become the primary physician. Unfortunately, many physicians have little experience with adults who have developmental problems. But if experienced physicians are available in the community, other parents can be a good source of information about them. Again, many of the suggestions Chapter 3 gives about choosing a pediatrician can also help you select a new physician for the adult with autism.

Do Adults and Children with Autism Have the Same Needs?

In many ways, adults and children have similar needs. To begin with, both need consistency among their many environments—at home, in school, and at the workplace. And like children with autism, adults with autism need individualized programs based upon their unique learning needs. They both require consistent, structured programs that teach them appropriate behavior, as well as training to improve their communication and self-care skills.

The difference between adults and children with autism is in the philosophy used to teach them. With children, the goal is usually to change behavior. With adults, however, the focus should be on working with what you've got—trying to channel and direct ingrained problem behavior into more appropriate types of behavior. For example, if years of training have not succeeded in eliminating hand flapping in a young adult with autism, he might be taught instead to pick up a magazine and flip through its pages whenever he feels compelled to flap his hands. A similar strategy might be used for an adult who cannot control a compulsion to arrange the objects in his bathroom. To refocus his energy, teachers might make him responsible for organizing the bathrooms where he lives.

Just as a child's program does, an adult's program should include training in communication, self-care, social skill development, controlling impulses, and following directions. But for most adults with autism, training in academic skills such as pure math and science should be phased out and replaced by training in the functional life skills needed for survival in the adult world. "Survival Academic Skills" should include reading signs, following simple written directions, understanding time concepts, handling money, and writing one's name. As you will hear often, the work to build these important skills should begin in childhood. And later on, both residential and employment programs for adults with autism should continue to build on these skills in order to foster as much independence as possible.

Nurturing Independence

Most adults with autism have the potential to become contributing members of society. But they can only reach that potential through active training, beginning in childhood. We now know that, given the right environment—at work, in employment training, or at home—adults with autism can continue to learn and grow all their lives.

The Goal—A Fish Story

You have probably heard the proverb:

"If you *give* a person a fish, he will eat for a day. If you *teach* a person to fish, he will eat for a lifetime."

So it is with people with autism. The more they are capable of satisfying their own needs and wants, the happier they will be. Parents and professionals should therefore not just *give* care to adults with autism, they should *teach* them to care for themselves. As hard as it may be to insist that your child do things for himself, it is the only way he will become independent. Commit yourself now to finding and working with programs that will make a good fisherman out of your child when he becomes an adult. No one would claim that the road to independence is easy, but in the long run, it offers the best hope for a bright future for your child, your family, and yourself.

"As If"

In nurturing independence, the concept of "as if" is crucial to ensuring that young people are challenged to their full potential. The concept of "as if" is simple: if you treat an adult with autism *as if* he were capable of leading a productive adult life, the chances of him achieving that expectation are greatly improved. On the other hand, if you treat him *as if* he needs constant care, his skills and independence will decline. Your expectations, and the expectations of those who work with your child, will play a critical role in determining the degree of independence he achieves. First at home and at school, and then later in employment and residential programs, everyone must be treated *as if* they have the potential for living and working independently. That is the best way to ensure that greater opportunities open up for all adults with autism.

Learned Helplessness

Just as attitudes like "as if" can help pave the way to independence for an adult with autism, so too can other attitudes pose major stumbling blocks. One of the most harmful of these attitudes is the belief that adults should either be able to be productive *or* should receive welfare. In other words, people who can't care for themselves should get help. Yet care giving is the worst possible way to help adults with autism. When you give only care to an adult with autism, you are in fact teaching that adult to be helpless. This condition of "learned helplessness" reduces a person's skills, dignity, and sense of responsibility for his future. Care giving without expectations almost always results in the rapid deterioration of skills, such as shoe tying and self feeding, attained by the adult during his educational years.

A Supportive Environment

In order to gain the independence and skills necessary to function in the adult world, adults with autism need a special kind of supportive environment. They need an environment that strikes a balance between the need to encourage—even force—them to be productive at home and at work and the need to provide them with enough care and structure to help them feel secure and less anxious. This type of supportive environment is equally important in both residential placement and in employment training. So whether you are evaluating a potential home or a potential job opportunity for your child, remember that the *learning* environment is critical, and that for people with autism, *every* environment—good or bad—is a learning environment. If all an agency provides is care, your child with autism will not be motivated to try to learn the skills needed for greater independence. Remember, merely providing care is not enough for people with autism; if the environment does not also nurture independence, it is not supportive.

Six key elements make up a supportive environment for people with autism:

1. **Individualized Planning.** All services provided to an adult with autism—from personal hygiene to job skills training—must be tailored to his specific needs and abilities. For example, if an adult with autism continues to have communication problems, specific, detailed training should be planned. The staff of the residential or employment program should be made up of professionals trained in working with people with autism and in providing a supportive environment.

2. **Commitment to Less Restrictive and More Normal Life Experiences.** The central goal of a supportive environment is to nurture independence in people with autism and to help them to become integrated into their community as much as possible. If the goal of any agency, school, or organization providing services to your child is different, you should question whether it offers a truly supportive environment or whether its methods actually encourage learned helplessness. Programs that provide too much care giving and not enough training cannot succeed in enabling adults with autism to achieve more normal lives.

A supportive environment will also strive to foster independence in *all* adults with autism, no matter what their abilities. Its programs should be available to all people with autism, from high-functioning, cooperative people to lower-functioning, less sociable people. No one should be denied services or be removed from the program because he is considered difficult. The commitment should be to individual success for each person served. Independence is not an "all-or-nothing" proposition; everyone should be given as much independence, responsibility, and opportunity as he can handle. In a supportive environment, trained professionals know when to help and when to watch. They know how to establish realistic, yet challenging goals.

3. **A Compatible Physical Environment.** At home and in the workplace, the physical environment—the building, rooms, and outside areas—should be compatible with your child's

preferences. For example, if noisy places disturb your child, then he should live and work in a quiet environment. A compatible environment is important because how your child reacts to the layout, color, shape, noise level, and even smell may affect his behavior or ability to learn. You are probably already sensitive to your child's likes and dislikes in these areas; you should make sure that your child's residential or employment training agency is sensitive too.

4. Remedial Programming. If your child is to achieve independence, there are several skills he must have. These skills are "functional"; they allow a person with autism to function as normally as possible in the real world. They include: 1) communication skills; 2) independent self-care skills; and 3) the ability to function without constant supervision. A residential or employment training agency should provide ***educational services*** to help your child learn new functional skills or to fill in gaps in his prior education. For example, because most adults with autism continue to need language and communication therapy, the agency should have language therapists on its staff. And if an adult with autism needs help in learning self-care skills, a personal-needs counselor should be available.

Remember, you need not—in fact you *must* not—wait until your child is an adult to start work on these essential skills. The sooner you accept your child's autism and begin to build these skills, the less remedial programming he will need as an adult. Teach your child domestic and self-care skills at home, and insist that he do as much as possible for himself—for example, take dishes to the sink, make his bed. In addition, make sure that your child's program at school focuses on the functional skills he will need later.

5. Commitment to Encouraging Appropriate Behavior. Success in achieving independence depends greatly on the person with autism, and in particular, on his behavior. If his behavior is not socially acceptable, he cannot achieve much real independence. An adult who has violent temper tantrums, for example, stands little chance of keeping a job or getting along with the other residents in a group home. A supportive environment, therefore, should work to improve the behavior of people with autism and to reduce inappropriate behavior.

6. Commitment to a Lifetime of Service. Because people with autism need a supportive environment throughout their lives, agencies should be committed to providing services for a lifetime. This may sound like a lot to ask, but consistency is a critical element in successfully nurturing independence in adults with autism. Because people with autism have difficulty coping with changes in their world, agencies should focus on long-term consistency and stability. Doing less can jeopardize years of progress.

As discussed earlier, *all* of your child's environments should be supportive. They should provide the care he needs in order to feel secure, but they should also continually challenge your child to become as independent as possible. A good rule of thumb is that for every time care is given to an adult with autism, three opportunities for training or learning should be offered. This holds true whether your child is at home, at work, or receiving education or employment training.

In evaluating adult programs and agencies in the future, you should make sure that each of the elements of a supportive environment outlined above is present. Do not, however, confuse the emphasis on nurturing independence with a free-form, unstructured environment for your child with autism. A supportive environment for adults with autism is still far more regimented and controlled than most people's environments. It is how the elements of control, growth, and care are balanced that distinguishes a supportive environment for adults with autism.

Employment Options: A Safety Net Approach

In the real world, grown-ups work. Besides paying the bills, work gives people a sense of accomplishment, pride, and self-esteem. Your child, too, should be able to reap these benefits of working.

Of course, because your child has autism, there will probably be limitations on the types of jobs he will be able to hold, and there will definitely be differences in the way he is trained for and placed on a job. In most areas, local vocational training agencies or state human services departments train people with disabilities and then search for suitable work for them. In many states, adults with autism receive the same services that adults with other disabilities receive. Sometimes the services provided everyone happen to be effective for people with autism, but too often they are not.

Unfortunately, in many areas employment programs provide only a combination of what amounts to adult day care with limited job skills training. Usually, this kind of program does not help adults with autism; they need more intensive training in a supportive environment. As a result, inadequate job skills or behavior problems may make it impossible for them to keep jobs, and they may suffer gaps in employment. In addition, they may continually have to wait to get back into training and to receive new placement help.

In the best employment programs, these problems can be avoided by using an approach known as the "safety net approach." The safety net approach is simply a continuing commitment to work with an adult with autism throughout his life. When a person has a gap in employment or needs retraining, the agency automatically accepts him back into its program. With a safety net approach, the adult with autism is able to return to an employment setting without first having to go to the back of the line for training or services. This approach to the continuing employment training needs of people with autism is gradually being accepted around the country.

Types of Employment

A wide variety of employment options are available today for adults with disabilities. These options are usually grouped into four types, according to the kinds of job skills and levels of independence they require. The types are: sheltered, secure, supported, and competitive employment.

Sheltered Employment. Sheltered employment offers the adult with autism a degree of job security. He works at a job site operated by the employment training agency, performing relatively simple tasks such as mail processing, collating, packaging, woodworking, or product assembly. He is paid for his work. In most programs, his co-workers may also have autism or some other condition. The program may offer training, but the amount of training can vary tremendously. Although sheltered workshops are quite common, they have one major drawback: the adult with autism may just stay in the sheltered workshop indefinitely, and may never be prepared for more independent work.

Secure Employment. Although secure employment involves basically the same kinds of work that sheltered employment does, it is fundamentally different in philosophy. Like sheltered employment, it offers structured work and a guaranteed job, but it also trains the adult with autism so he may eventually be able to work in a more independent and competitive workplace. The training focuses not only on improving job skills, but also on improving behavior. For example, staying with a task until finished, moving from one task to another, controlling impulses, working with less supervision, and improving communication and self-care skills are all important skills that secure employment should teach. Secure employment usually works best with adults more severely affected by autism and those who have had little or no employment training. It is always the better choice for adults who might otherwise work in a sheltered workshop.

Supported Employment. Supported employment is ideal for the adult with autism who has acceptable behavior and has learned the skills necessary to work in the competitive work force, yet still needs supervision to complete the job requirements. In this type of employment, one to four adults with autism work alongside nondisabled adults at a real job site, doing work such as stocking store shelves, pricing merchandise, assembling products, and cleaning offices. The adults with autism are supported by a job coach—a professional or volunteer employed by the employment training agency, not the employer. The job coach teaches the adults with autism the skills needed for the job, reinforces appropriate behavior while working to eliminate inappropriate behavior, supervises each person at work, provides for transportation to and from the job site, and helps maintain a good relationship between the employer and employees. The goal of supported employment is to help the adult with autism become increasingly independent so that he can work without a job coach.

Competitive Employment. Once an adult with autism has mastered both the job skills and the behavior necessary for completely independent work, he is ready for competitive employment. In competitive employment, a person works independently, comes and goes to work on his own, and does not need a job coach. Typical competitive work for an adult with autism includes word processing and data entry, mail sorting and delivery, office assistance, library help, janitorial services, and work in grocery stores. Currently, competitive employment for adults with autism is fairly uncommon. Only about 10 percent of adults with autism achieve this level of employment.

Competitive employment represents almost a graduation from a supportive environment, because the adult with autism no longer needs continuing supervision or training, and is able to function in the world independently. In a truly supportive environment, however, the agency always stands ready to help out if necessary. For example, if behavior problems cause trouble at work in a competitive setting, a job coach can be brought in to help. If problems persist, the person can return to work in a secure employment program, while continuing to receive training to improve both behavior and job skills. The agency never stops caring about the individual.

Secure, supported, and competitive employment programs are all usually designed to keep adults with autism and other disabilities continuously working at the highest level of independence they can handle. Consequently, they provide the adult with autism with the all-important supportive environment described earlier in this chapter. Sheltered workshops, on the other hand, do not foster independence or provide many opportunities for personal growth.

The preceding section provided an overview of the types of employment options usually available for adults with autism. But you need more than a general idea of what is out there. When it comes to employment programs, there is great variety from state to state in eligibility requirements, training methods, and placement success. And once your child turns twenty-one, you cannot expect someone to seek you out to offer services or even to explain what services are available. Long before your child finishes school, you should begin to search for employment services and, if necessary, to demand more appropriate services for your child. It is almost never too early to start this process of investigating options and of advocating for improved employment training services. Start by asking parents of adults with autism about the services available in your community. And, as discussed in Chapter 7, make sure that your child with autism receives training to build vocational skills as part of his educational program.

Residential Options: The Dark Ages

Since the early 1970s, federal, state, and local governments have been releasing people with disabilities of all kinds from institutions. The expectation behind this process of *deinstitutionalization* is that people with disabilities should lead happier, more productive lives once they are back in the community. While deinstitutionalization has proven to be moderately successful with people who are mentally retarded or mentally ill, it has been less successful for adults with autism—mainly because there just are not enough community residential placement options for people with autism. As a result, adults with autism still make up a large percentage of people living in institutions. Others wind up with ineffective placements, expensive placements, or even *no* placements. Because you will want to avoid these less-than-ideal placements for your child, the drawbacks of each are described below.

No Placement. In the United States today, many adults with autism simply have no residential placement. Most live at home with parents who either do not know about appropriate services for adults with autism or who are unwilling to have their son or daughter placed inappropriately. This situation can be explosive for both the adult with autism and his family, due to the daily stress of living with the behavior and learning problems associated with autism.

Inappropriate Placement. As mentioned earlier, many adults with autism are placed inappropriately in state institutions. Institutions are usually staffed by a variety of professionals, but, compared with other residential settings, there is a high resident/staff ratio. In most states, institutions house up to one thousand people. Additionally, because these institutions usually house people with many different disabilities, they seldom focus on the unique learning styles of adults with autism. These settings provide little opportunity for helping adults with autism develop greater independence. In fact, they tend to exacerbate the symptoms of autism and to contribute to the general deterioration of the skills and health of an adult with autism.

Ineffective Placement. Many adults with autism live in residential programs that are staffed by workers who are not skilled in providing a supportive environment. In addition, the staff members may use ineffective methods—methods that encourage learned helplessness—to try to teach skills, including behavior skills. Such programs primarily provide care rather than training, and do not help the adult with autism. Ineffective placements, like inappropriate placements, generally worsen the condition of the adult with autism.

Expensive Placement. There are a few high quality community-based residential placement options that provide the supportive environment adults with autism need to grow and learn. Unfortunately, because they are unique, they can be quite expensive, with costs ranging from $125,000 to $900,000 per year. And because these placements are not available in all states, there may not be any near the home of the parents of the adult with autism.

Types of Residential Settings

Recently, federal, state, and local agencies have begun to do something about the chronic lack of community-based residential options that has led to the conditions described above. These agencies have finally realized that *public* residential programs should offer disabled adults the same high quality services that private programs do. As a result, residential options for adults with autism have gradually begun to expand. Today, although too many adults with autism remain in institutions for lack of an appropriate placement in the community, there is increasing movement toward community living for *all* adults with autism. But remember, it will take constant advocacy from you and parents like you if this goal is to be met. Here is a summary of the common community-based living arrangements:

Community Group Homes. Over the past decade, there has been a dramatic increase in the number and type of community group homes for adults with all types of disabilities. These homes, which are usually located in residential neighborhoods, house from two to eight adults. During the day, residents typically leave the home to go to work or training. At home, a staff of qualified and trained professionals teaches the residents to take care of the house themselves, and often helps with the housekeeping as well. In many programs, the professional staff may also offer training in other areas, including communication, self-help, and behavior skills, but each program is different. Generally, the resident/staff ratio ranges from 1-to-1 to 2-to-3, so there is much supervision. Group homes are usually operated by city and county governments, local disability organizations such as ASA chapters, local ARCs, and others. Some group homes have only residents with autism, but more often group homes house people with a variety of disabilities. For adults with autism, a group home that is just for people with autism works better because the programming can be tailored specifically to their needs.

Supervised Apartments. A supervised apartment is basically just a small group home. Typically, there is only one supervised apartment per apartment building. The apartment is usually shared by two adults who require less daily supervision than residents of group homes. One to two days each week, a supervisor checks up on the residents and helps train them to care for themselves and the apartment. During the day, the residents go to work or training. Like group homes, supervised apartments for adults with autism work best if the other residents also have autism and if the program is tailored to their needs.

Skill Development Homes. A skill development home is a fairly recent variation on the group home or supervised apartment.

In this arrangement, an adult with a disability lives with a family that has been trained by an agency or organization in working with people with disabilities. In most cases, the host family is paid by the state. The host family treats the adult with autism like a member of the family, and teaches self-care, housekeeping, recreation, and leisure-time skills. Again, a skill development home works best if the training and approach are tailored to adults with autism.

Other Arrangements. In addition to the arrangements described above, there are many other ways of providing supportive and challenging living environments for adults with autism. For example, there are many residential schools and self-contained communities for adults with disabilities. The key elements—supervision, the number of residents, location, and programming—can vary tremendously from program to program. Thus, a program that is inappropriate or ineffective for one person may work quite well for another. No single approach works best for all people with autism.

What to Look for in Residential Programs

When you investigate residential options for your child, there are several things to look for and to look out for. The most important element, of course, is a commitment to the "supportive environment" that works best to encourage appropriate behavior, independent life skills, and employment skills in adults with autism. It is also important, however, to look for signs that the program is well managed.

To determine whether a program is supportive, look first at the staff. Are they trained in working with adults with autism? Do they focus on training people toward independence, treating the adults "as if" they have the potential to lead more normal lives in the community? Is there at least one staff member for every three adults with autism? Secondly, look at the program itself. Is it challenging enough for your child? Does it focus on providing opportunities for being out in the community, including food shopping, bowling, field trips, and even community service? Or does the program appear to be ineffective?

Ineffective programs are actually fairly easy to spot. One of the surest signs is what is know as "couch potato behavior." Couch potato behavior—sitting and vegetating in front of the T.V.—is all too common in some residential programs. It represents a program's lack of commitment to do what it takes to promote skills and independence, and can only result in deterioration of the residents' skills.

Besides looking for signs that a program is supportive, you should also look for signs that it is well managed. For example, you should examine the physical condition of furniture and of the house, apartment, or building; ask the program administrators about staff turnover rates; and form your own impressions about the overall atmosphere of the residence. Is it clean? Is the food tasty and nutritious? Is there any privacy? All of these elements are important indicators of how seriously a program takes the happiness and well-being of its residents.

Unfortunately, there is no cookbook recipe for finding the right residential program. Just as every adult with autism is unique, so too is every program. It can help you to talk to parents of other residents to find out whether they think the home is an effective environment for their child. Remember, though, what works well for one person may not work as well for another. You should look for a program with the approach to teaching, training, behavior control, and activity that works best for *your* child. You can refer to the list of characteristics of an appropriate educational program at the end of Chapter 7 for a summary of what to look for in any program for adults with autism.

Easing the Transition to Employment and Independent Living

Letting go of a child is never easy. No parent is ever quite prepared for the day his child moves out to live on his own or to begin work. For parents of adults with autism, letting go can be especially hard—not only because of the years they have spent providing intense care, but also because of the added stress of searching for adequate residential and employment programs for their child.

Perhaps most disturbing to parents of children with autism are the feelings of abandonment and guilt that move in when their child moves out. Often parents feel as if they have "given up" on their child by putting someone else in charge of his daily care. They may also feel useless now that they are no longer solely responsible for their child's welfare.

The best antidote for these feelings is to acknowledge ahead of time that your child will have to leave home someday and that he likely will require some type of secure living arrangement all his adult life. If you acknowledge this need early on, you can not only anticipate how you will feel, but you can also plan ahead for residential and employment placements. And if you plan ahead, you will be able to choose the most appropriate programs for your child. This will help you to feel better *and* to be a better advocate for quality services in your child's program.

If you do not consider residential placement until there is a family crisis, you may find the options painfully limited. The best programs frequently have long waiting lists. So it is important to plan early for your child's eventual residential placement in order to secure the best possible program for him when he becomes an adult.

Once your child has moved out, you, like all parents, will have to adjust to the "empty nest." Finding new family roles and going back to old jobs, hobbies, or activities helps. But what helps most is the passage of time and the discovery that your child can—and will—continue to grow now that he's out in the real world. Again, if you are prepared for the feelings you will have when your adult with autism leaves home, it will be easier to cope with them.

You must also be prepared to help your child cope with his feelings. For the adult with autism, entry into community living and employment training can be traumatic. New surroundings, activities, people, and expectations can all create great stress and make the adjustment lengthy and difficult. With the right help, however, most adults with autism can make the adjustment.

The best way for you to help with the transition is to "desensitize" your child *before* the change occurs. For at least a month before he moves into a residential program or begins job training, take him on daily visits to the place where he will be living or working. Go inside to show him what he will be doing and introduce him to the staff and other participants in the program. Talk with him reassuringly about what is going to happen. This will help your child get used to the idea ahead of time.

What the Future Holds

At the start of this chapter, I said I intended to write not only about today, but also about the tomorrow parents and professionals who care about people with autism can create. Briefly, here is what I see for the future:

1. **Greater Independence for Adults with Autism.** As more and more parents and professionals realize that people with autism can continue to learn throughout their lives, there will be greater and better efforts to teach adults with autism the skills they need to live independently.

2. **Increasingly More Sociable People with Autism.** As we learn more about how to teach children with autism, programs will become more successful in teaching appropriate social behavior. In turn, this improved social behavior will help increase residential and employment opportunities for all people with autism.

3. **Expanded Residential Placements.** More group homes and supervised apartments—the residential placements best suited to adults with autism—will be established, and their services will be more tailored to the needs of adults with autism.

4. **Improved Employment Training.** More employment training programs will provide the continual training the adult with autism needs, and will be there to help between jobs with retraining and new job placements.

5. **Greater Employment Opportunities.** Improved education and programming plus more social behavior will result in a generation of people with autism who have better skills, and as a result, increased employment options.

These goals *are* within our grasp. Over the last twenty-five years, significant progress has been made in the care, education, and training of people with autism, and we are still making headway today. As I said at the beginning of the chapter, it is simply impossible to predict what life will be like for any child with autism when he is an adult.

Remember, the progress that can do so much to improve life for people with autism depends in large part on the commitment and hard work of parents and professionals. Only constant advocacy can achieve our goals. For many other conditions—from Down syndrome to mental illness—advocacy has yielded excellent results. Clearly, doing nothing is the surest way to ensure no progress is made; advocacy by parents, professionals, and organizations is the only guarantee of a better future for people with autism.

Conclusion

Currently, good services for adults with autism—services provided in a supportive environment—are scarce. There are, however, some excellent examples of what a quality program can be. The Autism Society of America, based in Washington, D.C., has identified these quality programs in its *Directory of Programs Serving Children and Adults with Autism*, which is listed in the references at the end of this chapter. The Autism Society has also been very helpful in influencing federal legislation and in advocating for children and adults with autism in this country and abroad.

Armed with the knowledge that an effective national advocacy organization for children and adults with autism exists, parents and professionals should gain strength. There is hope for a brighter tomorrow for adults with autism, but only if everyone works together. Advocates, parents, and professionals must put aside their many differences and rise above the controversies that seem perpetually to plague the field of autism. They must focus instead on the pragmatic issues—the development of employment services, community-based residential services, and effective educational programs. With one voice, they must advocate for more programs like the few model programs presently available, and for appropriate, lifetime services for all adults with autism.

Parents will not obtain the best services just because they want them. Professionals will not be able to offer the best services just because there is a need for them. Parents, professionals, and organizations must *all* work together, guiding and buoying each other when necessary, to ensure that these services come to be.

One final message—a message that is too often forgotten by parents in the day-to-day struggle and frustration of raising a child with autism. There is hope.

References

Holmes, David L. *Establishing Group Homes for Adults with Autism.* Princeton, NJ: The Eden Press, 1985.

Kiernan, W.E., and J.A. Stark. *Pathways to Employment for Adults with Developmental Disabilities.* Baltimore: Paul H. Brookes, 1986.

Lauries, K.R., ed. *Directory of Programs Serving Children and Adults with Autism.* 5th ed. Washington, D.C.: The Autism Society of America, 1985.

Shostack, A.L. *Group Homes for Teenagers.* New York: Human Sciences Press, 1987.

Storm, K., and Holmes, D.L. "Factors Involved in Programming for Adolescents and Adults with Autism." In *Children Grow Up: Autism in Adolescents and Adults,* edited by K. Meyers and B. Griesman. Lawrenceville, NJ: COSAC Press, 1986.

Summers, J.A., ed. *The Right to Grow Up.* Baltimore: Paul H. Brookes, 1986.

Parent Statements

Not too long ago my son took a four-day vacation in the mountains. What's more, he paid for it out of his own earnings. Big deal you say? For that severely handicapped young man, you bet it was. And for my wife and me, it was a major triumph. You see, my son is autistic, epileptic, and deaf. He cannot talk, but he can stuff shoe pad inserts into plastic packages and box them neatly—and get paid for his efforts. Yet four years ago, he was self-destructive, totally withdrawn, and unable to communicate. Today he knows a dozen signs; he can tell others what he wants and needs.

Looking at a picture of my son at work, I realized how far my son has come. My son's early years were quite difficult for all of us and we never really knew what the future held. Now, we can see what faith and hard work have accomplished together.

It's scary when I think about Janet becoming a teenager. It's scary because there's not enough time.

I see other kids and I say, "Hmm, do you think it's going to be like this?" We're fearful of the social interaction. That's why we're working the way we're working, because that's what's not being dealt with at all—that whole social thing is irrelevant to the educators. To them, math and reading are education.

I worry about the future a lot, because I think she can handle it academically, but it's the social aspects and the behavior and everything else that the real world is all about.

This is not fact, it's only my feelings, but I don't have time to think too much about the long term except to wonder whether he'll be happy and self-sufficient. I know that he will possibly have social problems—interaction problems—later on, but I can't dwell on that.

The main thing I hope is that she's independent at doing whatever she's doing and she's happy doing it. If she doesn't go to college, fine.

I just hope she knows right from wrong.

That's my biggest hope, that Scott is self-sufficient.

It would be nice if she knew how to manage her own life, how to do something. It's so scary. I just hate to think that for the rest of her life she will look at television and just vegetate. That would just be a crime to me.

I have thoughts—maybe they're way off base—but having a girl, I have thoughts that she might be sexually taken advantage of. And the fact that she's so trusting about things makes me worry, too. I think about drugs and I think about things that other regular people have to deal with.

I remember when I was a kid, I used to think vocational education was for "dummies." Having a child with autism has really changed my perceptions. I'm not expecting a miracle or anything, but I really hope vocational education will be Carl's ticket to self-sufficiency.

You've got to remember that a lot of the things that seem cute when your child is an adorable little kid aren't going to seem nearly so cute when he's a full-grown man.

Self-sufficiency—I think that's my major worry.

Even though our son is eighteen, he has just recently learned to respond positively to affection. It's so gratifying to have him initiate, as well as return a hug and kiss, that sometimes we forget that his age may make such public displays seem inappropriate. As an example, we were in a museum when my husband and son shared a spontaneous bear hug. A female guard approached and sternly informed my husband that "such behavior was not allowed in this hall." My husband, who was able to gather his wits a lot faster than I could have, innocently asked her to point out the hall where "such behavior" would be tolerated.

There just doesn't seem to be any growth in residential services. Meanwhile, I'm getting older and I'm not sure I can keep up the energy level I could when I was younger. We need to get these services in place now.

Glossary

Adaptive behavior—The ability to adjust to new environments, tasks, objects, and people, and to apply new skills to those new situations.

Advocacy—Supporting or promoting a cause. Speaking out.

Advocacy groups—Organizations that work to protect the rights and opportunities of handicapped children and their parents.

Anticonvulsant—A drug used to control seizures. Even though all seizures are not convulsions, this term is commonly used.

Applied behavior analysis—A method of teaching designed to analyze and change behavior in a precisely measurable and accountable manner. Also called behavior modification.

ARD Committee (Admission, Review, and Dismissal Committee)—This committee is made up of teachers and other professionals. It is responsible for the *admission* of children to special education, *review* of the progress of children in special education programs, and *dismissal* of children from special education.

Assessment—Process to determine a child's strengths and weaknesses. Includes testing and observations performed by a team of professionals and parents. Usually used to determine special education needs. Term is used interchangeably with *evaluation*.

Attention—The ability to concentrate on a task.

Attention span—The amount of time one is able to concentrate on a task. Also called *attending* in special education jargon.

Auditory—Relating to the ability to hear.

Babbling—The sound a baby makes when he combines a vowel and consonant and repeats them over and over again (e.g., ba-ba-ba, ga-ga-ga).

Behavior modification—*See* Applied behavior analysis.

Beneficiary—The person indicated in a trust or insurance policy to receive any payments that become due.

Cause-and-effect—The concept that actions create reactions.

Cerebral palsy—Brain damage caused at birth or shortly thereafter. Affects the motor areas of the brain.

Childhood schizophrenia—A major psychiatric disorder, probably with multiple causes. Symptoms include disturbances in form and content of thought, perception, emotions, sense of self, volition, relationship to the external world, and psychomotor behavior. Childhood schizophrenia is very rare.

Cognition—The ability to know and understand the environment.

Competitive employment—Jobs which pay workers at least minimum wage to produce valued goods or services, and which are performed in settings that include nondisabled workers.

Convulsion—Involuntary contractions of the muscles. A seizure.

Cost-of-care liability—The right of a state providing care to a handicapped person to charge for the care and to collect from the handicapped person's assets.

Cue—Input that prompts a person to perform a behavior or activity.

Development—The process of growth and learning during which a child acquires skills and abilities.

Developmental disability—A handicap or impairment originating before the age of eighteen which may be expected to continue indefinitely and which constitutes a substantial disability. Such conditions include pervasive developmental disorders, autism, cerebral palsy, and mental retardation.

Developmental milestone—A developmental goal that functions as a measurement of developmental progress over time.

Developmentally delayed—A person whose development is slower than normal.

Diagnostic and Statistical Manual of Mental Disorders (DSM III-R)—A manual published by the American Psychiatric Association (APA) which describes all of the diagnostic criteria and the systematic descriptions of various mental disorders.

Discretionary trust—A trust in which the trustee (the person responsible for governing the trust) has the authority to use or not use the trust funds for any purpose, as long as funds are expended only for the beneficiary.

Disinherit—To deprive someone of an inheritance. Parents of handicapped children may do this to prevent the state from imposing cost-of-care liability on their child's assets.

Dispute resolution procedures—The procedures established by law and regulation for the fair resolution of disputes regarding a child's special education.

Dopamine—One of the neurotransmitters.

Due process hearing—Part of the procedures established to protect the rights of parents and special-needs children during disputes under Public Law 94–142. These are hearings before an impartial person to review the identification, evaluation, placement, and services by a handicapped child's educational agency.

Early development—Development during the first three years of life.

Early intervention—The specialized way of interacting with infants to minimize the effects of conditions that can delay early development.

Echolalia—A parrot-like repetition of phrases or words just heard (immediate echolalia), or heard hours, days, weeks, or even months ago (delayed echolalia).

Education for All Handicapped Children Act—The federal law that guarantees all handicapped children the right to a free appropriate public education. It is Public Law 94-142.

EEG—*See* Electroencephalogram.

Electroencephalogram (EEG)—The machine and test used to determine levels of electrical discharge from nerve cells.

Engagement—The ability to remain focused and interactive with (or responsive to) a person or object.

Epilepsy—A recurrent condition caused by abnormal electrical discharges in the brain that causes seizures.

Estate planning—Formal, written arrangements for handling the possessions and assets of people after they have died.

Etiology—The study of the cause of disease.

Evaluation—*See* Assessment.

Expressive language—The ability to use gestures, words, and written symbols to communicate.

Extinction—A procedure in which reinforcement of a previously reinforced behavior is withheld.

Fine motor—Relating to the use of the small muscles of the body, such as those in the hands, feet, fingers, and toes.

Fragile-X syndrome—A genetic condition in which one part of the X-chromosome has a defect. The condition causes mental retardation.

Genetic—Inherited.

Generalization—Transferring a skill taught in one place, or with one person, to other places and people.

Graduated guidance—Systematically and gradually reducing the amount of physical guidance used.

Gross motor—Relating to the use of the large muscles of the body.

Handicapped—Refers to people who have some sort of disability, including physical disabilities, mental retardation, sensory impairments, behavioral disorders, learning disabilities, and multiple handicaps.

Hepatitis—An inflammation of the liver.

Hyperactivity—A specific nervous-system-based difficulty which makes it hard for a person to control muscle (motor) behavior.

Identification—The determination that a child should be evaluated as a possible candidate for special education services.

IEP—Individualized Education Program. The written plan that describes what services the local education agency has promised to provide your child.

Imitation—The ability to observe the actions of others and to copy them in one's own actions. Also known as modeling.

Input—Information that a person receives through any of the senses (vision, hearing, touch, feeling, smell) that helps that person develop new skills.

Insistence on sameness—A tendency in many people with autism to become upset when familiar routines are changed.

Interdisciplinary team—A team of professionals who evaluate your child and then develop a comprehensive summary report of his or her strengths and needs.

Interpretive—The sessions during which parents and teachers review and discuss the results of a child's evaluation.

I.Q. (Intelligence Quotient)—A measure of cognitive ability based on specifically designed standardized tests.

Language—The expression and understanding of human communication.

Least restrictive environment—The requirement under Public Law 94–142 that handicapped children receiving special education must be made a part of a regular school to the fullest extent possible. Included in the law as a way of ending the traditional practice of isolating handicapped children.

Local Education Agency (LEA)—The agency responsible for providing educational services on the local (city, county, and school district) level.

Luxury trust—A trust that describes the kind of allowable expenses in a way that excludes the cost of care in state-funded programs in order to avoid cost-of-care liability.

Mainstreaming—The practice of involving handicapped children in regular school and preschool environments.

Malnutrition—Nutritional intake that is insufficient to promote or maintain growth and development.

Medicaid—A joint state and federal program that offers medical assistance to people who are entitled to receive Supplementary Security Income.

Medicare—A federal program that provides payments for medical care to people who are receiving Social Security payments.

Mental retardation—Below normal mental function. Children who are mentally retarded learn more slowly than other children, but "mental retardation" itself does not indicate a specific level of mental ability. The level of mental function may not be identifiable until a much later age.

Modeling—*See* Imitation.

Motor—Relating to the ability to move oneself.

Motor planning—The ability to think through and carry out a physical task.

Multihandicapped—Having more than one handicap.

Neuroleptic—Medicine which produces symptoms resembling those of diseases of the nervous system.

Neurologist—A physician specializing in medical problems associated with the brain and spinal cord.

Neurotransmitter—The chemical substance between nerve cells in the brain which allows the transmission of an impulse from one nerve to another.

Occupational therapist (O.T.)—A therapist who specializes in improving the development of fine motor and adaptive skills.

Oral motor—Relating to the movement of muscles in and around the mouth.

Parent-professional partnership—The teaming of parents and teachers (or doctors, nurses, or other professionals) to work together to facilitate the development of babies and children with special needs.

Perseveration—Repetitive movement or speech that is thought to be created by the person's own inner preoccupations.

Physical therapist (P.T.)—A therapist who works with motor skills.

Pincer grasp—The use of the thumb and forefinger to grasp small objects.

Placement—The selection of the educational program for a child who needs special education programs.

Prompt—Input that encourages a child to perform a movement or activity. *See* Cue.

Public Law 94–142—*See* Education for All Handicapped Children Act.

Punishment—A consequence that is applied following a behavior to reduce the probability of that behavior occurring again. Punishment can be very mild (a frown or scolding), more moderate (a brief time-out), or very severe (electric shock to reduce life-threatening behavior).

Receptive language—The ability to understand spoken and written communication as well as gestures.

Reinforcement—Providing a pleasant consequence (positive reinforcement) or removing an unpleasant consequence (negative reinforcement) after a behavior in order to increase or maintain that behavior.

Related services—Services that enable a child to benefit from special education. Related services include speech, occupational, and physical therapies, as well as transportation.

Respite care—Skilled adult- or child-care and supervision that can be provided in your home or the home of a care-provider. Respite care may be available for several hours per week or for overnight stays.

Screening test—A test given to groups of children to sort out those who need further evaluation.

SEA—The State Education Agency.

Secure employment—Vocational training that prepares adults with disabilities to enter the work force. The training is designed specifically to teach the skills needed to survive and succeed in supported or competitive employment situations.

Seizure—Abnormal electrical discharges in nerve cells in the brain.

Self-help—The ability to take care of one's self, through such skills as eating, dressing, bathing, and cleaning. Begins early with awareness, responsiveness, and participation in self-help activities.

Sensory ability—The ability to process sensations, such as touch, sound, light, smell, and movement.

Sheltered employment—Employment in work settings where all workers have disabilities, are continually supervised, and are paid less than minimum wage. There is no expectation for workers to move on to more independent, integrated employment.

Social ability—The ability to function in groups and to interact with people.

Special education—Specialized instruction based on educational disabilities determined by a team evaluation. It must be precisely matched to educational needs and adapted to the child's learning style.

Special needs—Needs generated by a person's handicap.

Speech/language pathologist—A therapist who works to improve speech and language skills, as well as to improve oral motor abilities.

S.S.D.I.—Social Security Disability Insurance. This money has been paid into the Social Security system through payroll deductions on earnings. Disabled workers are entitled to these benefits. People who become disabled before the age of twenty-two may collect S.S.D.I. under a parent's account, if the parent is retired, disabled, or deceased.

S.S.I.—Supplemental Security Income is available for low-income people who are disabled, blind, or aged. S.S.I. is based on need, not on past earnings.

Stereotypy (stereotypic behavior)—Purposeless movements such as hand flapping which are repetitive and odd.

Stimulant—A psychotropic drug such as Ritalin and Dexedrine often used to control hyperactivity in children.

Stimulus—A physical object or environmental event that *may* have an effect upon the behavior of a person. Some stimuli are internal (earache pain), while others are external (a smile from a loved one).

Supported employment—Paid employment for people with developmental disabilities for whom competitive employment at or above minimum wage is unlikely. Employment is supported by any activity—a job coach, for example—designed to keep the worker employed.

Support trust—A trust that requires that funds be expended to pay for the beneficiary's expenses of living, including housing, food, and transportation.

Sutures—Stitches, used to close a wound.

Symptomatic—Having a cause that is identified.

Tactile—Relating to touch.

Tardive dyskinesia—Involuntary movements of the mouth, tongue, and lips can occur and may be associated with choreo-atheroid (purposeless, quick, jerky movements that occur suddenly) movements of the trunk and limbs. Some medications prescribed for autism contribute to the development of this condition.

Therapist—A trained professional who works to overcome the effects of developmental problems.

Uniform Gifts to Minors Act (UGMA)—A law that governs gifts to minors. Under the UGMA, gifts become the property of the minor at age eighteen or twenty-one.

Vestibular—Pertaining to the sensory system located in the inner ear that allows that body to maintain balance and enjoyably participate in movement such as swinging and roughhousing.

Visual motor—the skill required to carry out a task such as putting a puzzle piece into a puzzle or a key into a keyhole.

Vocational training—Training for a job. Learning skills to perform in the workplace.

Reading List

This Reading List is designed especially for parents of children with autism. Because children with autism are much like "normal" children in some respects, child-raising books and general family health books are also included.

This list does not pretend to be complete. There are other useful books available. Check with your library or bookstore, as well as with the parent groups listed in the Resource Guide.

Chapter 1

Cohen, D.J., and A. Donnellan, eds. *Handbook of Autism and Pervasive Developmental Disorders.* New York: Wiley, 1987. A professional text presenting the most current research and thinking in autism. The biological bases chapters are particularly strong. May be too technical for some parents.

Lauries, K.R., ed. *Directory of Programs Serving Children and Adults with Autism.* 5th ed. Washington, D.C.: National Society for Children and Adults with Autism, 1985. Lists programs serving people with autism in the United States. Slightly outdated at this point, but still useful.

Melton, David. *Promises to Keep: A Handbook for Parents of Learning Disabled, Brain-Injured, and Other Exceptional Children.* New York: Franklin Watts, 1984. A good general guide to raising and caring for special-needs children.

Moore, Cory. *A Reader's Guide for Parents of Children with Mental, Physical, or Emotional Disabilities.* Rockville, MD: Woodbine House, 1990. A comprehensive, annotated reading list for all subjects related to developmental disabilities. A valuable resource.

Paluszny, M. *Autism: A Practical Guide for Parents and Professionals.* Syracuse: Syracuse University Press, 1979. A useful book for parents, describing the history and treatment of children with autism. Somewhat outdated.

Schopler, E., and G.B. Mesibov. *Current Issues in Autism Series.* 6 vols. New York: Plenum, 1983–88. This series covers a wide range of areas of professional concern in autism. It is by far the most comprehensive series to date, covering such topics as families, neurobiological issues, social behavior, communication problems, and adults with autism. Written for professionals, but parents may find certain chapters useful.

Schopler, E., and G.B. Mesibov. *Diagnosis and Assessment in Autism.* New York: Plenum Press, 1988. Written for a professional audience, this book presents our current understanding of autism, as well as controversies.

Chapter 2

Having a Brother Like David. The Minneapolis Children's Center, 2525 Chicago Ave., South Minneapolis, MN 55404. A story written for young children about a small boy whose brother David has autism.

Kushner, H.S. *When Bad Things Happen to Good People.* New York: Avon, 1981. A biographical account of a rabbi and his family following the death of their son from a rare disease. A moving and compassionate work.

Murphy, Albert T. *Special Children, Special Parents: Personal Issues with Handicapped Children.* Englewood Cliffs, NJ: Prentice Hall, 1981. A look into the emotions of parents of handicapped children. Includes many statements by parents.

Perske, Robert. *Hope for Families: New Directions for Parents of Persons with Retardation or Other Disabilities.* Nashville: Abingdon Press, 1981. A compassionate and philosophical book for parents about adjusting to a handicapped child.

Chapter 3

Batshaw, Mark L., and Yvonne M. Perret. *Children with Handicaps: A Medical Primer.* Baltimore: Paul H. Brookes, 1981. A layman's medical book about birth defects and other medical conditions of children.

Dalldorf, J.S. "Medical Needs of the Autistic Adolescent." In *Autism in Adolescents and Adults,* edited by E. Schopler and G. Mesibov. New York: Plenum, 1983. Discusses specific medical concerns of adolescents and young adults with autism.

LaCamera, R.G., and A.C. LaCamera. "Routine Health Care." In *Handbook of Autism and Pervasive Developmental Disorders,* edited by D.J. Cohen and A. Donnellan. New York: Wiley, 1987. Describes medical concerns and treatments, as well as controversies, for children and adults with autism. Technical.

Reisner, Helen. *Children with Epilepsy: A Parents Guide.* Kensington, MD: Woodbine House, 1988. A useful book for parents of children with autism who also have seizures.

Wing, L. *Autistic Children: A Guide for Parents and Professionals.* New York: Brunner/Mazel, 1985. Written for parents, this book contains some useful information about medical issues.

Chapter 4

Azrin, N., V. Besalel, R.V. Hall, and M. Hall, eds. *How to Teach Series.* Austin, TX: Pro-Ed, 1980–82. This series contains several short guidebooks which will help develop behavioral teaching skills for use at home and in the community. The language is not too technical, and there are useful exercises for practicing what you've learned. *Please note:* problems that persist, or problems presenting a danger to your child or others, require consultation with a professional who specializes in the behavioral treatment of autism. The Resource Guide will help you identify those professionals. Useful titles in this series include: "How to Select Reinforcers" (#1001); "How to Use Systematic Attention and Approval" (#1002); "How to Use Planned Ignoring Extinction" (#1003); "How to Use Time Out" (#1004); "How to Use Shaping" (#1006); "How to Use Reprimands" (#1008); "How to Use Incidental Teaching for Elaborating Language" (#1010); "How to Use Positive Practice" (#1012); "How to Teach through Modeling and Imitation" (#1016).

Baker, B.L., and A.J. Brightman. *Steps to Independence.* Baltimore: Paul H. Brookes, 1989. An excellent, how-to guide for parents on teaching basic skills and managing behavior problems.

Foxx, R.M., and N.H. Azrin. *Toilet Training the Retarded.* Champaign, IL: Research Press, 1973. The procedures described in this book form the core of most successful toilet training programs for children with developmental disabilities. The language is somewhat technical, but readable. Parents experiencing considerable difficulty toilet training their child may want to consult a professional trained in this area.

Patterson, G.R. *Living with Children.* Champaign, IL: Research Press, 1976. This is an excellent little book about child behavior management, written especially for parents. While it does not deal exclusively with children with autism, the ideas presented are applicable in many cases.

Patterson, G.R. *Families.* Champaign, IL: Research Press, 1975. A slightly more technical, and more detailed, version of *Living with Children.*

Chapter 5

Featherstone, Helen. *A Difference in the Family: Life with a Disabled Child.* New York: Basic Books, 1980. A highly compassionate account of one family's journey on the road to acceptance of their child's severe handicaps. Highly recommended.

Christopher, William, and Barbara Christopher. *Mixed Blessings.* Nashville: Abingdon Press, 1989. A moving, personal account about raising a child with autism.

Goldfarb, L.A., M.J. Brotherson, J.A. Summers, and A.P. Turnbull. *Meeting the Challenge of Disability or Chronic Illness: A Family Guide.* Baltimore: Paul H. Brookes, 1986. A book for families that focuses on the process of solving challenges created by disability. While not specifically about autism, this book is valuable as a generic guide to coping.

Grandin, Temple, and Margaret Scariano. *Emergence: Labeled Autistic.* Novato, CA: Arena Press, 1986. A personal account of growing up with autism, written by a young woman with high-functioning autism. An exceptional book.

Meyer, Donald J., Patricia F. Vadasy, and Rebecca R. Fewell. *Living with a Brother or Sister with Special Needs: A Book for Sibs.* Seattle, WA: University of Washington Press, 1985. An excellent introduction to disabilities for siblings. Reviews specific disabilities and discusses what it is like to be a sibling of a special-needs child. Recommended.

Park, Clara Claiborne. *The Siege: The First Eight Years of an Autistic Child with an Epilogue, Fifteen Years Later.* New York: Atlantic Monthly Press, 1982. A mother's account of her family's experiences raising a daughter with autism. A classic, and highly recommended.

Patterson, Gerald R. *Living with Children: New Methods for Parents and Teachers.* Champaign, IL: Research Press, 1976. A parents' lesson book of techniques for dealing with children.

Powell, Thomas H., and Peggy Ahrenhold Ogle. *Brothers & Sisters: A Special Part of Exceptional Families.* Baltimore: Paul H. Brookes, 1985. A detailed, clinical examination of the siblings of exceptional children. The book primarily reviews research on the subject.

Schleifer, Maxwell J., and Stanley D. Klein, eds. *The Disabled Child and the Family: An Exceptional Parent Reader.* Boston: The Exceptional Parent Press, 1985. A collection of articles from "Exceptional Parent" magazine covering a wide range of topics related to having a handicapped person in the family.

Spence, Eleanor. *The Devil Hole.* New York: Lothrop, Lee, & Shepard, 1977. This engaging novel of an Australian family spans the four-year period beginning shortly before the birth of Carl, who has autism. Carl's different behavior, the reactions of observers, and the consequent disruptive effect and emotional problems for parents and siblings are skillfully and perceptively presented. Appropriate for siblings aged 12–15.

Chapter 6

Brodzinsky, D., A. Gormly, and S.R. Ambron. *Lifespan Human Development.* New York: Holt, Rinehart & Winston, 1987. This book describes the basics of normal human development across the lifespan and would be useful to parents and professionals alike who wish to brush up on the fundamentals of human growth.

DeMyer, M.K. *Parents and Children in Autism.* New York: Wiley, 1979. Dr. DeMyer describes her research on developmental changes in children with autism. Although aimed at professionals, the book may prove to be of interest to parents as well.

White, Burton L. *The First Three Years of Life.* Revised Edition. New York: Prentice Hall Press, 1985. One of the classics on child development, covering the first three years of life.

Wing, L. *Autistic Children: A Guide for Parents and Professionals.* New York: Brunner/Mazel, 1985. This book written for parents has useful suggestions for dealing with developmental problems of children and adults with autism.

Chapter 7

Anderson, Winifred, Stephen Chitwood, and Deidre Hayden. *Negotiating the Special Education Maze.* Kensington, MD: Woodbine House, 1989. A step-by-step guide to help parents make sure their children receive appropriate special education services under P.L. 94–142.

Association of Retarded Citizens. *The Partnership: How to Make It Work.* Arlington, TX: ARC National Research and Demonstration Institute, 1977. A short pamphlet about the relationship between parents and the professionals providing services to a handicapped child.

Cutler, Barbara Coyne. *Unraveling the Special Education Maze: An Action Guide for Parents.* Champaign, IL: Research Press, 1981. A guide for parents to dealing with the special education system and to being a good advocate for their child.

Shore, Kenneth. *The Special Education Handbook.* New York: Teachers College Press, 1986. Excellent, comprehensive book written for parents by a school psychologist. Explains the special education process clearly.

Wuerch, B.B., and L.M. Voeltz. *Longitudinal Leisure Skills for Severely Handicapped Learners: The Ho'onanea Curriculm Component.* Baltimore: Paul H. Brookes, 1982. This book describes lifelong leisure skills for people with severe handicaps, and how to teach them.

Chapter 8

Apolloni, Tony, and Thomas P. Cooke. *A New Look at Guardianship: Protective Services That Support Personalized Living.* Baltimore: Paul H. Brookes, 1984. This book reviews the options for providing future support for handicapped persons.

Budoff, Milton, and Alan Orenstein. *Due Process in Special Education: On Going to a Hearing.* Cambridge, MA: Brookline Books, 1982. A thorough book that examines due process procedures in special education.

Moore, Ralph J., Jr. *Handbook on Estate Planning for Families of Developmentally Disabled Persons in Maryland, the District of Columbia, and Virginia.* Baltimore: Maryland State Planning Council on Developmental Disabilities, 3rd edition, 1989. A guide to estate planning for parents of exceptional children. Although written for the laws of two states and the District of Columbia, the legal principles are generally applicable to all states.

Russell, L.M. *Alternatives: A Family Guide to Legal and Financial Planning for the Disabled.* Evanston, IL: First Publications, 1983. Discusses how to plan for a child with mental disabilities. Covers wills, trusts, government benefits, taxes, and financial planning.

Scheiber, Barbara, and Cory Moore. *Practical Advice to Parents: A Guide to Finding Help for Children with Handicaps.* Washington, D.C.: Closer Look, Parents' Campaign for Handicapped Children and Youth and Association for Retarded Citizens, 1983. A brief guide to obtaining services for handicapped children, including medical care, education, and financial assistance.

Shrybman, James A. *Due Process in Special Education.* Rockville, MD: Aspen Systems Corp., 1982. A detailed legal guide to the law and special education, including IEP, appeals, and due process hearings.

United States Department of Education. *"To Assure the Free Appropriate Public Education of All Handicapped Children": Annual Report to Congress on the Implementation of The Education of the Handicapped Act.* Office of Special Education and Rehabilitative Services, United States Department of Education, annual. The annual report about Public Law 94–142, and about what is being done, or not being done, to carry out its purpose.

Chapter 9

Biklen, Douglas. *Let Our Children Go: An Organizing Manual for Advocates and Parents.* Syracuse, NY: Human Policy Press, 1979. A handbook for organizing a grassroots campaign to improve the treatment and education of exceptional children.

Children's Defense Fund. *It's Time to Stand Up for Your Children: A Parent's Guide to Child Advocacy.* Washington, D.C.: Children's Defense Fund. A 48–page booklet that discusses just what its title suggests. Available from Children's Defense Fund, 122 C St., N.W., Washington, D.C. 20001.

Des Jardins, Charlotte. *How to Organize an Effective Parent/Advocacy Group and Move Bureaucracies.* Chicago: Coordinating Council for Handicapped Children, 1980. A handbook on organizing parent advocacy groups and working for change in educational services for handicapped children.

Dickman, Irving, and Sol Gordon. *One Miracle at a Time: How to Get Help for Your Disabled Child.* New York: Simon and Schuster, 1985.

Shields, Craig V. *Strategies: A Practical Guide for Dealing with Professionals and Human Service Systems.* Richmond Hill, Ontario: Human Services Press, 1987.

Chapter 10

Bruinicks, R.H., and K.C. Lakin. *Living and Learning in the Least Restrictive Environment.* Baltimore: Paul H. Brookes, 1985. A book that discusses the social changes in America that have resulted in greater integration into the community of people with disabilities. Primarily written for professionals, but should also be of interest to parents and other family members.

Christian, W.P., G.T. Hannah, and T.J. Glahn, eds. *Programming Effective Human Services: Strategies for Institutional Change and Client Transition.* New York: Plenum, 1984. Chapters in this book describe various innovative approaches to managing and implementing services for people with severe handicaps. May be too technical for some.

Holmes, David L. *Establishing Group Homes for Adults with Autism.* Princeton, NJ: Eden Press, 1985. Describes problems and solutions in starting up a group home.

Lauries, K.R., ed. *Directory of Programs Serving Children and Adults with Autism.* 5th ed. Washington, D.C.: National Society for Children and Adults with Autism, 1985. Lists programs serving people with autism in the United States. Slightly outdated at this point, but still useful.

McKee, L., and V. Blacklidge. *An Easy Guide for Caring Parents: Sexuality and Socialization.* Contra Costa, CA: Planned Parenthood of Contra Costa, 1981. This easy-to-read guide explains how to discuss issues concerning sexuality with young adults with mental retardation.

Summers, J.A., ed. *The Right to Grow Up: An Introduction to Adults with Developmental Disabilities.* Baltimore: Paul H. Brookes, 1986. A book for professionals addressing the needs of families and individuals with disabilities in the transition from school-based services to adult services. Issues explored include residential and vocational services, sexuality, leisure and recreation, aging, and federal laws and policies.

Turnbull, H.R., A.P. Turnbull, G.J. Bronicki, J.A. Summers, and C. Roeder-Gordon. *Disability and the Family: A Guide to Decisions for Adulthood.* Baltimore: Paul H. Brookes, 1989. A guide for parents on legal, financial, and residential issues confronting families with a special-needs member.

Magazines and Newsletters

Advocate. The Autism Society of America, 1234 Massachusetts Ave., NW, Ste. 1017, Washington, D.C. 20005. Especially informative! Free with membership in ASA.

The ARC. Association of Retarded Citizens of the U.S., 2501 Avenue J, Arlington, TX 76006 (817/640–0204). News and information on mental retardation and the activities of the national office of the ARC and its affiliates.

Augmentive Communication News. One Surf Way, Suite 215, Monterey, CA 93940. Newsletter on products, research, and policy regarding augmentive communication with disabled people.

Autism Research Review International. Institute for Child Behavior Research, 4182 Adams Ave., San Diego, CA 92116. A quarterly newsletter of up-to-date information from the bio-medical and educational literature on autism. Articles published are of interest and value to both parents and professionals concerned with the care of children with autism.

Closing the Gap. P.O. Box 68, Henderson, MN 56044 (612/248–3294). Bimonthly newsletter on microcomputer technology for persons with severe handicaps. Publishes a comprehensive resource guide yearly.

Disabled U.S.A. President's Committee on Employment of the Handicapped; 1111 20th St., N.W., 6th Fl., Washington, D.C. 20036. Reports progress in opportunities for people with disabilities and developments in rehabilitation employment.

Especially Grandparents. King County ARC, 2230 Eighth Ave., Seattle, WA 98121. A newsletter that contains articles on topics of concern to grandparents of special-needs children, designed to help them cope with the special challenges facing them.

Exceptional Parent. 605 Commonwealth Ave., Boston, MA 02215 (617/526–8961). Magazine focusing on timely topics which affect the lives of parents of children with handicaps.

Journal of Autism and Developmental Disorders. Plenum Publishing Corp., 227 W. 17th St., New York, NY 10011. Inquire about special price for ASA members.

Network News. National Network of Parent Centers, 312 Stuart St., 2nd Fl., Boston, MA 02116. Provides information on educational advocacy issues and topics of concern to leaders of parent centers.

Newsletter. NICHY, Box 1492, Washington, D.C. 20013. A topical newsletter on issues of importance to people living or working with children with special needs. Free subscription.

OSERS News in Print. Office of Special Education and Rehabilitative Services, 330 C St., S.W., 3018 Switzer Building, Washington, D.C. 20202. Includes various resources and other information for those concerned with the needs of people with handicaps.

Pacesetter Newsletter. Parent Advocacy Coalition for Educational Rights (PACER), 4826 Chicago Ave., Minneapolis, MN 55417. A quarterly newsletter for parents interested in special education issues.

Residual Autism Newsletter. 3701 W. 108th Place, Crown Point, IN 46307. The newsletter for parents of high functioning children with autism.

Sibling Information Network Newsletter. Connecticut's University Affiliated Program, School of Education, The University of Connecticut, Box U–64, Room 227, Storrs, CT 06268. Covers research and literature reviews, meetings, family relationships, and other information of interest to siblings.

Resource Guide

National Organizations

The national organizations listed below provide a variety of services that can be of help to you and your child with autism. For further information about any of these organizations, call or write and request a copy of their newsletter or other publications.

American Association of University
Affiliated Programs for Persons with
Developmental Disabilities (AAUAP)
8630 Fenton St., Ste. 410
Silver Spring, MD 20910
301/588–8252
A network of university-based and university-affiliated centers that diagnose and treat people with developmental disabilities such as autism. Consult the Local Organizations list for the AAUAP program nearest you.

Autism Society of America
8601 Georgia Ave., Ste. 503
Silver Spring, MD 20901
301/565–0433; 800/3–AUTISM
A national organization of parents and professionals established to promote a better understanding of autism, to encourage the development of services, to support research related to autism, and to advocate on the behalf of people with autism and their families. Maintains the ASA Information and Referral Service, which acts as a clearinghouse for information about autism and services for people with autism. Publishes the *Advocate*, a bimonthly newsletter, and a National Directory of Programs Serving Children and Adults with Autism. Coordinates a national network of affiliated local chapters (see the Local Organizations list). For the location of the state or local chapter nearest you, call the 800 number listed above. Formerly known as the National Society for Children and Adults with Autism (NSAC).

ASA International Affairs Committee
Autism Training Center
Old Main 316
Marshall University
Huntington, WV 25755
304/696–2332
Seeks to increase awareness of autism internationally through the dissemination and coordination of information and the exchange of information between parents

and professionals internationally. Can provide information about international programs.

The Association for Persons with Severe Handicaps (TASH)
11201 Greenwood Ave. N
Seattle, WA 98133
206/361–8870
Professional/parent organization that works for a dignified lifestyle for all people with severe handicaps through legal and educational advocacy. Publishes a newsletter and a professional journal.

Association for Retarded Citizens (ARC)
500 E. Border St.
Ste. 300
Arlington, TX 76010
817/261–6003
A grassroots national organization of retarded persons and their advocates. Publishes information about all types of mental retardation, advocates on behalf of retarded persons, and supports an extensive national network of local associations. See the Local Organizations list for the chapter nearest you.

Autism Services Center
P.O. Box 507
605 9th St.
Huntington, WV 25710
304/525–8014
Established to provide training, consulting services, advocacy, and information to those concerned with the welfare and care of people with autism. Operates a free National Autism Hotline; charges for other services.

Bazelon Center
1101 15th St., NW, Ste. 1212
Washington, D.C. 20005
202/467–5730
A public interest law firm (formerly the Mental Health Law Project) which conducts test cases to defend the rights of people with mental disabilities.

Center on Human Development
Division of Special Education and Rehabilitation
Clinical Services Building
College of Education
Eugene, OR 97403–1211
Can provided information on employment options for developmentally disabled people.

Children's Defense Fund
25 E St., N.W.
Washington, D.C. 20001
800/424–9602 (202/628–8787 in D.C.)
A legal organization that lobbies and brings test cases to court to expand the rights of children, including those of handicapped children.

Council for Exceptional Children
1920 Association Dr.
Reston, VA 22091
703/620–3660
A national organization with approximately 1,000 local chapters concerned with the educational needs of exceptional children. Publishes *The Exceptional Parent* magazine and performs computer searches.

Institute for Child Behavior Research
4182 Adams Ave.
San Diego, CA 92116
Contact: Bernard Rimland, Ph.D., Director
A major function of this institute is to provide parents and professionals with information about the value of the various treatments available for children with autism. Has an extensive publications list.

International Rett Syndrome Association
9121 Piscataway Rd., Ste. 2–B
Clinton, MD 20735
301/856–3334
Contact: Kathy Hunter, President
An organization of parents of children with Rett Syndrome and professionals. Offers support to parents, collects and distributes information, assists in identifying children with Rett Syndrome, and promotes research related to Rett Syndrome. Publishes a newsletter.

Joseph P. Kennedy, Jr., Foundation
1350 New York Ave., N.W.
Suite 500
Washington, D.C. 20005
202/393–1250
This foundation created and founded the Special Olympics. Also runs the "Let's Play to Grow" program, which sponsors events for parents and infants that encourage early play activities.

Kids on the Block
9385 C Gerwig Lane
Columbia, MD 21406
410/290–9095; 800/368–KIDS
This is a performing arts puppet show that gears its shows to school-aged children. The puppets have a variety of handicaps including autism.

National Fragile X Foundation
1441 York St., Ste. 215
Denver, CO 80206
800/688–8765
Supports education, diagnosis, and research in Fragile X syndrome. Publishes *The Fragile X Foundation Newsletter.*

National Information Center
for Children & Youth with Disabilities (NICHCY)
Box 1492
Washington, D.C. 20013
800/999–5599
NICHCY was established to provide practical advice on locating educational programs and other kinds of special services for handicapped children and youth. Parents can call or send in requests for free information on a wide range of subjects, including autism.

National Organization on Disability (NOD)
910 16th St., N.W., Suite 600
Washington, D.C. 20006
202/293–5960
A national data bank of information on disabilities and related issues.

National Rehabilitation Information Center
4407 Eighth St., N.E.
Washington, D.C. 20017
Can provide information on employment opportunities for disabled adults.

Parent Educational Advocacy Training Center
228 Pitt St., Suite 300
Alexandria, VA
703/836–2953
Trains parents to serve as educational advocates for their special-needs children. Offers a five-session course ("Next Steps: Planning for Employment") to prepare parents for their roles as career education advocates.

Parentele: An Alliance of Parents and Friends
Networking for Those with Special Needs
310 S. Jersey St.
Denver, CO 80224
Contact: Elaine Clearfield
An organization dedicated to networking and information sharing with representatives in each state.

Rehabilitation Research and Training Center
Virginia Commonwealth University
1314 W. Main St.
Richmond, VA 23284–0001
Can provide information about employment for people with severe developmental disabilities.

Sibling Information Network
1776 Ellington Rd.
S. Windsor, CT 06074
203/648–1205
A clearinghouse of information on the disabled and their families with a concentration on siblings. Publishes a quarterly newsletter containing reviews, resource information, and discussions of family issues.

Siblings for Significant Change
105 E. 22nd St.
New York, NY 10010
212/420–0430
A sibling membership organization that provides information, workshops, and conferences to increase public awareness of the needs of children with handicaps and their families.

Special Olympics
1350 New York Ave., N.W.
Suite 500
Washington, D.C. 20005
202/628–3630
An international program of physical fitness, sports training, and athletic competition for mentally retarded children and adults. Accommodates competitors at all ability levels by assigning them to "competition divisions" based on age and actual performance.

TEACCH (Treatment and Education of Autistic and Related Communication Handicapped Children and Adults)
Division TEACCH, CB# 7180
310 Medical School Wing E
Chapel Hill, NC 27599–7180
919/966–2174
Contact: Eric Schopler, Ph.D., Director
A comprehensive community-based program for persons with autism. Through North Carolina's five regional TEACCH centers, provides diagnostic evaluation, individualized treatment, parent and professional training, and consultation.

Technical Assistance for Parent Programs (TAPP)
95 Berkeley St., Ste. 104
Boston, MA 02116
617/482–2915
Contact: Martha Ziegler, Director
TAPP provides technical assistance for programs that provide information and training for parents of children with disabilities. Assistance is provided through the following regional centers:

Parent Information Center
155 Manchester St.
P.O. Box 1422
Concord, NH 03301
603/224-6299
Contact: Judith Raskin, Director

Parent Advocacy Coalition for
Educational Rights (PACER)
4826 Chicago Ave., South
Minneapolis, MN 55417–1055
800/53–PACER (MN only)
612/827–2966
Contact: Marge Goldberg or Paula
Goldberg, Directors

Parents Educating Parents
Georgia/ARC
1851 Ram Runway, Ste. 104
College Park, GA 30337
404/761–2745
Contact: Mildred Hill, Director

Parents Advocating Vocational
Education (PAVE)
6316 S. 12th St.
Tacoma, WA 98645
800–5–PARENT (WA only)
206/565–2266
Contact: Martha Gentili, Director

Local Organizations

The following list contains addresses, phone numbers, and names of contact people for public and private agencies in each state that provide certain kinds of assistance to people with special needs and their families. We wish to thank the National Information Center for Handicapped Children & Youth (NICHCY) and the Autism Society of America (ASA) for contributing much of this information.

Here are brief descriptions of the types of organizations this list includes:

The State Department of Education is the agency responsible for providing education to school-aged children, including special education services to children with autism. In many states, the Department of Education also administers early intervention programs for special-needs children aged 0–2, and preschool programs for those aged 3–5. If it does not, it can refer you to the agency that does.

The State Vocational Rehabilitation Agency provides medical, therapeutic, educational, counseling, training, and other services needed to prepare people for work. The state agency will refer you to the local office nearest you.

The State Mental Retardation Program provides funding, in some states, for residential and day programs for children and adults with mental retardation. In other states, the State Mental Retardation Program can direct you to the appropriate funding agency.

The Developmental Disabilities Council provides funding for direct services for people with developmental disabilities. Most provide services such as diagnosis, evaluation, information and referral, social services, group homes, advocacy, and protection.

The Protection & Advocacy Agency is a legal organization established to protect the rights of people with disabilities. It can supply information about the educational, health, residential, social, and legal services available for children with autism in your state.

American Association of University Affiliated Programs (AAUAP) are federally funded centers that offer services to parents of children with special needs. They are a good source of the multidisciplinary diagnostic team described in Chapter 1.

Parent Programs include privately and publicly funded groups that offer support, information, and referral services to parents of children with special needs.

Autism Society of America (ASA) Chapters are local affiliates of the national organization that provide support and information to parents of children with autism, and direct them to resources and people in their area who can help them.

Association of Retarded Citizens (ARC) Chapters and their many programs are essential resources for parents whose children with autism also have mental retardation. Each state's ARC is listed below, but there are also many local branches. To locate the branch nearest you, contact your state ARC or check your telephone book under "Association for Retarded Citizens" or "ARC," or look under the name of your city, county, region, state, or state capital (e.g., "Montgomery County ARC").

ALABAMA

Student Instructional Services
State Department of Education
1020 Monticello Ct.
Montgomery, AL 36117–1901
205/261–5099
Contact: Ann Ramsey, Coordinator

Program for Exceptional Children & Youth [Ages 3–5]
Dept. of Education
1020 Monticello Ct.
Montgomery, AL 36117
205/261–5099
Contact: James Wald

Crippled Children's Services [Ages 0–2]
Dept. of Education
P.O. Box 1586
2129 E. South Blvd.
Montgomery, AL 36111–0586
205/281–8780
Contact: Christine Kendall, Director

Div. of Rehabilitation & Crippled Children's Services
Dept. of Education
P.O. Box 11586
2129 E. South Blvd.
Montgomery, AL 36111
205/281–8780
Contact: Lamona Lucas, Director

Department of Mental Health & Mental Retardation
200 Interstate Park Dr.
P.O. Box 3710
Montgomery, AL 36193
205/271–9295
Contact: Larry Latham, Assoc. Commissioner

Community Programs
Dept. of Mental Health/Mental Retardation
200 Interstate Park Dr.
P.O. Box 3710
Montgomery, AL 36193–5001
205/271–9253
Contact: Mary Lee Rice, Director

Alabama Developmental Disabilities Planning Council
P.O. Box 3710
Montgomery, AL 36193–5001
205/271–9278
Contact: Joan Hannah, Director

Alabama Developmental Disabilities Advocacy Program
P.O. Drawer 2847
The University of Alabama
Tuscaloosa, AL 35487–2847
205/348–4928
Contact: Suellen Galbraith, Director

Sparks Center for Developmental & Learning Disorders
University of Alabama at Birmingham
1720 Seventh Ave., South
Birmingham, AL 35233
205/934–5471
Contact: Dr. Gary Myers, Director

Special Education Action Committee, Inc.
P.O. Box 161274
Mobile, AL 36616–2274
205/478–1208; 800/222–7322 (In AL)
Contact: Carol Blades, Director

Alabama State Society
Autism Society of America
1211 Nancy Ford Rd.
Hartsell, AL 35640
205/773–3733
Contact: Jackie Harper, Pres.

Northern Alabama Chapter
Autism Society of America
11308 Hillwood Dr., S.E.
Huntsville, AL 35803
205/539–5552
Contact: Howard Henrikson, Pres.

Birmingham Area Chapter
Autism Society of America
4825 Lincrest Dr.
Birmingham, AL 35222
205/599–5277
Contact: Marvin Thornton, Pres.

Mobile Alabama Chapter
Autism Society of America
6463 Zeigler Blvd.
Mobile, AL 36608
205/344–2811
Contact: Jo Ann Wetzel, Pres.

Association for Retarded Citizens of Alabama
444 S. Decatur
Montgomery, AL 36104
205/262–7688
Contact: Douglas Sandford, Exec. Dir.

ALASKA

Office of Special Services
Department of Education
Pouch F
Juneau, AK 99811
907/465–2970
Contact: William S. Mulnix, Director

Office of Special Services & Supplemental Programs [Ages 3–5]
Dept. of Education
P.O. Box F
Juneau, AK 99811
907/465–2970
Contact: Christine Niemi, Director

Dept. of Health & Social Services [Ages 0–2]
1231 Gambell St.
Anchorage, AL 99501
907/278–3841
Contact: Karen Lamb, ILP Education Specialist

Div. of Vocational Rehabilitation
Dept. of Education
Pouch F, Mail Stop 0581
State Office Building
Juneau, AK 99811
907/465–2814
Contact: Keith Anderson, Director

Developmental Disabilities Section
Div. of Mental Health & Developmental Disabilities
Dept. of Health & Human Services
Pouch H–04
Juneau, AK 99811
Contact: Christine Hagmeier, Acting Dir.

Child & Adolescent Mental Health
Div. of Mental Health & Developmental Disabilities
Dept. of Health & Social Services
Pouch H–04
Juneau, AK 99811
907/465–3370
Contact: John Vandenberg, Coordinator

Developmental Disabilities Planning Council
600 University Ave., Suite B
Fairbanks, AK 99709–3651
907/479–6507
Contact: Dorothy Truran, Director

Advocacy Service of Alaska
325 E. Third Ave., 2nd Fl.

Anchorage, AK 99501
907/274–3658
Contact: David Maltman, Director

Alaska Parent Coalition
7530 Blackberry
Anchorage, AK 99502

Special Education Parent Team
210 Ferry Way, Ste. 200
Juneau, AK 99801
907/586–6806
Contact: Linda Griffith

Alaska State Chapter
Autism Society of America
1060 Serrano Dr.
Wasilla, AK 99687
907/376–1224
Contact: Kay Freimuth, President

Alaska Association for Retarded Citizens
2211–A Arca Dr.
Anchorage, AK 99506
907/277–6677
Contact: Mary Jane Starlings

AMERICAN SAMOA

Special Education
Dept. of Education
Pago Pago, American Samoa 96799
684/633–1323
Contact: Jane French, Director

Special Education Div. [Ages 3–5]
Dept. of Education
Box 434
Pago Pago, AS 96799
684/633–1323
Contact: Linda Avegalio, Director

Vocational Rehabilitation
American Samoa Govt.
P.O. Box 3492
Pago Pago, AS 96799
684/633–1805
Contact: Ken Galea'i, Director

Independent Living Program
Office of Manpower Resources
Territory of American Samoa
Fagatoga 97699
Contact: Tanya Huff, Director

American Samoa Developmental Disabilities Council
P.O. Box 3823
Pago Pago, AS 96799
684/633–2919
Contact: Matau Taele, Exec. Dir.

Client Assistance & Protection & Advocacy Program
P.O. Box 3407
Pago Pago, AS 96799
684/633–2418
Contact: Minareta Thompson, Director

ARIZONA

Special Education Section
Dept. of Education
1535 W. Jefferson
Phoenix, AZ 85007
602/255–3183
Contact: Kay Lund, Deputy Associate Superintendent

Div. of Special Education [Ages 3–5]
Dept. of Education
1535 W. Jefferson
Phoenix, AZ 85007
602/542–3183
Contact: JoAnn Woodley, Preschool Coordinator

Div. of Developmental Disabilities [Ages 0–2]
Dept. of Economic Security
P.O. Box 6123–791A
Phoenix, AZ 85005
602/258–0419
Contact: Marlene Morgan, Coordinator

Rehabilitation Services Bureau
Dept. of Economic Security
1300 W. Washington St.
Phoenix, AZ 85007
602/542–3332
Contact: James Griffith, Admin.

Div. of Developmental Disabilities
Department of Economic Security
P.O. Box 6760
Phoenix, AZ 85005
602/255–5775
Contact: Lyn Rucker, Assis. Director

Program for Youths & Adolescents
Div. of Behavioral Health Services
Dept. of Health Services
411 N. 24th St.
Phoenix, AZ 85008
602/220–6478
Contact: Stephen Perkins, Coordinator

Governor's Council on
Developmental Disabilities
1717 W. Jefferson
P.O. Box 6123
Phoenix, AZ 85007
602/255–4049
Contact: Rita Charron, Director

Arizona Center for Law in the
Public Interest
363 N. First Ave., Suite 100
Phoenix, AZ 85003
602/252–4904
Contact: Kevin Lanigan, Exec. Dir.

Dine' Center for Human Development
Navajo Community College
Tsaile, AZ 86556
602/724–3351
Contact: Loren Sekayumptewa, Exec. Dir.

Pilot Parent Partnerships
2150 E. Highland Ave., No. 105
Phoenix, AZ 85016
602/468–3001
Contact: Mary Slaughter, Director

Pima County Chapter
Autism Society of America
5201 E. 28th St.
Tucson, AZ 85711
602/294–0493
Contact: Georgia Bolton, President

Greater Phoenix Chapter
Autism Society of America
4912 West Evans
Glendale, AZ 85306
602/843–4731
Contact: Pat Peck, President

Association for Retarded
Citizens of Arizona
5610 S. Central
Phoenix, AZ 85040
602/243–1787

ARKANSAS

Special Education Section
Dept. of Education
Education Building, Room 105–C
Little Rock, AR 72201
501/682–4221
Contact: Dr. Diane Sydoriak, Assoc. Dir.

Special Education Section [Ages 3–5]
Dept. of Education
4 Capitol Mall, Room 105–C
Little Rock, AR 72201
501/682–4222
Contact: Mary Kay Curry

Div. of Developmental Disabilities Services [Ages 0–2]
Dept. of Human Services
P.O. Box 1437
7th & Main Sts.
Little Rock, AR 72203–1437
501/682–8705
Contact: Kellie Jennings, Early Intervention Coordinator

Div. of Rehabilitation Services
Dept. of Human Services
P.O. Box 3781
7th & Main Sts.
Little Rock, AR 72203
501/682–6708

Developmental Disabilities Services
Department of Human Services
Suite 400, Waldon Building
7th & Main Sts., 5th Fl.
Little Rock, AR 72201

501/682–8662
Contact: Ann Majure, Deputy Director

Adolescent Inpatient Unit
Arkansas State Hospital
4313 W. Markham St.
Little Rock, AR 72201–4096
501/686–9100
Contact: Dr. Barry Pipkin

Governor's Developmental Disabilities Planning Council
4815 W. Markham St.
Little Rock, AR 72201
501/661–2589
Contact: Cindy Hartsfield, Director

Advocacy Services, Inc.
1120 Marshall St., Ste. 311
Little Rock, AR 72202
501/371–2171
Contact: Nan Ellen East, Exec. Dir.

Arkansas Coalition for the Handicapped
519 E. Capitol
Little Rock, AR 72202
501/376–3420
Contact: Bonnie Johnson, Director

FOCUS, Inc.
2917 King St., Ste. C
Jonesboro, AR 72401
501/935–2750
Contact: Barbara Semrau

Parent-to-Parent
Union Station Square, Ste. 406
Little Rock, AR 72201
501/375–4464
Contact: Sheri Shepherd, Coordinator

Autism Society of Arkansas
Autism Society of America
13200 St. Charles Blvd.
Little Rock, AR 72211
Contact: Charlene Prousnitzer, President

Association for Retarded Citizens of Arkansas
Union Station Square, Ste. 406
Little Rock, AR 72201
501/375–4464
Contact: Nancy Sullivan, Exec. Dir.

CALIFORNIA

Special Education Div.
California Department of Education
P.O. Box 944272
Sacramento, CA 94244–2720
916/323–4768
Contact: Patrick Campbell, Director

Infant/Preschool Unit [Ages 3–5]
Special Education Div.
Dept. of Education
721 Capitol Mall
Sacramento, CA 95814
916/324–8417
Contact: Nancy Obley-Kilborn

Early Intervention Program [Ages 0–2]
Dept. of Developmental Services
1600 9th St., Room 310
Sacramento, CA 95814
916/324–2090
Contact: Julie Jackson, Asst. Deputy Dir.

Dept. of Rehabilitation
Health & Welfare Agency
830 K Street Mall
Sacramento, CA 95814
916/445–3971
Contact: P. Cecilio Fontanoza, Dir.

Dept. of Developmental Services
Health & Welfare Agency
1600 9th St., N.W., 2nd Floor
Sacramento, CA 95814
916/323–3131
Contact: Gary Macomber, Director

Special Populations Branch
Dept. of Mental Health
1600 9th St.
Sacramento, CA 95814
916/323–9289
Contact: Betsy Burke, Director

State Council on Developmental Disabilities
1507 21st St., Room 320
Sacramento, CA 95814–5220
916/322–8481
Contact: James Bellotti, Director

California Protection & Advocacy, Inc.
2131 Capitol Ave.
Sacramento, CA 95816
916/447–3324; 800/952–5746
Contact: Albert Zonca, Exec. Dir.

Mental Retardation & Developmental Disability Program
University of California at Los Angeles
760 Westwood Plaza
Los Angeles, CA 90024
213/825–0395
Contact: Dr. James Simmons, Director

Center for Child Development & Developmental Disorders
University Affiliated Training Program
Children's Hospital of Los Angeles
4650 Sunset Blvd.
Los Angeles, CA 90027
213/669–2151
Contact: Dr. Wylda Hammond, Director

Team of Advocates for Special Kids (TASK)
18685 Santa Ynez
Fountain Valley, CA 92708
714/962–6332
Contact: Joan Tellefsen

Parents Helping Parents
535 Race St., Ste. 220
San Jose, CA 95126
408/288–5010
Contact: Florene Poyadue

DREDF
2212 6th St.
Berkeley, CA 94710
415/644–2555
Contact: Pam Steneberg

Disability Services Matrix
P.O. Box 6541
San Rafael, CA 94903
415/499–3877
Contact: Joan Kilburn

Autism Society of California
812 J St., Ste. 48
Sacramento, CA 95814
916/441–1243
Contact: Marie White, President

Central California Chapter
Autism Society of America
17557 W. McKinley
Kerman, CA 93630
209/846–9227
Contact: Marianne Shubin, Pres.

Desert Communities Chapter
Autism Society of America
P.O. Box 1182
Sugarloaf, CA 92836
714/585–7062
Contact: Peter Rodriguez, Pres.

Kern County Chapter
Autism Society of America
6504 Edgemont
Bakersfield, CA 93306
805/831–8897
Contact: Phyllis Gutierrez, Pres.

Los Angeles Chapter
Autism Society of America
2213 Midvale Ave.
Los Angeles, CA 90064
213/559–5664; 213/475–5167
Contact: Ms. Toby Ahrenberg, Pres.

Long Beach/San Gabriel Chapter
Autism Society of America
3424 Bellflower Blvd.
Long Beach, CA 90815
213/425–6850
Contact: Mary Preble, President

Sacramento Chapter
Autism Society of America
4325 Frizell Ave.
Sacramento, CA 95842
916/338–3833
Contact: Helen Richard, Pres.

San Diego Chapter
6260 Childs Ave.
San Diego, CA 92139
619/267–3383
Contact: Alison Blake, Pres.

San Francisco Bay Area Chap.
Autism Society of America
1154 Alicante Dr.
Pacifica, CA 94044
415/359–2561
Contact: Sylvia Fabris, Pres.

Santa Clara County Chapter
Autism Society of America
2865 Thomas Grove
Morgan Hill, CA 95037
415/948–6834; 415/779–5020
Contact: Carole Friis, President

Ventura County Chapter
Autism Society of America
P.O. Box 1752
Ventura, CA 93002
805/642–0366
Contact: Melinda Abel, Pres.

Association for Retarded Citizens of California
1510 J St., Ste. 180
Sacramento, CA 95814
916/441–3322
Contact: Frederic Hougardy, Exec. Dir.

COLORADO

Special Education Services Unit
Department of Education
201 E. Colfax Ave.
Denver, CO 80203
303/866–6694
Contact: Dr. Brian McNulty, Director

Special Education Div. [Ages 3–5]
Dept. of Education
201 E. Colfax Ave., Rm. 301
Denver, CO 80203
303/866–6710
Contact: Elizabeth Soper, Coordinator

Early Childhood Education [Ages 0–2]
Dept. of Education
201 E. Colfax Ave.
Denver, CO 80203

Div. of Rehabilitation
Dept. of Social Services
1575 Sherman St., 4th Fl.
Denver, CO 80203
303/866–2866
Contact: Anthony Francavilla, Acting Director

Div. for Developmental Disabilities
3824 W. Princeton Circle
Denver, CO 80236
303/762–4550
Contact: Jeff Sandler, Director

Div. of Mental Health
Dept. of Institutions
3520 W. Oxford Ave.
Denver, CO 80236
303/762–4075
Contact: Hilde Wilkinson, Coordinator

Colorado Developmental Disabilities Council
777 Grant St., Ste. 410
Denver, CO 80203–3518
303/894–2345
Contact: William Gorman, Exec. Dir.

The Legal Center
455 Sherman St., Suite 130
Denver, CO 80203
303/722–0300
Contact: Mary Anne Harvey, Exec. Dir.

John F. Kennedy Child Development Center
University of Colorado Health Sciences Center
4200 E. Ninth Ave., Box C234
Denver, CO 80262
303/394–7224
Contact: Dr. Bonnie Camp, Director

Parents Education & Assistance for Kids (PEAK)
6055 Lehman Dr., Ste. 101
Colorado Springs, CO 80918
303/531–9400
Contact: Judy Martz or Barbara Buswell, Directors

Parent-to-Parent
Contact PEAK, above

Colorado Association for Autistic Persons
5031 W. Quarles Dr.
Littleton, CO 80123
303/979–5962
Contact: Diane Bucci, President

Association for Retarded Citizens of Colorado
Capitol Life Center, Ste. 750
1600 Sherman St.
Denver, CO 80203
303/832–2722
Contact: Jeffrey Strully, Exec. Dir.

CONNECTICUT

Bureau of Special Education & Pupil Personnel Services
State Department of Education
P.O. Box 2219
Hartford, CT 06102–2219
203/566–3561
Contact: Dr. Tom Gillung, Director

Early Childhood Unit [Ages 3–5]
Div. of Curriculum & Professional Development
Dept. of Education
P.O. Box 2219
Hartford, CT 06145
203/566–6586
Contact: Kay Halverson, Coordinator

Early Childhood Unit [Ages 0–2]
Dept. of Education
P.O. Box 2219
Hartford, CT 06145
203/566–6584
Contact: Virginia Volk, Coordinator

Div. of Rehabilitation Services
Board of Education
600 Asylum Ave.
Hartford, CT 06105
203/566–4440
Contact: Marilyn Campbell, Director

Department of Mental Retardation
90 Pitkin St.
East Hartford, CT 06108
203/528–7141
Contact: Brian Lensink, Commissioner

Dept. of Children & Youth Services
170 Sigourny St.
Hartford, CT 06115
203/566–8180
Contact: Dr. Robert Gossart

Developmental Disabilities Council
90 Pitkin St.
East Hartford, CT 06108
203/725–3829
Contact: Edward Preneta

Office of Protection & Advocacy for Handicapped & Developmentally Disabled Persons
90 Washington St., Lower Level
Hartford, CT 06106
203/566–7616; 800/842–7303
Contact: Eliot J. Dober, Exec. Dir.

Connecticut's University Affiliated Program on Developmental Disabilities
991 Main St.
East Hartford, CT 06108
203/282–7050
Contact: Director

Connecticut Parent Advocacy Center
P.O. Box 579
East Lyme, CT 06333
203/739–3089
Contact: Nancy Prescott, Director

Parent-to-Parent
Dept. of Pediatrics
University of Connecticut
The Exchange
Farmington, CT 06032

203/674–1485; 203–951–0045
Contact: Molly P. Cole

Newington Children's Hospital
181 East Cedar St.
Newington, CT 06111
Contact: Dr. Michael Powers

Connecticut State Society
Autism Society of America
18 Sidney Avenue
West Hartford, CT 06110
203/536–9576
Contact: Rena Gans, President

Naugatuck Valley Chapter
Autism Society of America
3 Cobbler Lane
New Milford, CT 06776
203/355–0230
Contact: Janice Orlander, Pres.

South Central Connecticut Chapter
Autism Society of America
87 Clinton Ave.
New Haven, CT 06513
203/772–3521
Contact: Ms. Edna Saavedra, Pres.

Association for Retarded Citizens of Connecticut
45 S. Main St.
West Hartford, CT 06107
203/233–3629
Contact: Margaret Dignoti, Exec. Dir.

DELAWARE

Exceptional Children/Special Programs Div.
Department of Public Instruction
P.O. Box 1402
Dover, DE 19903
302/736–5471
Contact: Dr. Carl Haltom, Director

Exceptional Children/Special Programs Div. [Ages 3–5]
Department of Public Instruction
P.O. Box 1402
Dover, DE 19903
302/736–4667
Contact: Barbara Humphreys, State Specialist

Exceptional Children/Special Programs Div. [Ages 0–2]
Department of Public Instruction
P.O. Box 1402
Dover, DE 19903
302/736–4557
Contact: Sheryl Parkhurst, State Supervisor

Div. of Vocational Rehabilitation
Dept. of Labor
321 E. 11th St.
Wilmington, DE 19801
302/571–2851
Contact: Anthony Sokolowski, Dir.

Div. of Mental Retardation
Dept. of Health & Human Services
Robins Building
802 Silver Lake Blvd.
Dover, DE 19901
302/736–4386
Contact: Thomas Pledgie, Director

Div. of Child Mental Health Services
Div. of Services for Children, Youth & Families
330 E. 30th St.
Wilmington, DE 19802
302/995–8369
Contact: Julian Taplin, Director

Developmental Disabilities Council
156 S. State St.
P.O. Box 1401
Dover, DE 19901
302/736–4456
Contact: James Linehan

Disabilities Law Program
144 E. Market St.
Georgetown, DE 19947
302/856–0038
Contact: Christine Long, Administrator

Parent Information Center of Delaware, Inc.
226 W. Park Place, Ste. 4–6
Newark, DE 19711
302/366–0152
Contact: Marie-Ann Aghazadian, Director

Parent-to-Parent
Contact Parent Information Center, above

Delaware State Chapter
Autism Society of America
11 Broadfield Dr.
Newark, DE 19713
302/737–2387
Contact: Elizabeth Allen, President

Delaware Autistic Program
144 Brennan Dr.
Newark, DE 19713
302/454–2202
Contact: Dr. Andrew Bondy, Director

Association for Retarded Citizens of Delaware
Tower Office Park
240 N. James St., Ste. B–2
Wilmington, DE 19804
302/996–9400
Contact: David Richard, Exec. Dir.

DISTRICT OF COLUMBIA

Div. of Special Education
D.C. Public Schools
10th & H Sts., N.W.
Washington, D.C. 20001
202/724–4018
Contact: Dr. Doris Woodson, Asst. Supt.

Logan Child Study Center [Ages 3–5]
3rd & G Sts., N.E.
Washington, D.C. 20002
202/724–4800
Contact: Robbie King, Coordinator

Office of EarlyChildhood Development [Ages 0–2]
Commission on Social Services
Randall Bldg., Ste. 224
First & I Sts., S.W.
Washington, D.C. 20024
202/727–5930
Contact: Virginia View, Program Manager

Vocational Rehabilitation Services Administration
Dept. of Human Resources
605 G. St., N.W.
Washington, D.C. 20001
202/727–3227
Contact: Katherine Williams, Acting Administrator

Dept. of Human Services
Commission on Social Services
Developmental Disabilities Administration
409 O St., N.W.
Washington, D.C. 20001
202/673–7678
Contact: George Smith, Administrator

Child/Youth Services Administration
D.C. Mental Health System
1875 Connecticut Ave., N.W., No. 1130
Washington, D.C. 20009
202/673–7773
Maresa Isaacs, Administrator

Developmental Disabilities State Planning Council
605 G St., N.W., Room 1108
Washington, D.C. 20001–3754
202/727–0904
Contact: Phyllis Bolden, Exec. Dir.

Information, Protection & Advocacy Center for Handicapped Individuals
300 I St., N.E., Suite 202
Washington, DC 20002
202/547–8081
Contact: Yetta Galiber, Exec. Dir.

Georgetown University Child Development Center
Bles Bldg., Room CG–52
3800 Reservoir Rd., N.W.

Washington, D.C. 20007
202/687–8635
Contact: Dr. Phyllis Magrab, Director

Parents Reaching Out Services, Inc.
1900 Massachusetts Ave., S.E.
Washington, D.C. 20003
202/546–8847
Contact: Gloria Stokes, Director

District of Columbia Chapter
Autism Society of America
234 Newcomb St., S.E. #709
Washington, D.C. 20032
202/574–3230
Contact: Sandra Cunningham, Pres.

Association of Retarded Citizens of D.C.
900 Varnum St., N.E.
Washington, D.C. 20017
202/636–2950
Contact: Vincent Gray

FLORIDA

Bureau of Education for Exceptional Students
Dept. of Education
Knott Building
Tallahassee, FL 32399
904/488–1570
Contact: Diane Gillespie, Bureau Chief

Bureau of Education for Exceptional Children [Ages 3–5]
Dept. of Education
Knott Building
Tallahassee, FL 32399
904/488–2054
Contact: Landis Stetler, Director

Office of Early Intervention
Dept. of Education
Knott Building
Tallahassee, FL 32399
904/488–4830
Contact: Nancy Thomas, Administrator

Div. of Vocational Rehabilitation
Dept. of Labor & Employment Security
1709–A Mahan Dr.
Tallahassee, FL 32399
904/488–6210
Contact: Calvin Melton, Director

Developmental Services Program Office
Dept. of Health & Rehabilitative Services
1311 Winewood Blvd.
Building 5, Room 215
Tallahassee, FL 32301
904/488–4257
Contact: Kingsley Ross, Director

Mental Health Services, Children's Program
Alcohol, Drug Abuse, & Mental Health Program Office
1317 Winewood Blvd.
Tallahassee, FL 32301
904/487–2415
Contact: Devon Hardy, Administrator

Florida Developmental Disabilities Planning Council
1317 Winewood Blvd.
Tallahassee, FL 32301
904/488–4180
Contact: Joseph Krieger, Exec. Dir.

Advocacy Center for Persons with Disabilities
2661 Executive Center Circle, W.
Clifton Building, Ste. 209
Tallahassee, FL 32301
904/488–9070
Contact: Jonathan Rossman, Director

Mailman Center for Child Development
University of Miami School of Medicine
P.O. Box 016820 – D–820
Miami, FL 33101
305/547–6635
Contact: Dr. Robert Stempfel, Director

Parent Education Network of Florida, Inc.
2215 E. Henry Ave.
Tampa, FL 33610
813/238–6100
Contact: Linda Pitts, Director

Parent-to-Parent of Florida, Inc.
P.O. Box 1362
Thonotosassa, FL 33590–1362
813/986–3899
Contact: Susan Duwa

Florida Society for Children
& Adults with Autism
Autism Society of America
202 Avenue E, N.W.,
Winter Haven, FL 33880
819/299–8133
Contact: Ann Wills, Pres.

Central Florida Chapter
Autism Society of America
4301 Kasper Dr.
Orlando, FL 32806
305/896–1774
Contact: James Baumann, Pres.

Autism Society of America
Southwest Florida Chapter
1456 Lynwood Ave.
Fort Meyers, FL 33901
813/332–5395
Contact: Richard Bashaw, Pres.

First Coast Autistic Society
Autism Society of America
385 Perthshire Dr.
Jacksonville, FL 32216
904/272–8988
Contact: Carol Monroe, Pres.

Florida Panhandle Chapter
Autism Society of America
349 Holmes Blvd.
Fort Walton Beach, FL 32548
904/862–8942
Contact: Janice Copeland, President

Gulf Coast Florida Chapter
Autism Society of America
1484 52nd Ave., N.E.
St. Petersburg, FL 33702
813/521–1561
Contact: Anne Dinapoli, Pres.

North Central Florida Chapter
Autism Society of America
2210 N.W. 6th Pl.
Gainesville, FL 32603
904/376–2867; 904/392–3611
Contact: Dr. Ralph Maurer, Pres.

Polk Autism Chapter
Autism Society of America
219 Riggins St.
Lakeland, FL 33801
813/688–8877
Contact: Bettye Hunter, President

South Florida Chapter
Autism Society of America
3325 Oak Dr.
Hollywood, FL 33021
305/651–2706
Contact: Barbara Gershun, Pres.

Association for Retarded Citizens of Florida
411 E. College Ave.
Tallahassee, FL 32301
904/681–1931
Contact: Chris Shuh

GEORGIA

Div. of Exceptional Students
Dept. of Education
1970 Twin Towers East
Atlanta, GA 30334
404/656–2425
Contact: Dr. Joan A. Jordan, Director

Dept. of Education [Ages 3–5]
1970 Twin Towers East
Atlanta, GA 30334
404/656–2426
Contact: Rae Ann Redman, Consultant
for Preschool Education

Mental Retardation Services [Ages 0–2]
Div. of Mental Health & Mental Retardation
878 Peachtree St., Ste. 310
Atlanta, GA 30309–3999
404/894–6329
Contact: Ralph McCuin, Director

Div. of Rehabilitation Services
Dept. of Human Resources
878 Peachtree St., N.E., Rm. 706
Atlanta, GA 30309
404/894–6670
Contact: Thomas Gaines, Director

Mental Retardation Services
Div. of Mental Health & Mental Retardation
Dept. of Human Resources
878 Peachtree St., N.E.
Atlanta, GA 30309
404/894–6313
Contact: Charles Kimber, Deputy Dir.

Child & Adolescent Mental Health Services
Div. of Mental Health & Mental Retardation
878 Peachtree St., N.E., No. 315
Atlanta, GA 30309–3999
404/894–6559
Contact: Ruth Coody, Director

Georgia Council on Developmental Disabilities, 6th Floor
878 Peachtree St., N.E.
Atlanta, GA 30309–3917
404/894–5790
Contact: Zebe Schmitt, Director

Georgia Advocacy Office, Inc.
Suite 811
1447 Peachtree St., N.E.
Atlanta, GA 30309
404/885–1447; 800/282–4538
Contact: Pat Powell, Exec. Dir.

University Affiliated Program of Georgia
570 Aderhold Hall
Athens, GA 30602
404/542–1685
Contact: Dr. Richard Talbott, Exec. Dir.

Georgia Retardation Center
University Affiliated Program
4770 N. Peachtree Rd.
Atlanta, GA 30338
404/393–7089
Contact: Jane Brown, Acting Coordinator

Parents Educating Parents (PEP)
Georgia ARC
1851 Ram Runway, Ste. 104
College Park, GA 30337
404/761–2745
Contact: Mildred Hill, Director

Parent-to-Parent of Georgia, Inc.
1644 Tullie Circle, N.E.
Atlanta, GA 30329
404/636–1449
Contact: Cathy Spraetz, Exec. Dir.

Georgia Chapter
Autism Society of America
540 Willow Knoll
Marietta, GA 33367
404/451–0954; 404/953–2907
Contact: Kirby Pruett, President

Association for Retarded Citizens of Georgia
1851 Ram Runway, Ste. 104
College Park, GA 30337
404/761–3150

GUAM

Special Education Div.
Dept. of Education
P.O. Box DE
Agana, GU 96910
671/472–8703, Ex. 375
Contact: Steve Spencer, Acting Director

Special Education Div. [Ages 3–5]
Dept. of Education
P.O. Box DE
Agana, GU 96910
671/472–8703, Ex. 375
Contact: Faye Mata, Director

Dept. of Vocational Rehabilitation
122 Harmon Plaza, Rm B–201
Harmon Industrial Park, GU 96911
671/646–9468
Contact: Rosa Salas, Director

Guam Developmental Disabilities Council
c/o Life Skills Center
284 E. Hospital Loop
Tamuning, GU 96911
809/646–8691
Contact: Roseanne Ada, Administrator

The Advocacy Office
P.O. Box 8830
Tamuning, GU 96911
671/646–9026
Contact: Edward del Rosario, Dir.

HAWAII

Special Education Section
Department of Education
3430 Leahi Ave.
Honolulu, HI 96815
808/737–3720
Contact: Margaret Donovan, Administrator

Special Health Needs Branch [Ages 0–2]
Dept. of Health
741 Sunset Ave.
Honolulu, HI 98616
808/732–3197
Contact: Alan Taniguchi, Chief

Vocational Rehabilitation & Services for the Blind
Dept. of Social Services
P.O. Box 339
Honolulu, HI 96809
808/548–4769
Contact: Toshio Nishioka, Administrator

Community Services for the Developmentally Disabled
741A Sunset Ave.
Honolulu, HI 96816
808/732–0935
Contact: Ethel Yamane, Director

Children's Mental Health Services Branch
3627 Kilauea Ave., Ste. 101
Honolulu, HI 96816
808/735–5242
Contact: David Foster, Chief

State Planning Council for Developmental Disabilities
P.O. Box 3378
Honolulu, HI 96801–3378
808/548–5994
Contact: Diana Tizard, Exec. Sec.

Protection & Advocacy Agency
1580 Makaloa St., Ste. 1060
Honolulu, HI 96814
808/949–2922
Contact: Patty Henderson, Exec. Dir.

Special Parent Information Network
335 Merchant St., Rm. 353
Honolulu, HI 96813
808/548–2648

Hawaii Chapter
Autism Society of America
7398 Ainanani St.
Honolulu, HI 96825
808/395–2702
Contact: Vickie Kirihara, Pres.

Association for Retarded Citizens of Hawaii
3989 Diamond Head Rd.
Honolulu, HI 96816
808/737–7995
Contact: Ahmad Saidin, Exec. Dir.

IDAHO

Special Education Div.
Department of Education
Len B. Jordan Building
650 W. State St.
Boise, ID 83720–0001
208/334–3940
Contact: Martha Noffsinger, Supervisor

Special Education Div. [Ages 3–5]
Department of Education
Len B. Jordan Building
650 W. State St.
Boise, ID 83720–0001
208/334–3940

Bureau of Developmental Disabilities [Ages 0–2]
Dept. of Health & Welfare
450 W. State St., 10th Fl.
Boise, ID 83720
208/334–5531
Contact: Paul Swatsenbarg, Chief

Div. of Vocational Rehabilitation
State Board for Voc. Rehab.
650 W. State St., Rm. 150
Boise, ID 83720
208/334–3390
Contact: George Pelletier, Administrator

Bureau of Adult & Child Development
Div. of Community Rehabilitation
Dept. of Health & Welfare
450 W. State, 19th Floor
Boise, ID 83720
208/334–5531
Contact: Paul Swatsenbarg, Chief

Idaho State Council on Developmental Disabilities
450 West State
Boise, ID 83720
208/334–5509
Contact: John D. Watts

Idaho's Coalition of Advocates for the Disabled, Inc.
1409 W. Washington
Boise, ID 83702
208/336–5353
Contact: Brent Marchbanks, Director

Idaho Parents Unlimited (IPUL)
6816 Fernwood Dr.
Boise, ID 83709
208/377–2199
Contact: Martha Gilgen

ILLINOIS

Dept. of Special Education
State Board of Education
100 N. First St.
Springfield, IL 62777
217/782–6601
Contact: Edward Sontag, Director

Dept. of Special Education [Ages 3–5]
State Board of Education
100 N. First St.
Springfield, IL 62777
217/782–6601
Contact: Sandra Crews, Special Education Specialist

Dept. of Special Education [Ages 0–2]
State Board of Education
100 N. First St.
Springfield, IL 62777
217/782–6601
Contact: Jonah Deppe, Early Childhood Specialist

Dept. of Rehabilitation Services
State Board of Vocational Education & Rehabilitation
623 E. Adams St.
P.O. Box 19429
Springfield, IL 62794
Contact: Philip Bradley, Acting Director

Dept. of Mental Health & Developmental Disabilities
402 Stratton Office Building
Springfield, IL 62706
217/782–7395
Contact: William Murphy, Deputy Dir.

Institute for Juvenile Research
907 S. Wolcott
Chicago, IL 60612
312/996–1733
Contact: Lee Combrinck-Graham, Dir.

Illinois Developmental Disabilities Planning Council
840 S. Spring St.
Springfield, IL 62706
217/782–9696
Contact: Carl Suter, Exec. Dir.

Protection & Advocacy, Inc.
175 W. Jackson, Suite A–2103
Chicago, IL 60604
312/341–0022
Contact: Zena Naiditch, Director

University Affiliated Facility for Developmental Disabilities
University of Illinois at Chicago
1640 W. Roosevelt Rd.
Chicago, IL 60608
312/413–1647
Contact: Dr. David Braddock, Director

Coordinating Council for Handicapped Children
20 E. Jackson Blvd., Room 900
Chicago, IL 60604
312/939–3513
Contact: Charlotte Des Jardins

Designs for Change
220 S. State St., Room 1900
Chicago, IL 60604
312/922–0317
Contact: Donald Moore, Director

Direction Service of Illinois
730 E. Vine, Rm. 107
Springfield, IL 62703
217/523–1232; 800/634–8540 (In IL)
Contact: Merle Wallace

Illinois State Society
Autism Society of America
2200 S. Main St., Ste. 317
Lombard, IL 60148
312/963–1964; 312/691–1270
Contact: Jan Welborn, President

Central Illinois Chapter
Autism Society of America
1208 S. Philo Road
Urbana, IL 60060
217/344–6920
Contact: Beverly Pryor, President

Greater Chicago Area Chap.
Autism Society of America
1507 Clinton Pl.
River Forest, IL 60305
312/346–6700
Contact: Mary Stamatakos, Pres.

Joliet Area Chapter
Autism Society of America
411 The Lane
Hinsdale, IL 60521
312/920–8557
Contact: Phyllis Plekavic, Pres.

Northeast Illinois Chapter
Autism Society of America
1812 Buckingham
Mundelein, IL 60060
312/566–0945
Contact: Maura & Carl Bodo, Pres.

Peoria Chapter
Autism Society of America
2904 W. Parkwood
Peoria, IL 61614
309/691–7005
Contact: Judy Corrigan, Pres.

Southern Illinois Chapter
Autism Society of America
R.R. No. 1
Ashley, IL 62808
618/485–6641
Contact: Evelyn Brehm, Acting Pres.

Association for Retarded Citizens of Illinois
700 S. Federal St., Ste. 123
Chicago, IL 60605
312/922–6932
Contact: Donald Moss, Exec. Dir.

INDIANA

Div. of Special Education
Dept. of Education
State House, Rm. 229
Indianapolis, IN 46204
317/269–9462
Contact: Paul Ash, Director

Early Intervention Project [Ages 0–2]
Div. of Developmental Disabilities
Dept. of Mental Health
47 S. Pennsylvania, Ste. 401A
Indianapolis, IN 46204
317/232–2291
Contact: Doree Bedwell, Director

Dept. of Human Services [Vocational Rehabilitation]
251 N. Illinois St.
P.O. Box 7083
Indianapolis, IN 46207
317/232–1139
Contact: Jean Merritt, Commissioner

Div. of Developmental Disabilities
Dept. of Mental Health
117 E. Washington St.
Indianapolis, IN 46204–3637
Contact: Jack S. Collins, Director

Div. of Special Program Services
Dept. of Mental Health
117 E. Washington St.
Indianapolis, IN 46204–3637
317/232–7840
Contact: Ray Benson, Director

Governor's Planning Council on Developmental Disabilities
117 E. Washington St.
Indianapolis, IN 46204–3614
317/232–7820
Contact: Suellen Jackson-Boner, Dir.

Indiana Advocacy Services
850 N. Meridian St., Suite 2–C
Indianapolis, IN 46204
317/232–1150; 800/622–4845
Contact: Mary Lou Haynes, Exec. Dir.

Riley Child Development Center
Indiana University School of Medicine
702 Barnhill Dr.
Indianapolis, IN 46223
317/274–8167
Contact: Dr. Ernest Smith, Director

Institute for the Study of Developmental Disabilities
2853 E. Tenth St.
Bloomington, IN 47405
812/335–6508
Contact: Dr. Henry Schroeder, Director

Task Force on Education for the Handicapped, Inc.
833 Northside Blvd.
Building 1, Rear
South Bend, IN 46617
219/234–7101
Contact: Richard Burden, Director

Indiana Parent Information Network
2107 E. 65th St.
Indianapolis, IN 46220
317/232–2291
Contact: Donna Olson

Central Indiana Chapter
Autism Society of America
6035 Forest View Dr.
Indianapolis, IN 46208
317/253–1821
Contact: Bev Purdue, President

Elkhart Area
Autism Society of America
249 Homan Ave.
Elkhart, IN 45616
219/294–2137
Contact: Kay Ann Kunter, Pres.

Northwest Indiana Chapter
Autism Society of America
1931 Loganberry Lane
Crown Point, IN 46307
219/886–2484
Contact: Mary Ann Mrozoski

Three Rivers Chapter
Autism Society of America
13219 McDuffee Rd.
Charubusco, IN 46723
219/747–6151
Contact: Richard Cahoon, Pres.

Wabash Valley Chapter
Autism Society of America
20 N. 9th St.
West Terre Haute, IN 47885
812/238–4361
Contact: Patricia McFarlin, Pres.

Association for Retarded Citizens of Indiana
110 E. Washington St., 9th Fl.
Indianapolis, IN 46204
317/632–4387
Contact: John Dickerson, Exec. Dir.

IOWA

Special Education Div.
Department of Public Instruction
Grimes State Office Building
Des Moines, IA 50319
515/281–3176
Contact: Frank Vance, Director

Bureau of Special Education [Ages 0–5]
Dept. of Education
Grimes State Office Building
Des Moines, IA 50319–0146
515/281–3176
Contact: Joan T. Clary, ECSE Consultant

Div. of Vocational Rehabilitation Services
Dept. of Public Instruction
510 E. 12th St.
Des Moines, IA 50319
515/281–4154
Contact: Jerry Starkweather, Administrator

Div. of Mental Health Resources
Dept. of Social Services
Hoover State Office Building
Des Moines, IA 50319
515/281–6003
Contact: Charles Palmer, Director

Governor's Planning Council for Developmental Disabilities
Dept. of Human Services
Hoover Building, 5th Floor
Des Moines, IA 50319
515/281–5646
Contact: Karen Perlowski, Director

Iowa Protection & Advocacy Service, Inc.
3015 Merle Hay Rd., Suite 6
Des Moines, IA 50310
515/278–2502
Contact: Mervin L. Roth, Director

Iowa University Affiliated Facility
Div. of Developmental Disabilities
University Hospital School
The University of Iowa
Iowa City, IA 52242
319/353–6390
Contact: Dr. Alfred Healy, Director

Iowa Exceptional Parent Center
33 N. 12th St.
P.O. Box 1151
Fort Dodge, IA 50501
515/576–5870
Contact: Carla Lawson, Director

Parent-to-Parent
Contact Iowa Exceptional Parent Center, above

Iowa State Society
Autism Society of America
715 E. Locust
Des Moines, IA 50309
319/824–3296
Contact: Keith Hall, Pres.

East Central Iowa Chapter
Autism Society of America
P.O. Box 4724
Cedar Rapids, IA 52407
Contact: Meg Oberreuter, Pres.

Quad Cities Iowa Chapter
Autism Society of America
1505 W. 34th St.
Davenport, IA 52806
319/386–6359
Contact: Connie Toland, Pres.

Siouxland Iowa Chapter
Autism Society of America
1915 West Street
Sioux City, IA 51103
Contact: Barbara Refro, Pres.

Association for Retarded Citizens of Iowa
715 E. Locust

Des Moines, IA 50309
515/283–2358
Contact: Mary Etta Lane, Exec. Dir.

KANSAS

Department of Education
120 E. 10th St.
Topeka, KS 66612
913/296–4945
Contact: James E. Marshall, Director of Special Education

Special Education Administration [Ages 3–5]
Dept. of Education
120 E. 10th St.
Topeka, KS 66612
913/296–3869
Contact: Betty Weithers

Coordinating Council on Early Childhood Developmental Services [Ages 0–2]
Landon State Office Bldg.
900 S.W. Jackson, 10th Fl.
Topeka, KS 66620–0001
913/296–1329
Contact: Judy Moler, Exec. Coordinator

Rehabilitation Services
Dept. of Social & Rehabilitation Services
300 S.W. Oakley, 2nd Fl.
Topeka, KS 66606
913/296–3911
Contact: Gabriel Faimon, Commissioner

Dept. of Social & Rehabilitative Services
State Office Building, 5th Floor
Topeka, KS 66612
913/296–3471
Contact: Special Asst. to Commissioner

Child & Adolescent Mental Health Programs
SRS/MH & RS
506 N. State Office Building
Topeka, KS 66612
913/296–3774
Contact: David Topp, Director

Kansas Planning Council on Developmental Disabilities
State Office Building
5th Floor North
Topeka, KS 66612
913/296–2608
Contact: John Kelly, Exec. Dir.

Kansas Advocacy & Protection Services
513 Leavenworth St., Suite 2
Manhatten, KS 66502
913/776–1541; 800/432–8276
Contact: Joan Strickler, Exec. Dir.

Kansas University Affiliated Facility
Children's Rehabilitation Unit
Kansas University Medical Center
39th & Rainbow Blvd.
Kansas City, KS 66103
913/588–5900
Contact: Dr. Joseph Hollowell, Director

Kansas University Affiliated Facility
348 Haworth Hall
University of Kansas
Lawrence, KS 66045
913/864–4950
Contact: Jean Ann Summers, Director

Kansas University Affiliated Facility
2601 Gabriel
Parsons, KS 67357
316/421–6550
Contact: Joseph Spradlin, Director

Families Together, Inc.
4125 S.W. Gage Ctr. Dr., Ste. 200
Topeka, KS 66604
913/267–6343
Contact: Patricia Gerdel, Director

Family Together
1111 W. 59th Terrace
Shawnee, KS 66203
913/268–8200
Contact: Brent Glazier, Exec. Dir.

Kansas State Society
Autism Society of America
6311 Marjorie Lane
Wichita, KS 67209
316/682–1023
Contact: Glen Zumwalt, Pres.

Johnson Wyandotte County Chap.
Autism Society of America
12766 Circle Dr.
Shawnee, KS 66216
913/471–2262
Contact: Mary Russell, President

Topeka-Lawrence Chapter
Autism Society of America
3215 W. 11th St.
Topeka, KS 66604
913/234–4638
Contact: Gloria Olson, Pres.

Wichita Chapter
Autism Society of America
630 S. Byron
Wichita, KS 67209
316/6832–1023
Contact: Judy Pollard

Association for Retarded Citizens of Kansas
1111 W. 59th Terrace
Shawnee, KS 66203
913/268–8200
Contact: Brent Glazier, Exec. Dir.

KENTUCKY

Office of Education for Exceptional Children
Department of Education
Capitol Plaza Tower, 8th Floor
Frankfort, KY 40601
502/564–4970
Contact: Vivian Link, Assoc. Superintendent

Office of Education for Exceptional Children [Ages 3–5]
Capitol Plaza Tower, 8th Floor
Frankfort, KY 40601
502/564–4970
Contact: Maggie Chiara, EC Consultant

Infant & Toddler Program
Dept. of Mental Health & Mental Retardation Services
275 E. Main St.
Frankfort, KY 40621
502/564–7700
Contact: Jim Henson, Coordinator

Office of Vocational Rehabilitation
Dept. of Education
Capitol Plaza Tower, 9th Fl.
Frankfort, KY 40601
502/564–4566
Contact: Carroll Burchett, Assoc. Superintendent

Div. of Mental Retardation
Dept. for Mental Health & Mental Retardation Services
275 E. Main St.
Frankfort, KY 40621
502/564–7700
Contact: Charlie Bratcher, Director

Children & Youth Services Branch
Dept. for Mental Health & Mental Retardation Services
275 E. Main St., 1st Fl. East
Frankfort, KY 40621
502/564–7610
Contact: Richard Alleva, Manager

Kentucky Developmental Disabilities Planning Council
Bureau of Health Services
275 E. Main St.
Frankfort, KY 40621
502/564–7841
Contact: Richard Eversman, Director

Office for Public Advocacy
Div. for Protection & Advocacy
1264 Louisville Rd.
Frankfort, KY 40601
502/564–2967; 800/373–2988
Contact: Gayla O. Peach, Director

Interdisciplinary Human Development Institute
University Affiliated Facility
University of Kentucky
114 Porter Building
730 South Limestone
Lexington, KY 40506–0205
606/257–1714
Contact: Dr. Melton Martinson, Director

Kentucky Special Parent Involvement Network
318 W. Kentucky St.
Louisville, KY 40203
502/587–5717
Contact: Paulette Logsdon, Director

Directions Service Center
Blue Grass Area Chapter
1450 Newtown Pike
Lexington, KY 40511
606/233–9370
Contact: Jenny Mayberry, Director

Kentucky State Society
Autism Society of America
P.O. Box 37011
Louisville, KY 40204
502/566–5678
Contact: Alice Boyer, President

Association for Retarded Citizens of Kentucky
833 E. Main
Frankfort, KY 40601
502/875–5225
Contact: President

LOUISIANA

Special Educational Services
Dept. of Education
P.O. Box 94064, 9th Fl.
Baton Rouge, LA 70804–9064
504/342–3631
Contact: Paulette Thomas, Assistant Superintendent

Office of Special Education Services [Ages 0–5]
Dept. of Education
P.O. Box 94064, 9th Fl.
Baton Rouge, LA 70804–9064
504/342–3631
Contact: Terry Arikol, Acting Dir.

Div. of Vocational Rehabilitation
Office of Human Development
1755 Florida Blvd.
P.O. Box 94371
Baton Rouge, LA 70804
504/342–2285
Contact: Alton Toms, Director

Office of Mental Retardation
Dept. of Health & Human Resources
721 Government St., Room 308
Baton Rouge, LA 70802
504/342–6811
Contact: Rose Forest, Deputy Asst. Secretary

Div. of Special Programs
Office of Mental Health
Dept. of Health & Human Resources
P.O. Box 4049, 655 N. 5th St.
Baton Rouge, LA 70821
504/342–2540
Contact: Martha Forbes, Director

Louisiana State Planning Council on Developmental Disabilities
721 Government St., Room 201
Baton Rouge, LA 70802–6029
504/342–6804
Contact: Anne E. Farber

Advocacy Center for the Elderly & Disabled
1001 Howard Ave, Suite 300A
New Orleans, LA 70113
504/522–2337; 800/662–7705
Contact: Lois V. Simpson, Exec. Dir.

Human Development Center
Louisiana State University
Medical Center
Building 138
1100 Florida Ave.
New Orleans, LA 70119
504/942–8202
Contact: Dr. Robert Crow, Director Children's Center

Louisiana State University
Medical Center
3730 Blair
Shreveport, LA 71103
318/227–5108
Contact: Clydie Mitchell, Director

Project PROMPT
United Cerebral Palsy of Greater New Orleans
1500 Edwards Ave., Suite O
Harahan, LA 70123
504/734–7736
Contact: Sharon Duda, Director

Parent Linc
200 Henry Clay Ave.
New Orleans, LA 70118
504/899–9511, Ex. 268
Contact: John Hill

Louisiana State Society
Autism Society of America
100 Parsonage Lane
Lafayette, LA 70503
318/984–6234; 504/295–3721
Contact: Laura Robertson, Pres.

Acadian Chapter
Autism Society of America
100 Parsonage Lane
Lafayette, LA 70503
318/232–4418
Contact: Laura Robertson, Pres.

Baton Rouge Society
Autism Society of America
1334 Brook Hollow
Baton Rouge, LA 70810
504/291–4213
Contact: Pranab Chondhury, Pres.

CENLA's Society for Autistic Children
Autism Society of America
4102 Castle Rd.
Alexandria, LA 71303
318/487–6876
Contact: James Palmer, President

Greater New Orleans Chapter
Autism Society of America
4769 St. Roch Ave.
New Orleans, LA 70122
504/288–0050
Contact: Kathy Walsh, President

Louisiana Bayou Chapter
Autism Society of America
20 Winfield Blvd.
Houma, LA 70360
504/868–2365
Contact: Lora Wendell, Pres.

North Lake Chapter
Autism Society of America
P.O. Box 848
Mandeville, LA 70470–0848
504/893–4575
Contact: I. John Hornsby, Jr.

North Louisiana Chapter
Autism Society of America
P.O. Box 44005
Shreveport, LA 71134
318/869–3269
Contact: Tom Palczynski, Pres.

Southwest Louisiana Chapter
Autism Society of America
1011 6th St.
Lake Charles, LA 70601
318/436–0169
Contact: Ann Hart Miller

Greater New Orleans Chapter
Autism Society of America
3400 Kent Avenue, C107
Metaire, LA 70006
Contact: Linda Landry, Pres.

Association for Retarded Citizens of Louisiana
658 St. Louis St.
Baton Rouge, LA 70802
504/383–0742
Contact: Pat Davies, Exec. Dir.

MAINE

Div. of Special Education
Department of Educational & Cultural Services

State House, Station 23
Augusta, ME 04333
207/289–5953
Contact: David N. Stockford, Director

Early Childhood Services [Ages 0–5]
Div. of Special Education
Department of Educational & Cultural Services
State House, Station 23
Augusta, ME 04333
207/289–5950
Contact: Susan Mackey-Andrews

Bureau of Rehabilitation Services
Dept. of Health & Welfare
32 Winthrop St.
Augusta, ME 04330
207/289–2266
Contact: Pamela Tetley, Director

Dept. of Mental Health & Mental Retardation
411 State Office Bldg.
Station 40
Augusta, ME 04333
207/289–4220
Contact: Ron Welch, Assoc. Commissioner

Bureau of Children with Special Needs
Dept. of Mental Health & Mental Retardation
411 State Office Bldg., Rm. 424
Augusta, ME 04333
207/289–4250
Contact: Robert Durgan, Director

Developmental Disabilities Council
State Office Building, STA 139
Augusta, ME 04330
207/289–4213
Contact: Peter Stowell, Exec. Dir.

Advocates for the Developmentally Disabled
2 Mulliken Ct
P.O. Box 5341
Augusta, ME 04330
207/289–5755; 800/452–1948
Contact: Laura Petovello, Exec. Dir.

University Affiliated Handicapped Children's Program
Eastern Maine Medical Center
417 State St., Box 17
Bangor, ME 04401
207/945–7584
Contact: Dr. James Hirschfeld, Director

Special-Needs Parent Information Network (SPIN)
P.O. Box 2067
Augusta, ME 04330
207/582–2504; 800/325–0220 (In ME)
Contact: Deborah Guimont, Dir.

Maine State Chapter
Autism Society of America
P.O. Box 597
Gardiner, ME 04345
207/582–7727
Contact: Don Brann, President

MARYLAND

Div. of Special Education
Department of Education
200 W. Baltimore St.
Baltimore, MD 21201
301/659–2489
Contact: Richard Steinke, Director

Program Development & Assistance Branch [Ages 3–5]
Div. of Special Education
200 W. Baltimore St.
Baltimore, MD 21201
301/333–2495
Contact: Sheila Draper, Chief

Infant & Toddlers Program
118 N. Howard, Ste. 608
Baltimore, MD 21201
301/225–4190
Contact: Carol Ann Baglin, Director

Div. of Vocational Rehabilitation
Dept. of Education
200 W. Baltimore St.
Baltimore, MD 21201
301/333–2294
Contact: James Jeffers, Assistant State Superintendent

Developmental Disabilities Administration
Dept. of Health & Mental Hygiene
201 W. Preston St.
4th Floor, O'Connor Building
Baltimore, MD 21201
301/225–5600
Contact: Lois Meszaros, Director

Div. of Child & Adolescent Services Unit
Mental Hygiene Administration
Dept. of Health & Mental Hygiene
201 W. Preston St.
Baltimore, MD 21201
303/225–6649
Contact: Jack Myhill, Chief

Maryland Developmental Disabilities Planning Council
One Market Place, Box 10
201 W. Preston St.
Baltimore, MD 21201
301/333–3688
Contact: Gertrude Jeffers, Dir.

Maryland Disability Law Center
2510 St. Paul St.
Baltimore, MD 21218
301/333–7600
Contact: Steve Ney, Director

Kennedy Institute for Handicapped Children
707 North Broadway
Baltimore, MD 21205
301/550–9000
Contact: Dr. Gary Goldstein, President

Parent Support Network
Infants & Toddlers Program
118 N. Howard, Ste. 608
Baltimore, MD 21201
301/225–4190
Contact: Carol Ann Baglin, Director

Parent-to-Parent
Dept. of Education
200 W. Baltimore St.
Baltimore, MD 21201
301/333–2478; 800/383–6523
Contact: Marjorie Shulbank, Information & Referral Specialist

Maryland State Society
Autism Society of America
1701 Treehouse Court
Annapolis, MD 21401
301/263–0875
Contact: Diane Smear, Pres.

Anne Arundel Society
Autism Society of America
2 Revell Rd.
Severna Park, MD 21146
301/267–2337
Contact: Mary Preiser, Pres.

Baltimore-Chesapeake Society
Autism Society of America
626 Norhurst Way
Catonsville, MD 21228
301/744–8331
Contact: Fran Lerner, Pres.

Montgomery County Chapter
Autism Society of America
13413 Norden Dr.
Silver Spring, MD 20906
301/871–6239
Contact: Dorothy Lattner, Pres.

Prince Georges County Chapter
Autism Society of America
9104 Third Street
Lanham, MD 20706
Contact: Mr. & Mrs. Wm. Mitchell

Community Services for Autistic Adults and Children (CSAAC)
751 Twinbrook Parkway
Rockville, MD 20851
301/762–1650
Contact: Director

Association for Retarded Citizens of Maryland
5602 Baltimore National Pike
Suite 200
Baltimore, MD 21228
301/744–0255
Contact: William Baber, Exec. Dir.

MASSACHUSETTS

Div. of Special Education
Department of Education
1385 Hancock St., 3rd Fl.
Quincy, MA 02169–5183
617/770–7468
Contact: Mary Beth Fafard, Director

Early Childhood Special Education [Ages 3–5]
Dept. of Education
1385 Hancock St.
Quincy, MA 02169
617/770–7476
Contact: Elizabeth Shaefer, Director

Early Childhood Developmental Services Units [Ages 0–2]
Div. of Family Health Services
Dept. of Public Health
150 Tremont St.
Boston, MA 02111
617/727–5090
Contact: Andrea W. Shuman

Massachusetts Rehabilitation Commission
20 Park Plaza, Statler Office Bldg.
Boston, MA 02116
617/727–2172
Contact: Elmer Bartels, Commissioner

Dept. of Mental Retardation
160 N. Washington St.
Boston, MA 02114
617/727–5608
Contact: Mary McCarthy, Commissioner

Child-Adolescent Services
Dept. of Mental Health
160 N. Washington St.
Boston, MA 02114
617/727–9850
Contact: Joan Mikula, Asst. Commissioner

Mass. Developmental Disabilities Planning Council
600 Washington St., Room 670
Boston, MA 02111–1704
617/727–4178
Contact: Randy Chaffin, Exec. Dir.

Developmental Disabilities Law Center for Massachusetts
11 Beacon St., Ste. 925
Boston, MA 02108
617/723–8455
Contact: Richard Howard, Exec. Dir.

Developmental Evaluation Clinic
Children's Hospital Medical Center
300 Longwood Ave.
Boston, MA 02115
617/735–6509
Contact: Dr. Allen Crocker, Dir.

Shriver Center University Affiliated Facility
200 Trapelo Rd.
Waltham, MA 02254
617/642–0001
Contact: Dr. Philip Reilly, Dir.

Statewide Parent Information Network (SPIN)
Federation for Children with Special Needs
312 Stuart St., 2nd Floor
Boston, MA 02116
617/482–2915; 800/331–0688 (In MA)
Contact: Artie Higgins, Director

Parent-to-Parent
1249 Boylston St.
Boston, MA 02215
617/266–4520
Contact: Cindy Politch, Parent Support Coordinator

Massachusetts State Chapter
Autism Society of America
508 Hancock Street

Fall River, MA 02221
Contact: Barbara Dominique

Massachusetts North Shore Chap.
Autism Society of America
184 Lafayette St.
Salem, MA 01970
617/774–1225
Contact: June Kalman, President

Western Mass. Autism Society
Autism Society of America
53 Williamsburg Drive
Longmeadow, MA 01106
413/567–1119
Contact: Katherine Papazoglou, Pres.

Community Resources for People with Autism
27 School St.
Springfield, MA 01105
413/732–1169

Association for Retarded Citizens of Massachusetts
217 South St.
Waltham, MA 02154
617/891–6270

MICHIGAN

Special Education Services
Michigan Dept. of Education
P.O. Box 30008
Lansing, MI 48909
517/373–9433
Contact: Dr. Edward Birch, Director

Special Education Services [Ages 3–5]
Michigan Dept. of Education
P.O. Box 30008
Lansing, MI 48909
517/373–8215
Contact: Jan Baxter, Supervisor

Early Childhood Education [Ages 0–2]
Dept. of Education
P.O. Box 30008
Lansing, MI 48909
517/373–8483
Contact: Jacquelyn Thompson, Consultant

Bureau of Rehabilitation
Dept. of Education
101 Pine St., 4th Fl.
P.O. Box 30010
Lansing, MI 48909
517/373–3391
Contact: Peter Griswold, Director

Bureau of Community Residential Services, Program Development Policy & Standards
Dept. of Mental Health
Lewis Cass Building, 6th Fl.
Lansing, MI 48913
517/373–2900
Contact: Ben Censoni, Deputy Director

Children's Program Standards Unit
Dept. of Mental Health
320 Walnut Blvd.
Lansing, MI 48913
517/373–0451
Contact: Paul Vander Velde, Director

Michigan Developmental Disabilities Council
Lewis Cass Building, 6th Floor
Lansing, MI 48926
517/373–0341
Contact: Elisabeth Ferguson, Exec. Dir.

Michigan Protection & Advocacy Service
109 W. Michigan, Suite 900
Lansing, MI 48933
517/487–1755
Contact: Elizabeth Bauer, Exec. Dir.

University Affiliated Facility
Developmental Disabilities Institute
Wayne State University
University Health Center, 6E
4201 St. Antoine
Detroit, MI 48201
313/577–2654
Contact: Director

Citizens Alliance to Uphold Special Education (CAUSE)
313 S. Washington Square, Lower Level
Lansing, MI 48933
517/485–4084; 800/221–9105
Contact: Cheryl Chilcote, Exec. Dir.

"Parents Are Experts" Project
United Cerebral Palsy Assn. of Metropolitan Detroit
17000 W. 8 Mile Rd., Ste. 380
Southfield, MI 48075
313/557–5070
Contact: Edith Sharp, Coordinator

Peer Support Project
530 W. Ionia St., Ste. C
Lansing, MI 48933
517/487–9260
Contact: Mary Marin

Michigan State Chapter
Autism Society of America
530 W. Ionia St., Ste. C
Lansing, MI 48933
517/487–9260; 800/223–6722
Contact: Julie Dickerson, President

Berrien County Autism Society
P.O. Box 316
Eau Claire, MI 49111
616/926–7356
Contact: Terry Briney, President

Flint Area Chapter
Autism Society of America
1115 Kennebec
Grand Blanc, MI 48439
313/694–3576
Contact: James Showkeir, Pres.

Grand Rapids Chapter
Autism Society of America
1005 Evelyn, N.E.
Grand Rapids, MI 49505
616/364–4743
Contact: Barb Denhoe, Pres.

Jackson Chapter
Autism Society of America
5308 Ridgewood Vista
Jackson, MI 49201
517/764–1508
Contact: Carolyn Sipes, Pres.

Kalamazoo-Battle Creek Chap.
Autism Society of America
2730 Bach Avenue
Portage, MI 49002
616/327–1395
Contact: Sherrie Bennett, Pres.

Lansing Area Chapter
Autism Society of America
416 North Okemos
Mason, MI 48854
517/676–4611
Contact: Wanda Weston, Pres.

Macomb/St. Clair Chapter
Autism Society of America
41664 Cimmaron
Mr. Clemens, MI 48044
313/263–4526
Contact: Danny Albers, Pres.

Monroe Chapter
Autism Society of America
3367 Springdale
Lambertville, MI 48144
313/856–4627
Contact: Susan Cameron, Pres.

Muskegon Area Chapter
Autism Society of America
545 Eugene Ave.
Muskegon, MI 49441
616/798–7813
Contact: Linda Eckerman, Pres.

Northwest Michigan Chapter
Autism Society of America
Route 1, Box 288A
Thomsonville, MI 49683
616/378–2396
Contact: Joe Ferrer, Pres.

Oakland County Chapter
Autism Society of America
16179 Beverly Rd.
Birmingham, MI 48009
313/646–6315
Contact: Anne Sanderson, Pres.

Saginaw Bay Area Chapter
Autism Society of America
2050 S. River Road.
Saginaw, MI 48603
517/781–2401
Contact: Al & Gloria Gonzales, Pres.

UPSAC
Autism Society of America
141 New Delta
Manistique, MI 49854
906/341–5812
Contact: Stuart Proctor, Pres.

Van Buren County Chapter
Autism Society of America
23313 44th Ave.
Mattawan, MI 49071
616/668–2307
Contact: William Steger, Pres.

Washtenaw County Chapter
Autism Society of America
7992 Grand Street
Dexter, MI 48130
313/426–3744
Contact: Harry Valentine, Pres.

Wayne County Chapter
Autism Society of America
9263 Brookline
Plymouth, MI 48170
313/455–8835
Contact: Pauline Kahn, Pres.

West Shore Area Chapter
Autism Society of America
6882 Georgetown
Hudsonville, MI 49426
616/669–2218
Contact: Paul Zupon, Pres.

Association for Retarded Citizens of Michigan
313 S. Washington, Ste. 310
Lansing, MI 48933
517/487–5426
Contact: Marjorie Mitchell, Exec. Dir.

MINNESOTA

Special Education Section
Dept. of Education
813 Capitol Square Building
550 Cedar St.
St. Paul, MN 55101–2233
612/296–1793
Contact: Dr. Norena Hale, Manager

Early Childhood Program [Ages 3–5]
Dept. of Education
Capitol Square Building, Rm. 830
550 Cedar St.
St. Paul, MN 55101
612/297–3619
Contact: Sandy Fink, Consultant

Interagency Planning Project for Youth & Children with Handicaps [Ages 0–2]
827 Capitol Square Building
550 Cedar St.
St. Paul, MN 55101
612/296–7032
Contact: Jan Rubenstein, Coordinator

Div. of Vocational Rehabilitation
Dept. of Jobs & Training
390 N. Robert St., 5th Fl.
St. Paul, MN 55101
612/296–1822
Contact: William Niederloh, Asst. Commissioner

Div. for Persons with Developmental Disabilities
Dept. of Public Works
Centennial Office Building, 5th Fl.
St. Paul, MN 55155
612/297–1241
Contact: Ed Skarnulis, Director

Child/Adolescent Services
Centennial Office Bldg.
658 Cedar St., 4th Fl.

St. Paul, MN 55155
612/296–2710
Contact: John Sykora, Director

Minnesota Developmental Disabilities Planning Council
658 Cedar St., Room 300
St. Paul, MN 55101
612/296–4018
Contact: Colleen Wieck, Exec. Dir.

Legal Aid Society of Minneapolis
222 Grain Exchange Building
323 Fourth Ave., South
Minneapolis, MN 55415
612/332–7301
Contact: Steve Scott, Director

Minnesota University Affiliated Program on Developmental Disabilities
University of Minnesota
6 Pattee Hall
Minneapolis, MN 55455
612/624–4848
Contact: Dr. Robert Bruininks, Director

Parent Advocacy Coalition for Educational Rights (PACER)
4826 Chicago Ave., South
Minneapolis, MN 55417–1055
612/827–2966; 800/53–PACER (In MN)
Contact: Marge Goldberg or Paula Goldberg, Directors

Pilot Parents
201 Ordean Bldg.
Duluth, MN 55802
218/726–4745
Contact: Lynne Frigaard

Southwest Minnesota Chapter
Autism Society of America
1605 N.W. 22nd St.
Rochester, MN 55901
507/289–7980
Contact: Val Koster, President

Twin Cities Chapter
Autism Society of America
253 E. 4th St.
St. Paul, MN 55101
612–224–0346
Contact: Julie Brown, President

West Metro Chapter
Autism Society of America
5624 73rd Ave., North
Brooklyn Park, MN 55429
612/560–5330
Contact: John Makepeace, Pres.

Association for Retarded Citizens of Minnesota
3225 Lyndale Ave., South
Minneapolis, MN 55408
612/827–5641
Contact: Sue Abnerholden, Exec. Dir.

MISSISSIPPI

Bureau of Special Services
Dept. of Education
P.O. Box 771
Jackson, MS 39205–0771
601/359–3490
Contact: Dr. Walter H. Moore, Dir.

Bureau of Special Services [Ages 3–5]
Dept. of Education
P.O. Box 771
Jackson, MS 39205–0771
Contact: Marie Catherine Jones, Consultant

Children's Medical Program [Ages 0–2]
State Board of Health
P.O. Box 1700
2423 N. State St.
Jackson, MS 39215–1700
601/960–7613
Contact: Sam Valentine, Dir.

Dept. of Vocational Rehabilitation
P.O. Box 1698
Jackson, MS 39215
601/354–6825
Contact: Morris Selby, Director

Bureau of Mental Retardation
Dept. of Mental Health
1500 Woolfolk Building
Jackson, MS 39201
601/359–1290
Contact: Roger McMurtry, Director

Div. of Children & Youth Services
Dept. of Mental Health
1101 Robert E. Lee Bldg.
239 N. Lamar St.
Jackson, MS 39201
601/359–1568
Contact: Lucy Leslie, Director

Developmental Disabilities Planning Council
1307 Woolfolk State Office Bldg.
Jackson, MS 39201
601/359–1290
Contact: Ed C. Bell, Director

Mississippi Protection & Advocacy System for Developmental Disabilities, Inc.
4793B McWillie Dr.
Jackson, MS 39206
601/981–8207
Contact: Rebecca Floyd, Exec. Dir.

Mississippi University Affiliated Program
University of Southern Mississippi
Southern Station, Box 5163
Hattiesburg, MS 39406–5163
601/266–5163
Contact: Dr. Robert Campbell, Director

Association of Developmental Organizations of Mississippi
6055 Highway 18 South, Ste. A
Jackson, MS 39209
601/922–3210; 800/231–3721 (In MS)
Contact: Anne Presley, Director

Mississippi Parent/Family Network
Route 1, Box 119
New Site, MS 38859
601/728–5121
Contact: Kathy Odle, Director

Mississippi Chapter
Autism Society of America
2205 Napoleon
Pearl, MS 39208
601/939–2863; 601/359–1386
Contact: Bill Colvin, President

Gulf Coast Chapter
Autism Society of America
P.O. Box 558
Long Beach, MS 39560
601/769–4530
Contact: Ron Bishop, President

Association for Retarded Citizens of Mississippi
Woodland Hills Bldg.
3000 Old Canton Rd., Ste. 510
Jackson, MS 39216
601/362–4830
Contact: Linda Bond, Director

MISSOURI

Div. of Special Education
Dept. of Elementary & Secondary Education
P.O. Box 480
Jefferson City, MO 65201
314/751–4909
Contact: Dr. John Heskett, Coordinator

Div. of Special Education
Dept. of Elementary & Secondary Education [Ages 3–5]
P.O. Box 480
Jefferson City, MO 65201
314/751–0185
Contact: Melody Friedeback, Asst. Dir.

Section of Special Education [Ages 0–2]
Dept. of Elementary & Secondary Education
P.O. Box 480
Jefferson City, MO 65102
314/751–2965
Contact: John Heskett, Coordinator

Div. of Vocational Rehabilitation
Dept. of Education
2401 E. McCarty St.

Jefferson City, MO 65101
314/751–3251
Contact: Don L. Gann, Asst. Commissioner

Div. of Mental Retardation & Developmental Disabilities
Dept. of Mental Health
2002 Missouri Blvd.
P.O. Box 687
Jefferson City, MO 65102
314/751–4054
Contact: Gary Sluyter, Director

Children & Youth Services
Dept. of Mental Health
P.O. Box 687
1915 Southridge Dr.
Jefferson City, MO 65102
314/751–4122
Contact: Linda Roebuck, Coordinator

Missouri Planning Council for Developmental Disabilities
P.O. Box 687
Jefferson City, MO 65102
314/751–4054
Contact: Kay Conklin, Coordinator

Missouri Protection & Advocacy Service
925 S. Country Club Dr., Unit B
Jefferson City, MO 65109
314/893–3333; 800/392–8667
Contact: Carol Larkin, Director

University Affiliated Program for Developmental Disabilities
University of Missouri at Kansas City
Institute for Human Development
2220 Holmes St.
Kansas City, MO 64108
816/276–1770
Contact: Dr. Carl Calkins, Director

Missouri Parents Act (MPACT)
1722 W. South Glenstone, Ste. 125
Springfield, MO 65804
417/882–7434
Contact: Marianne Toombs, Director

Missouri Parents Act (MPACT)
625 Euclid, Room 225
St. Louis, MO 63108
Contact: Margaret Taber, Director

Florissant Valley Chapter
Autism Society of America
1520 Keeven Lane
Florissant, MO 63031
314/831–3019
Contact: Sherry Ann Margrabe, Pres.

St. Louis Chapter
Autism Society of America
1653 Twin Oaks Drive
Arnold, MO 63010
314/878–4650
Contact: Sandy Kownacki, Pres.

Southwest Missouri Chapter
Autism Society of America
533 W. Pearl
Aurora, MO 65605
417/678–5151
Contact: George Woodward, Pres.

Western Missouri Area Chapter
Autism Society of America
937 Oak Ridge Dr.
Blue Springs, MO 64015
Contact: Marsha Chipman, Pres.

MONTANA

Office of Public Instruction
State Capitol, Rm. 106
Helena, MT 59620
406/444–4429
Contact: Robert Runkel, Director of Special Education

Dept. of Educational Services [Ages 3–5]
Office of Public Instruction
State Capitol
Helena, MT 59620
406/444–4428
Contact: Marilyn Pearson

Management Operations /Bureau [Ages 0–2]
Developmental Disabilities Div.
Dept. of Social & Rehabilitative Services
P.O. Box 4210
Helena, MT 59604
406/444–2995
Contact: Mike Henshew, Chief

Rehabilitative Services Div.
Dept. of Social & Rehabilitative Services
P.O. Box 4210
Helena, MT 59601
406/444–2590
Contact: Margaret Bullock, Administrator

Div. of Developmental Disabilities
Dept. of Social & Rehabilitative Services
P.O. Box 4210
111 Sanders, Room 202
Helena, MT 59604
406/444–2995
Contact: Dennis Taylor, Administrator

Developmental Disabilities
Planning Council
P.O. Box 4210
Helena, MT 59601
406/449–8325
Contact: Greg Olsen, Director

Montana Advocacy Program
1410 8th Ave.
Helena, MT 59601
406/444–3889; 800/245–4743
Contact: Kris Bakula, Exec. Dir.

Montana Center for Handicapped Children
Eastern Montana College
1500 N. 30th St.
Billings, MT 59101–0298
406/657–2312
Contact: Dr. Michael Hagen, Director

Montana University Affiliated Program
33 Corbin Hall
University of Montana
Missoula, MT 59812
406/243–5467
Contact: Dr. Richard Offner, Director

Parents, Let's Unite for Kids
Eastern Montana College
Montana Center for Handicapped Children
1500 N. 30th St.
Billings, MT 59101–0298
406/657–2055; 800–222–PLUK (In MT)
Contact: Katherine Kelker, Director

Parent-to-Parent
Contact Parents, Let's Unite for Kids, above

Montana State Chapter
Autism Society of America
3125 Avenue F
Billings, MT 59102
406/656–8053
Contact: Mary Lou Sweeney, Pres.

Association for Retarded Citizens of Montana
7 Willowbend Dr.
Billings, MT 59102
Contact: Leona Neufeld, Pres.

NEBRASKA

Special Education Branch
Dept. of Education
Box 94987
301 Centennial Mall South
Lincoln, NE 68509
402/471–2471
Contact: Gary M. Sherman, Director

Special Education Section [Ages 3–5]
Dept. of Education
P.O. Box 94987
Lincoln, NE 68509
402/471–2471
Contact: Jan Thelen, Coordinator

Div. of Rehabilitation Services
Dept. of Education
P.O. Box 94987
301 Centennial Mall, 6th Fl.
Lincoln, NE 68509

402/471–3645
Contact: Jason Andrew, Asst. Commissioner

Office of Mental Retardation
Dept. of Public Institutions
P.O. Box 94728
Lincoln, NE 68509
402/471–2851, Ex. 5110
Contact: Dave Evans, Director

Governor's Planning Council on Developmental Disabilities
2550 Ewing, Rm. 506
P.O. Box 95007
Lincoln, NE 68509–5007
402/471–2337
Contact: Mary Gordon, Director

Nebraska Advocacy Services
522 Lincoln Center Building
215 Centennial Mall South
Lincoln, NE 68508
402/474–3183
Contact: Timothy Shaw, Exec. Dir.

Meyer Children's Rehabilitation Institute
University of Nebraska Medical Center
444 S. 44th St.
Omaha, NE 68131–3795
402/559–6430
Contact: Dr. Bruce Buehler, Director

Autism Society of Nebraska
Autism Society of America
7516 Hayes Circle
Ralston, NE 68127
402/339–5844
Contact: Mrs. Terri Bennett, Pres.

Association for Retarded Citizens of Nebraska
521 S. 14th St., Ste. 211
Lincoln, NE 68508
402/475–4407
Contact: Ginger Clubine, Exec. Dir.

NEVADA

Special Education Branch
Dept. of Education
400 W. King St./Capitol Complex
Carson City, NV 89710
702/885–3140
Contact: Dr. Jane Early, Director

Special Education Branch [Ages 3–5]
Dept. of Education
400 W. King St./Capitol Complex
Carson City, NV 89710
702/885–3140
Contact: Sharon Palmer

Nevada Mental Health Institute [Ages 0–2]
Dept. of Human Resources
480 Galletti Way
Sparks, NV 89431
702/789–0284
Contact: Marilyn Walter, Grants Project Administrator

Rehabilitation Div.
Dept. of Human Resources
State Capitol Complex
505 E. King St.
Carson City, NV 89710
702/885–4440
Contact: Delbert Frost, Administrator

Mental Hygiene
Mental Retardation Div.
Gilbert Building
1001 N. Mountain St., Ste. 1H
Carson City, NV 89710
702/885–5943
Contact: Brian Lakren, Acting Administrator

Northern Nevada Child & Adolescent Mental Health Programs
Child & Adolescent Services
2655 Enterprise Rd.
Reno, NV 89512
702/789–0300
Contact: Wilford W. Beck

Planning Council for Developmental Disabilities
c/o Dept. of Rehabilitation
505 E. King St., Room 502
Carson City, NV 89710–0001
702/885–4440
Contact: Michael Becker, Planning Specialist

Office of Protection & Advocacy
2105 Capurro Way, Ste. B
Sparks, NV 89431
702/789–0233; 800/992–5715
Contact: Holli Elder, Project Director

Nevada Specially Trained Effective Parents (N–STEP)
Nevada Association for the Handicapped
6200 W. Oakey Blvd.
Las Vegas, NV 89102
702/870–7050
Contact: Vince Triggs, Director

Project ASSIST: A Direction of Service Nevada
CHANCE Parent Project
3015 Heights Dr.
Reno, NV 89503
702/747–0669; 800/522–0066

Association for Retarded Citizens of Nevada
680 S. Bailey St.
Fallon, NV 89406
702/423–4760
Contact: Frank Weinrauch, Exec. Dir.

NEW HAMPSHIRE

Special Education Bureau
Dept. of Education
101 Pleasant St.
Concord, NH 03301–3860
603/271–3741
Contact: Robert Kennedy, Director

Office of Special Education [Ages 0–5]
Dept. of Education
101 Pleasant St.
Concord, NH 03301–3860
603/271–3741
Contact: Luzanne Pierce

Div. of Mental Health & Developmental Services
Dept. of Health & Welfare
State Office Park South
105 Pleasant St.
Concord, NH 03301
603/228–5010
Contact: Richard Lepore, Assistant Div. Director

Philbrook Center for Children & Youth
121 S. Fruit St.
Concord, NH 03301
603/224–6531, Ex. 2365
Contact: William Wheeler, Superintendent

New Hampshire Developmental Disabilities Council
Concord Center, 10 Ferry St.
Concord, NH 03301–2425
603/271–3236
Contact: Director

Disabilities Rights Center
P.O. Box 19
Concord, NH 03302–0019
603/228–0432
Contact: Donna Woodfin, Director

Parent Information Center
155 Manchester St.
P.O. Box 1422
Concord, NH 03301
603/224–6299
Contact: Judith Raskin, Director

Parent-to-Parent
Parent Information Center
P.O. Box 1422
Concord, NH 03301–1422
602/224–7005
Contact: Terry Ohlson

New Hampshire State Society
Autism Society of America
Box 35
Merrimack, NH 03054

603/424–5957
Contact: David Hackett, Pres.

Association for Retarded Citizens of New Hampshire
10 Ferry St., Box 4
The Concord Center
Concord, NH 03301
603/228–9092
Contact: Christine Nicolleta

NEW JERSEY

Div. of Special Education
Dept. of Education
225 W. State St., CN 500
Trenton, NJ 08625
609/633–6833
Contact: Jeffrey Osowski, Director

Early Childhood Education [Ages 0–5]
Div. of Special Education
Dept. of Education
225 W. State St., CN 500
Trenton, NJ 08625
609/633–6951
Contact: Noreen Gallagher, Manager

Div. of Vocational Rehabilitation
Dept. of Labor & Industry
1005 Labor & Industry Bldg., CN 398
John Fitch Plaza
Trenton, NJ 08625
609/292–5987
Contact: George Chizmadia, Director

Div. of Developmental Disabilities
Dept. of Human Services
222 S. Warren St.
Capital Place One
Trenton, NJ 08625
609/292–3742
Contact: Eddie Moore, Director

Bureau of Children's Services
Div. of Mental Health & Hospitals
13 Roszel Rd., 2nd Fl.
Princeton, NJ 08540
609/987–2005
Contact: Joyce B. Wale, Asst. Chief

New Jersey Developmental Disabilities Council
108–110 N. Broad St., CN 700
Trenton, NJ 08625
609/292–3745
Contact: Catherine Rowan, Exec. Dir.

Dept. of Public Advocate
Office of Advocacy for the Developmentally Disabled
Hughes Justice Complex, CN850
Trenton, NJ 08625
609/292–9742; 800/792–8600
Contact: Sara Wiggins-Mitchell, Dir.

University Affiliated Facility
University of Medicine & Dentistry of New Jersey
Robert W. Johnson Medical School
675 Hoes Lane
Piscataway, NJ 08854–5635
201/463–4447
Contact: Dr. Deborah Spitalnick, Director

NJ Council of Organizations & Schools for Autistic Children and Adults (COSAC)
123 Franklin Corner Rd.
Lawrenceville, NJ 08648
609/895–0190
Contact: Nancy Richardson, Exec. Director

Involve New Jersey, Inc.
26C 2 East Second St.
Moorestown, NJ 08057
609/778–0599
Contact: Mary Callahan, Director

Statewide Parent Advocacy Network (SPAN)
516 N. Ave., East
Westfield, NJ 07090
201/654–7726
Contact: Diana Cuthbertson, Exec. Dir

Parents & Children Together Organized for Family Learning (PACTO)
178 Barracks St.
Perth Amboy, NJ 08861
201/324–2451
Contact: Jose Oliva, Director

New Jersey Self-Help Clearinghouse
St. Clare-Riverside Medical Ctr.
Pocono Rd.
Denville, NJ 07834
201/625–9565; 800/367–6274 (In NJ)
Contact: Edward Madara, Director

New Jersey State Society
Autism Society of America
4 Buffalo Run
East Brunswick, NJ 08816
201/251–0024
Contact: Norman Greenberg, Pres.

Central New Jersey Chapter
Autism Society of America
24 Pinebrook Drive
Neptune, NJ 07753
201/532–1469; 201/922–9052
Contact: Helmuth Kaunzinger

Douglass Chapter
Autism Society of America
R.R. 3, Box 82
Califon, NJ 07830
201/832–7918
Contact: Pam Purcell, President

Mercer Chapter
Autism Society of America
76 Jersey St.
Trenton, NJ 08611
609/921–2626
Contact: Stanley Zalenski, Pres.

Middlesex Central County Chap.
Autism Society of America
84 Fairmount Ave.
Chatham, NJ 07928
201/635–7275
Contact: Eugenia Ramsey, Pres.

Monmouth County Chapter
Autism Society of America
P.O. Box 336
Island Heights, NJ 08723
201/929–3084
Contact: Carmen Hart, President

Northeast New Jersey Chap.
Autism Society of America
31 Circle Ave.
Ridgewood, NJ 07450
201/848–8605
Contact: Joan Flicker, Pres.

Pace-South Jersey Chapter
Autism Society of America
816 Edge Park Dr.
Haddonfield, NJ 08033
609/428–5693
Contact: Arlene Fiorilli, Pres.

Association for Retarded Citizens of New Jersey
985 Livingston Ave.
North Brunswick, NJ 08902
201/246–2525
Contact: John Scagnelli, Exec. Dir.

NEW MEXICO

Special Education Unit
Dept. of Education
Educational Building
300 Don Gasper Ave.
Santa Fe, NM 87501–2786
505/827–6541
Contact: Jim Newby, Director

Special Education Unit [Ages 3–5]
Dept. of Education
Educational Building
300 Don Gasper Ave.
Santa Fe, NM 87501–2786
505/827–6541
Contact: Taran Tucker, Consultant

Developmental Disabilities Bureau [Ages 0–2]
Dept. of Health & Environment
P.O. Box 968
Santa Fe, NM 87504–0968
505/827–2575
Contact: Toby Hurtada

Div. of Vocational Rehabilitation
Dept. of Education
604 W. San Mateo
Santa Fe, NM 87503
505/827–3511
Contact: Ross Sweat, Director

Developmental Disabilities Bureau
Dept. of Health & the Environment
P.O. Box 968
Santa Fe, NM 87504–0968
505/827–0020, Ex. 0968
Contact: Steve Dossey, Chief

New Mexico Developmental Disabilities Planning Council
P.O. Box 968
Santa Fe, NM 87504–0968
505/827–2698
Contact: Eloisa Lobato, Acting Director

Protection & Advocacy System, Inc.
2201 San Pedro, N.E.
Building 4, Suite 140
Albuquerque, NM 87110
505/888–0111; 800/432–4682
Contact: James Jackson, Exec. Dir.

Parent Training & Support Program
Protection & Advocacy System
2201 San Pedro, NE
Building 4, No. 140
Albuquerque, NM 87110
505/888–0111
Contact: James Jackson, Dir.

Education for Parents of Indian Children with Special Needs (EPICS Project)
P.O. Box 788
Bernalillo, NM 87107
505/867–3396
Contact: Norman Segel, Director

Parents Reaching Out (PRO)
1127 University, N.E.
Albuquerque, NM 87102
505/842–9045; 800/524–5176 (In NM)
Contact: Sallie Van Curen, Exec. Dir.

New Mexico State Society
Autism Society of America
2617 Georgene Ave., N.E.
Albuquerque, NM 87112
505/294–2963
Contact: Martha Hayes, President

Association for Retarded Citizens of New Mexico
8210 La Mirada, N.E., Ste. 500
Albuquerque, NM 87109
Contact: Kermitt Stuve, Exec. Dir.

NEW YORK

Office for Education of Children with Handicapping Conditions
Dept. of Education
1073 Education Building Annex
Albany, NY 12234–0001
518/474–5548
Contact: Lawrence Gloekler, Director

Office for Education of Children with Handicapping Conditions [Ages 3–5]
Dept. of Education
1073 Education Building Annex
Albany, NY 12234–0001
518/474–8917
Contact: Michael Plotzker, Coordinator

Bureau of Child & Adolescent Health [Ages 0–2]
Dept. of Health
Corning Tower, Room 780
Albany, NY 12237
518/474–2084
Contact: Frank Zollo, Early Intervention Coordinator

Office of Vocational Rehabilitation
Dept. of Education
99 Washington Ave.
Albany, NY 12230
518/474–2714
Contact: Richard Switzer, Deputy Commissioner

Office of Mental Retardation & Developmental Disabilities
44 Holland Ave.
Albany, NY 12229
518/473–1997
Contact: Arthur Webb, Commissioner

Bureau of Children & Youth
Office of Mental Health
44 Holland Ave.
Albany, NY 12229
518/474–6902
Contact: Gloria Newton-Logsdon, Acting Associate Commissioner

New York State Developmental Disabilities Planning Council
Empire State Plaza, 10th Floor
Albany, NY 12223
518/474–3655
Contact: Isadora Mills, Exec. Dir.

N.Y. Commission on Quality of Care for the Mentally Disabled
99 Washington Ave.
Albany, NY 12210
518/473–4057
Contact: Clarence Sundram, Commissioner

University Affiliated Facility
Rose F. Kennedy Center
Albert Einstein College of Medicine
Yeshiva University
1410 Pelham Parkway,
South Bronx, NY 10461
212/430–2325
Contact: Dr. Herbert Cohen, Dir.

Robert Warner Rehabilitation Center
State University of New York at Buffalo
Children's Hospital of Buffalo
936 Delaware Ave.
Buffalo, NY 14209
716/878–7595
Contact: Dr. Robert Cooke, Director

Developmental Disabilities Center
St. Lukes/Roosevelt Hospital Center
Columbia University
College of Physicians & Surgeons
428 W. 59th St.
New York, NY 10019
212/554–6560
Contact: Madeline Appell, Director

University Affiliated Program for Developmental Disabilities
University of Rochester Medical Center
601 Elmwood Ave.
Rochester, NY 14642
716/275–2986
Contact: Phillip Davidson, Dir.

Institute for Basic Research in Developmental Disabilities
1050 Forest Hill Rd.
Staten Island, NY 10314
718/494–0600
Contact: Dr. Henryk Wisniewski, Dir.

Mental Retardation Institute
University Affiliated Facility
Westchester County Medical Center
Valhalla, NY 10595
914/285–8204
Contact: Ansley Bacon-Prue, Dir.

Advocates for Children of New York, Inc.
24–16 Bridge Plaza South
Long Island, NY 11101
717/729–8866
Contact: Norma Rollins, Director

Parents' Information Group/Parent Training Project
215 Bassett St.
Syracuse, NY 13210
315/478–0040
Contact: Deborah Olsen, Director

Parent Network Center
1443 Main St.
Buffalo, NY 14209
716/885–1004
Contact: Joan Watkins, Director

Parent-to-Parent
Senate Select Committee on the Disabled
Legislative Office Bldg.

Albany, NY 12247
518/455–2096
Contact: Marilyn Wessels, Director

Parent-to-Parent
Family Support Project for the Developmentally Disabled
North Central Bronx Hospital
3424 Kossath Ave.
Bronx, NY 10467
212/519–4796

New York State Society
Autism Society of America
Autistic of New York
10 Colvin Ave.
Albany, NY 12206
516/883–3989
Contact: Mary Flanagan

Bronx Chapter
Autism Society of America
3041 La Salle Ave.
Bronx, NY 10461
212/863–3070
Contact: Mary Ann Kenneally, Pres.

Brooklyn Chapter
Autism Society of America
225 Avenue S
Brooklyn, NY 11223
718/336–9533
Contact: Terry Sciamettia, Pres.

Broome County Chapter
Autism Society of America
4221 Sheryl Drive
Binghamton, NY 13095
607/772–8045; 607/798–8045
Contact: Stephanie Lockshin, Pres.

Central New York Chapter
Autism Society of America
418 Fellows Ave.
Syracuse, NY 13210
315/425–4380
Contact: Marty Clark, Pres.

Mid Hudson Chapter
Autism Society of America
Albany Post Rd.
Staatsburg, NY 12580
914/889–4176
Contact: John Persky, Pres.

Mohawk Valley Chapter
Autism Society of America
30 Wilbur Rd.
New Hartford, NY 13413
315/735–5797
Contact: Diana Williams, Pres.

Nassau/Suffolk Chapter
Autism Society of America
33 Beacon Hill Rd.
Port Washington, NY 11050
516/883–3989
Contact: Mary Flanagan, President

Queens Chapter
Autism Society of America
188–83 85th Rd.
Holliswood, NY 11423
718/776–8478
Contact: Edna Kleiman, Pres.

Rochester Area Chapter
Autism Society of America
160 Crawford Street
Rochester, NY 14620
716/244–9261
Contact: John Richter, Pres.

Rockland County Chapter
Autism Society of America
7 Fletcher Rd., Apt. E
Monsey, NY 10952
914/425–7268
Contact: Jan Kochmeister, Pres.

Staten Island Chapter
Autism Society of America
466 Jefferson Ave.
Staten Island, NY 10306
212/979–1307
Contact: Wilma Katz, President

Westchester Chapter
Autism Society of America
49 Cliffside Dr.
Yonkers, NY 10710
914/961–7956
Contact: Barbara Masur, President

Western New York Chapter
Autism Society of America
184 Fairlane Ave.
Tonawanda, NY 14150
716/834–3787
Contact: Angela Lagenor, Pres.

New York State Association for Retarded Children, Inc.
393 Delaware Ave.
Delmar, NY 12054
518/439–8311
Contact: Marc Brandt, Exec. Dir.

NORTH CAROLINA

Div. for Exceptional Children
Dept. of Public Instruction
Education Building, Rm. 442
116 W. Edenton
Raleigh, NC 27603–1712
919/733–3921
Contact: Lowell Harris, Director

Div. for Exceptional Children [Ages 3–5]
Dept. of Public Instruction
Education Building, Rm. 442
116 W. Edenton
Raleigh, NC 27611
919/733–3004
Contact: David Mills, Asst. Dir.

Mental Health, Mental Retardation & Substance Abuse Services [Ages 0–2]
Dept. of Human Resources
325 N. Salisbury St.
Raleigh, NC 27611
919/733–3654
Contact: Duncan Munn, Chief of Day Services

Div. of Vocational Rehabilitation Services
Dept. of Human Resources
620 North West St.
P.O. Box 26053
Raleigh, NC 27611
919/733–3364
Contact: Claude Myer, Director

Div. of Mental Health/Mental Retardation Services
Dept. of Human Services
Albemarle Building
325 Salisbury St.
Raleigh, NC 27611
919/733–3654
Contact: Patricia Porter

Child & Family Services
Mental Health, Mental Retardation & Substance Abuse Services
Dept. of Human Resources
325 N. Salisbury St.
Raleigh, NC 27611
919/733–0598
Contact: Lenore Behar, Special Assistant

North Carolina Council on Developmental Disabilities
1508 Western Blvd.
Raleigh, NC 27606–1359
919/733–6566
Contact: James W. Keene, Exec. Dir.

Governor's Advocacy Council for Persons with Disabilities
1318 Dale St., Ste. 100
Raleigh, NC 27605
919/733–9250
Contact: Lockhart Follin-Mace, Director

Clinical Center for the Study of Development & Learning
Biological Sciences Research Center 220H
University of North Carolina
Chapel Hill, NC 27514
919/966–1020
Contact: Dr. Melvin Levine, Director

Caswell/East Carolina University
Developmental Intervention & Research Institute
East Carolina University

Greenville, NC 27858
919/757–6164
Contact: C. Coble, J. Woodall, Directors

Exceptional Children's Advocacy Council
P.O. Box 16
Davidson, NC 28036
704/892–1321
Contact: Connie Hawkins, Director

Family & Infant Pre-School Program
Association for Retarded Citizens of N.C., Inc.
Western Carolina Center
300 Enola Rd.
Morganton, NC 28655
704/433–2661
Contact: Anita Hodges, Director

PARENTS Project
300 Enola Rd.
Morganton, NC 28655
704/433–2864
Contact: Anita Hodges, Director

Division TEACCH
Medical School Wing E
Chapel Hill, NC 27599
919/966–2174
Contact: Eric Schopler, Dir.

Autism Society of North Carolina
2216 Sanderford Rd.
Raleigh, NC 27610
919/821–4138
Contact: Betty Camp, President

Association for Retarded Citizens of North Carolina
16 Rowan St., P.O. Box 20545
Raleigh, NC 27619
919/782–4632
Contact: Mathew Johnsen, Exec. Dir.

NORTH DAKOTA

Special Education Div.
Dept. of Public Instruction
State Capitol
Bismarck, ND 58505–0164
701/224–2277
Contact: Gary Gronberg, Director

Special Education Div. [Ages 3–5]
Dept. of Public Instruction
State Capitol
Bismarck, ND 58505–6440
701/224–2277
Contact: Brenda Oas, Coordinator

Developmental Disabilities Div. [Ages 0–2]
Dept. of Human Services
State Capitol
Bismarck, ND 58505
701/224–2768
Contact: Shelby Niebergall

Dept. of Vocational Rehabilitation
State Board of Social Services
State Capitol Building
Bismarck, ND 58505
701/224–2907
Contact: Gene Hysjulien, Exec. Dir.

Developmental Disabilities Div.
Dept. of Human Services
State Capitol Building
Bismark, ND 58505
701/224–2768
Contact: Rob Graham, Acting Director

North Dakota Developmental Disabilities Council
Dept. of Human Services
State Capitol Building
Bismarck, ND 58505
701/224–2970
Contact: Tom Wallner, Director

Protection & Advocacy Project for the Developmentally Disabled
Governor's Council on Human Resources
State Capitol, 13th Floor
Bismarck, ND 58505
701/224–2972; 800/472–2670 (In ND)
Contact: Barbara Braun, Director

Pathfinder Services of North Dakota
P.O. Box 2087
Minot, ND 58701
701/268–3390
Contact: Katherine Erickson, Director

Parent-to-Parent
Contact Pathfinder Services, above

North Dakota State Society
Autism Society of America
1532 6th Ave., N.E.
Jamestown, ND 58401
701/251–1605
Contact: Amy Barnick, President

Association for Retarded Citizens of North Dakota
417½ E. Broadway, No. 9
P.O. Box 2776
Bismarck, ND 58502
701/223–5349
Contact: Dan Ulmer, Exec. Dir.

OHIO

Div. of Special Education
Dept. of Education
933 High St.
Worthington, OH 43085–4017
614/466–2650
Contact: Frank E. New, Director

Early Childhood Section [Ages 3–5]
Dept. of Education
65 S. Front St., Room 202
Columbus, OH 43266
614/466–0224
Contact: Jane Wiechel, Asst. Dir.

Div. of Maternal & Child Health [Ages 0–2]
State Dept. of Health
P.O. Box 118
Columbus, OH 43266–0118
614/466–3263
Contact: James Quilty, Chief

Rehabilitation Services Commission
400 E. Campus View Blvd.
Columbus, OH 43235
614/438–1210
Contact: Robert Rabe, Administrator

Dept. of Mental Retardation & Developmental Disabilities
State Office Tower
30 E. Broad St., Room 1284
Columbus, OH 43215
614/466–5214
Contact: Robert Brown, Director

Bureau of Children's Services
Dept. of Mental Health
30 E. Broad St., 11th Fl.
Columbus, OH 43215
614/466–2337
Contact: Patrick Canary, Chief

Ohio Developmental Disabilities Planning Council
30 E. Broad St., Rm. 1280
Columbus, OH 43215–3414
614/466–7203
Contact: Ken Campbell, Exec. Dir.

Ohio Legal Rights Service
8 E. Long St., 6th Floor
Columbus, OH 43215
614/466–7264; 800/282–9181 (In OH)
Contact: Carolyn Knight, Exec. Dir.

Affiliated Cincinnati Center for Developmental Disabilities
Pavilion Building
Elland & Bethesda Aves.
Cincinnati, OH 45229
513/559–4623
Contact: Dr. Jack Rubinstein, Dir.

The Nisonger Center
Ohio State University
McCampbell Hall
1581 Dodd Dr.
Columbus, OH 43210–1205
614/292–8365
Contact: Stephen Schroeder, Director

Tri-State Organized Coalition for Persons with Disabilities
SOC Information Center
106 Wellington Place, Lower Level

Cincinnati, OH 45219
513/381–2400
Contact: Cathy Heizman, Director

Ohio Coalition for the Education of Handicapped Children
933 High St., Ste. 106
Worthington, OH 43085
614/431–1307
Contact: Margaret Burley, Director

Parent-to-Parent
Contact Ohio Coalition for the Education of Handicapped Children, above

Ohio State Society
Autism Society of America
Ohio State University
751 Norhtwest Blvd.
Columbus, OH 43212
513/563–0753
Contact: Janet Clemmons

Central Ohio Chapter
Autism Society of America
320 W. 10th, Path. Dept. M352
Columbus, OH 43210
614/421–3881
Contact: Howard Newman, President

Cincinnati Chapter
Autism Society of America
3747 Renoir Pl.
Cincinnati, OH 45241
513/563–0753
Contact: Jennifer Brown, Pres.

Greater Akron Autism Society
4415 Leewood Rd.
Stow, OH 44224
216/686–1050
Contact: Joseph & Marilyn Henn, Presidents

Greater Cleveland Chapter
Autism Society of America
959 West Mile Dr.
Highland Heights, OH 44143
216/266–7180
Contact: Chuck Mintz, President

Youngstown Chapter
Autism Soceity of America
6149 Martha Dr.
Cortland, OH 44410
216/924–2076
Contact: Patricia Bloss, President

Association for Retarded Citizens of Ohio
360 S. 3rd St., Ste. 101
Columbus, OH 43215
614/228–4412
Contact: Carolyn Sidwell, Exec. Dir.

OKLAHOMA

Special Education Section
Dept. of Education
Oliver Hodge Memorial
Building, Room 215
Oklahoma City, OK 73105–4599
405/521–3352
Contact: Connie Siler, Director

Section for Exceptional Children [Ages 3–5]
Dept. of Education
2500 N. Lincoln Blvd., Ste. 263
Oklahoma City, OK 73105
405/521–3351
Contact: Karla Leatherman, Coordinator

Special Education Office [Ages 0–2]
Dept. of Education
Oliver Hodge Memorial
Building, Ste. 269
Oklahoma City, OK 73105
405/751–0065
Contact: Earlene Belling, Early Intervention Coordinator

Dept. of Human Services
Div. of Rehabilitation & Visual Services
P.O. Box 25352
Oklahoma City, OK 73125
405/424–4311, Ex. 2873
Contact: Jerry Dunlap, Asst. Dir.

Developmental Disabilities Services
Dept. of Human Services
P.O. Box 25352
Oklahoma City, OK 73125
405/521–3571
Contact: Deborah Rothe, Acting Director

Youth Community Services
Dept. of Mental Health
P.O. Box 53277
Capitol Station
Oklahoma City, OK 73152
405/271–7474
Contact: Marla Graham, Director

Oklahoma Developmental Disabilities Planning Council
Box 25352
Oklahoma City, OK 73125
405/521–2989
Contact: William Hilton, Director

Protection & Advocacy Agency
Osage Building, Room 133
9726 E. 42nd St.
Tulsa, OK 74146
918/664–5883
Contact: Dr. Bob VanOsdol, Director

Parents Reaching Out in Oklahoma (PRO-Oklahoma)
1917 S. Harvard Ave.
Oklahoma City, OK 73128
800/PL9–4142; 405/681–9710
Contact: Connie Motsinger, Director

Positive Reflections, Inc.
6141 N.W. Grand, Ste. 103
Oklahoma City, OK 73116
405/843–9114
Contact: Dana Baldridge or Nancy Thompson

Oklahoma State Society
Autism Society of America
316 Hoffman Drive
Norman, OK 73071
405/691–7502; 405/364–6415
Contact: Linda Fields, Pres.

OREGON

Special Education & Student Services Div.
Dept. of Education
700 Pringle Pkwy., S.E.
Salem, OR 97310
503/378–2677
Contact: Karen Brazeau, Assoc. Superintendent

Div. of Special Education [Ages 0–5]
Dept. of Education
700 Pringle Pkwy., S.E.
Salem, OR 97310
503/373–1484
Contact: Mike Barker, Coordinator

Vocational Rehabilitation Div.
Dept. of Human Resources
2045 Silverton Rd., N.E.
Salem, OR 97310
503/378–3850
Contact: Joil Southwell, Administrator

Program for Mental Retardation & Developmental Disabilities
Div. of Mental Health
Dept. of Human Resources
2575 Bittern St., N.W.
Salem, OR 97310
503/378–2429
Contact: James Toews, Assis. Admin.

Programs for Children & Adolescents
Mental Health Div.
2575 Bittern St., N.E.
Salem, OR 97310
503/378–2460
Contact: Faye Lindemann-Taylor, Coordinator

Oregon Developmental Disabilities
Planning Council
2575 Bittern St., N.E.
Salem, OR 97310–0001
503/378–2429
Contact: Clyde Muirhead, Planning Director

Oregon Advocacy Center
635 Board Trade Building
310 S.W. Fourth Ave., Ste. 625
Portland, OR 97204–2309
503/243–2081
Contact: Elam Lantz, Jr., Exec. Dir.

Center on Human Development
Clinical Services Building
College of Education
University of Oregon-Eugene
Eugene, OR 97403
503/686–3591
Contact: Dr. Hill Walker, Director

Crippled Children's Div.
Child Development & Rehabilitation Center
Oregon Health Sciences University
P.O. Box 574
Portland, OR 97207
503/279–8364
Contact: Dr. Gerald Smith, Director

Oregon COPE Project (Coalition in Oregon for Parent Education)
999 Locust St., N.E., No. 42
Salem, OR 97303
503/373–7477
Contact: Cheron Mayhall, Director

Parent-to-Parent
Contact Oregon COPE Project, above

Autism Council of Oregon
Autism Society of America
P.O. Box 13884
Salem, OR 97309
503/472–4850; 503/864–2410
Contact: Mary Anne Seaton, Pres.

Association for Retarded Citizens of Oregon
1745 State St.
Salem, OR 97301
503/581–2726
Janna Starr, Exec. Dir.

PENNSYLVANIA

Bureau of Special Education
Dept. of Education
333 Market St.
Harrisburg, PA 17126–0333
717/783–6913
Contact: James Tucker, Director

Bureau of Special Education [Ages 3–5]
Dept. of Education
333 Market St.
Harrisburg, PA 17126–0333
717/783–6913
Contact: Jill Lichty & Rick Price, Special Education Advisors

Bureau of Program Development & Policy [Ages 0–2]
Office of Mental Retardation
Health & Welfare Bldg., Rm. 302
Harrisburg, PA 17120
717/783–5758
Contact: Mel Knowlton, Dir.

Bureau of Vocational Rehabilitation
Dept. of Labor & Industry
Labor & Industry Bldg., Rm. 1300
7th & Forster Sts.
Harrisburg, PA 17120
717/787–5244
Contact: Joseph Snyder, Director

Dept. of Public Welfare
Health & Welfare Building, Rm. 302
Harrisburg, PA 17120
717/787–3700
Contact: Steve Eidelman, Deputy Secretary

Bureau of Children & Youth Services
Office of Mental Health
308 Health & Welfare Bldg.
Harrisburg, PA 17120
717/783–8335
Contact: Connie Dellmuth, Director

Developmental Disabilities Planning Council
Forum Building, Rm. 569
Commonwealth Ave.
Harrisburg, PA 17120
717/787–6057
Contact: David Schwartz, Exec. Dir.

Protection & Advocacy, Inc.
116 Pine St.
Harrisburg, PA 17101
717/236–8110; 800/692–7443
Contact: Kevin Casey, Exec. Dir.

Developmental Disabilities Program
Temple University
9th Floor, Ritter Annex
13th St. & Cecil Moore Ave.
Philadelphia, PA 19122
215/787–1356
Contact: Dr. Edward Newman, Director

Parents Union for Public Schools
401 N. Broad St., Room 916
Philadelphia, PA 19108
215/574–0337
Contact: Christine Davis, Director

Parent Education Network
240 Haymeadow Dr.
York, PA 17402
717/845–9722
Contact: Louise Thieme, Director

Parent-to-Parent
Contact Parent Education Network, above

Pennsylvania Chapter
Autism Society of America
500 Garden City Dr.
Monroeville, PA 15146
412/372–1443
Contact: Constance Torisky, Pres.

Cambria Chapter
Autism Society of America
384 Ridge View Lane
Conemaugh, PA 15909
Contact: Pauline Springer, Pres.

Greater Philadelphia Chapter
Autism Society of America
117 Cumberland Place
Bryn Mawr, PA 19010
215/342–2445
Contact: Reeva Golub & Dan Benau, Presidents

Greater Pittsburgh Chapter
Autism Society of America
500 Garden City Drive
Monroeville, PA 15146
412/856–7223
Contact: Connie Torisky, Pres.

Midwestern Pennsylvania Chapter
Autism Society of America
1612 Cloverdell Dr.
New Castle, PA 16101
412/654–4237
Contact: Linda S. Pacella, Pres.

Northwest Pennsylvania Chapter
Autism Society of America
5010 Dixson Dr.
Erie, PA 16509
814/868–3025
Contact: Marjorie Fischer, Pres.

Reading/Berks County Chapter
Autism Society of America
Box 171, R.D. No. 5
Reading, PA 19608
215/678–4806
Contact: Marianne Wersant, Pres.

Association for Retarded Citizens of Pennsylvania
123 Forster Place
Harrisburg, PA 17102
717/234–2621
Contact: W.A. West, Exec. Dir.

PUERTO RICO

Special Education Programs
Dept. of Education
Box 759
Hato Rey, PR 00919
809/764–8059

Contact: Lucila Torres Martinez, Asst. Sec. of Special Educ.

Early Childhood Educ. [Ages 3–5]
Dept. of Education
Box 759
Hato Rey, PR 00919
809/754–0094
Contact: Awilda Torres

Dept. of Health [Ages 0–2]
Maternal & Child Health Div.
Call Box 70184
San Juan, PR 00936
809/766–1616, Ex. 2146/2148
Contact: Carmen Aviles, Part H Coordinator

Div. de Rehabilitacion Vocacional
Dept. de Servcios Sociales
Apartado 1118
Hato Rey, PR 00919
809/725–1792
Contact: Angel Jimenez

Dept. of Social Services
P.O. Box 11398
Santurce, PR 00910
809/723–2127
Contact: Eva Alvarez de Orama, Asst. Sec. for Family Services

Developmental Disabilities Council
Box 9543
Santurce, PR 00908
809/722–0595
Contact: Maria Luisa Mendia, Dir.

Ombudsman for the Disabled, Governor's Office
Chardon Ave., No. 916
Hato Rey, PR 00936
809/766–2333
Contact: Nancy Nivef, Director

Associacion de Padres ProBienestar de Ninos Impedios de PR, Inc.
Box 21301
Rio Piedras, PR 00928
809/765–0345; 809/763–4665
Contact: Carmen Selles Vila, Director

Puerto Rico Society
Autism Society of America
G.P.O. Box 21301
Rio Piedras, PR 00928
Contact: Milagros Rodriguez, Pres.

RHODE ISLAND

Special Education Program Services Unit
Dept. of Education
Roger Williams Building, Rm. 209
22 Hayes St.
Providence, RI 02908
401/277–3505
Contact: Robert Pryhoda, Director

Special Education Program Services Unit [Ages 3–5]
Dept. of Elementary & Secondary Education
Roger Williams Bldg., Rm. 209
22 Hayes St.
Providence, RI 02908
401/277–3505
Contact: Amy Cohen, Preschool ECSE Consultant

Interagency Coordinating Council [Ages 0–2]
Dept. of Special Education
Rhode Island College
600 Mt. Pleasant Ave.
Providence, RI 02908
401/456–8599
Contact: Thomas Kochanek, Exec. Dir.

Vocational Rehabilitation
Dept. of Human Services
40 Fountain St.
Providence, RI 02903
401/421–7005
Contact: Sherri Campanelli, Administrator

Div. of Retardation
Dept. of Mental Health, Mental Retardation & Hospitals
Aime J. Forand Building
600 New London Ave.
Cranston, RI 02920
401/464–3234
Contact: Robert Carl, Jr., Exec. Dir.

Div. of Children's Mental Health Services
Dept. of Children & Their Families
610 Mt. Pleasant Ave.
Providence, RI 02908
401/457–4701

Rhode Island Developmental Disabilities Council
600 New London Ave.
Cranston, RI 02920
401/464–3191
Contact: Michael Slachek, Exec. Dir.

Rhode Island Protection & Advocacy System, Inc.
55 Bradford St., 2nd Floor
Providence, RI 02903
401/831–3150
Contact: Lind Katz, Exec. Dir.

Child Development Center
Rhode Island Hospital
593 Eddy St.
Providence, RI 02902
401/277–5581
Contact: Dr. Siegfried Pueschel, Dir.

Parent-to-Parent
R.I. Dept. of Education
22 Hayes St., Room 209
Providence, RI 02908
401/277–3505
Contact: Connie Susa, Parent Training Specialist

Rhode Island Society
Autism Society of America
128 Garden City Dr.
Cranston, RI 02920
401/942–7608
Contact: Robert R. Reidy, Pres.

Association for Retarded Citizens of Rhode Island
99 Vald Hill Rd.
Cranston, RI 02920
401/463–9191
Contact: James Healey, Exec. Dir.

SOUTH CAROLINA

Office of Programs for the Handicapped
Dept. of Education
Santee Building, A–24
100 Executive Center Dr.
Columbia, SC 29210
803/737–8710
Contact: Dr. Robert Black, Director

Programs for the Handicapped [Ages 3–5]
Dept. of Education
100 Executive Center Dr.
Santee Building, Ste. 210
Columbia, SC 29210
803/737–8710
Contact: Mary Ginn, State Plan Coordinator

Div. of Children's Health [Ages 0–2]
Dept. of Health & Environmental Control
2600 Bull St.
Columbia, SC 29201
803/734–4610
Contact: Eve Bogan, Program Administrator

Vocational Rehabilitation Dept.
1410 Boston Ave.
P.O. Box 15
West Columbia, SC 29171
803/734–4300
Contact: Joseph Dusenbury, Commissioner

Dept. of Mental Retardation
2712 Middleburg Dr.
P.O. Box 4706
Columbia, SC 29240
803/737–6444
Contact: Philip Massey, Commissioner

Mental Health Youth Services
Dept. of Mental Health
2414 Bull St., Box 485
Columbia, SC 29202
803/734–7856
Contact: Jerome Hanley, Director

S.C. Developmental Disabilities Planning Council
1205 Pendleton St., Rm. 404
Columbia, SC 29201–3731
803/758–8016
Contact: LaNelle DuRant, Exec. Dir.

S.C. Protection & Advocacy
System for the Handicapped, Inc.
3710 Landmark Dr., Ste. 208
Columbia, SC 29204
803/782–0639; 800/922–5225
Contact: Louise Ravenel, Exec. Dir.

University Affiliated Facility of South Carolina
Center for Developmental Disabilities
Benson Building, Pickens St.
University of South Carolina
Columbia, SC 29208
803/323–2244
Contact: Francys Travis, Director

Parents Reaching Out to Parents
220 Great North Rd.
Columbia, SC 29223
803/736–4595
Contact: Sue Slater, Director

South Carolina Chapter
Autism Society of America
P.O. Box 684
Effingham, SC 29541
803/563–4567
Contact: Audrey Horne

Association for Retarded Citizens of South Carolina
7412 Fairfield Rd.
Columbia, SC 29203
803/754–4763
Contact: John Beckley, Exec. Dir.

SOUTH DAKOTA

Section for Special Education
Dept. of Education
Kneip Office Building
700 N. Illinois St.
Pierre, SD 57501
605/773–3315
Contact: Dean Myers, Director

Section for Special Education [Ages 0–5]
Dept. of Education & Cultural Affairs
700 Governors Dr.
Pierre, SD 57501–3133
605/773–4693
Contact: Paulette Levisen

Dept. of Vocational Rehabilitation
700 N. Governors Dr.
Pierre, SD 57501
605/773–3195
Contact: John Madigan, Secretary

Office of Developmental Disabilities & Mental Health
Dept. of Social Services
Kneip Building
Pierre, SD 57501
605/773–3438
Contact: Thomas Scheinost, Administrator

South Dakota Advocacy Project
221 S. Central Ave.
Pierre, SD 57501
605/224–8294; 800/742–8108
Contact: Robert Kean, Exec. Dir.

South Dakota University Affiliated Facility
Center for Developmental Disabilities
USD School of Medicine
Vermillion, SD 57069
605/677–5311
Contact: Cecilia Rokusek, Acting Director

South Dakota Parent Connection
P.O. Box 84813
330 N. Main Ave., Ste. 301
Sioux Falls, SD 57118–4813
605/335–8844
Contact: Jeffrey Hayzlett, Director

Parent-to-Parent
Center for Developmental Disabilities
USD School of Medicine
414 E. Clark
Vermillion, SD 57069
605/677–5311

South Dakota Society
Autism Society of America
RR 1, Box 165
Elk Point, SD 57025
605/565–3450
Contact: Cathy Maynard, Pres.

Association for Retarded Citizens of South Dakota
P.O. Box 502
Pierre, SD 57501
605/224–8211
Contact: John Stengle, Exec. Dir.

TENNESSEE

Special Education Programs
Dept. of Education
103 Cordell Hull Building
Nashville, TN 37219
615/741–2851
Contact: Dr. JoLeta Reynolds, Assoc. Assistant Commissioner

Office for Special Education [Ages 0–2]
Dept. of Education
100 Cordell Hull Building
Nashville, TN 37219
615/741–2851
Contact: Sarah Willis, Part H. Coordinator

Div. of Vocational Rehabilitation
Dept. of Human Services
400 Deaderick St., 15th Fl.
Nashville, TN 37219
615/741–2019
Contact: Patsy Mathews, Asst. Commissioner

Dept. of Mental Health & Mental Retardation
Doctor's Building
706 Church St.
Nashville, TN 37219–5393
615/741–3803
Contact: James Foshee, Asst. Commissioner

Office of Children & Adolescent Services
Doctor's Building
706 Church St.
Nashville, TN 37219
615/741–3708
Contact: Duane Doidge, Director

Developmental Disabilities Planning Council
Doctor's Building, 3rd Fl.
706 Church St.
Nashville, TN 37219–5610
615/741–3807
Contact: Wanda Willis, Director

Effective Advocacy for Citizens with Handicaps (EACH)
P.O. Box 121257
Nashville, TN 37212
615/298–1080; 800/342–1660
Contact: Harriette Derryberry, Director

Child Development Center
University of Tennessee, Memphis
711 Jefferson Ave.
Memphis, TN 38105
901/528–6511
Contact: Dr. Gerald Golden, Director

Parents Offering Support to Other Parents (POSTOP)
801–A Teaberry Lane
Knoxville, TN 37912
615/691–2418
Contact: Ann Farr

Parents of Special Children
P.O. Box 3192

Murfreesboro, TN 37133
615/898–7525
Contact: Mary & Jim Goldsack

Tennessee State Society
Autism Society of America
2017 McClain Dr.
Knoxville, TN 37912
615/688–4929
Contact: Joseph Marshall, President

East Tennessee Chapter
Autism Society of America
2017 McClain Dr.
Knoxville, TN 37912
615/687–5090
Contact: Lee Bridges, President

Memphis Chapter
Autism Society of America
3264 Powers Road
Memphis, TN 38128
Contact: Kathleen Wickman, Pres.

Middle Tennessee Chapter
Autism Society of America
607 Davidson Rd.
Nashville, TN 37205
615/292–1579
Contact: Debora Carroll, Pres.

Association for Retarded Citizens of Tennessee
1805 Hayes, Ste. 100
Nashville, TN 37203
615/327–0294
Contact: Roger Blue, Exec. Dir.

TEXAS

Special Education Programs
Texas Education Agency
William B. Travis Bldg., Rm. 5–120
1701 N. Congress Ave.
Austin, TX 78701–2486
512/463–9414
Contact: Jill Gray, Director

Special Education Programs [Ages 3–5]
Texas Education Agency
William B. Travis Bldg.
1701 N. Congress Ave.
Austin, TX 78701
512/463–9414
Contact: Dainey Lege

Early Childhood Intervention Program [Ages 0–2]
Dept. of Health
1100 W. 49th St.
Austin, TX 78756
512/458–7673
Contact: Mary Elder, Administrator

Dept. of Mental Health & Mental Retardation
Box 12668, Capitol Station
Austin, TX 78711
512–465–4520
Contact: Jaylon Fincannon, Deputy Commissioner

Child/Adolescent Program
Dept. of Mental Health & Mental Retardation
Box 12668, Capitol Station
Austin, TX 78711
512/465–4657
Contact: Regenia Hicks, Program Specialist

Texas Planning Council for Developmental Disabilities
118 E. Riverside Dr.
Austin, TX 78704
512/445–8867
Contact: Roger Webb, Exec. Dir.

Advocacy, Inc.
7800 Shoal Creek Blvd.
Suite 171–E
Austin, TX 78752
512/454–4816; 800/252–9108
Contact: Exec. Dir.

University Affiliated Center
200 Treadway Plaza
6400 Harry Hines Blvd.
Dallas, TX 75235
214/688–7117
Contact: Dr. Mark Swanson, Director

Partnerships for Assisting Texans with Handicaps (PATH)
6465 Calder Ave., Ste. 202
Beaumont, TX 77707
409/866–4726
Contact: Janice Foreman, Director

Texas Parent Information Network
833 Houston Ave.
Austin, TX 78756
512/454–6694
Contact: Rona Stedtman

Texas State Society
Autism Society of America
1332 Cassia Way
San Antonio, TX 78232
512/494–1786
Contact: Ben Moore, President

Capital Area Texas Chapter
Autism Society of America
1711 Sylvan
Austin, TX 78741
512/442–5557
Contact: Ann Hardie, Pres.

Concho Valley Chapter
Autism Society of America
2528 Abilene
San Angelo, TX 76901
915/944–0452
Contact: Chuck Johnson, Pres.

Corpus Christi Chapter
Autism Society of America
325 Waverly
Corpus Christi, TX 75224
512/991–7933
Contact: John Buser, President

Dallas Chapter
Autism Society of America
5413 Redridge Rd.
Garland, TX 75042
214/690–1224
Contact: Carolyn Webster, Pres.

El Paso Chapter
Autism Society of America
4511 Frankfort
El Paso, TX 79903
915/532–6589
Contact: Al Bisconti, Pres.

Houston Chapter
Autism Society of America
11426 Pecan Creek
Houston, TX 77043
713/471–3330
Contact: Mrs. Renee Feldman, Pres.

Laredo Chapter
Autism Society of America
8725 Puerto Belo
Laredo, TX 78041
512/723–1318
Contact: Oscar Campos, President

Rio Grande Valley Chapter
Autism Society of America
P.O. Box 94
Olmito, TX 78575
512/350–4107
Contact: Kathryn Stanford, Pres.

San Antonio Chapter
Autism Society of America
5411 Vista Court
San Antonio, TX 78247
512/925–2321
Contact: Randy Asterman, Pres.

Tarrant County Chapter
121 W. Ridgegate Dr.
Garland, TX 75040
817/232–1742
Contact: Jerry Goodwin, Pres.

Association for Retarded Citizens of Texas
833 Houston St.
Austin, TX 78756
512/454–6694
Contact: Carmen Quesada, Exec. Dir.

UTAH

Special Education Section
State Office of Education
250 E. 5th, South
Salt Lake City, UT 84111–3204

801/538–7706
Contact: Steve Kukic, Director

Special Education Section [Ages 3–5]
State Office of Education
250 E. 5th, South
Salt Lake City, UT 84111
801/538–7708
Contact: John Killoran

Handicapped Children's Services [Ages 0–2]
State Dept. of Health
P.O. Box 16650
Salt Lake City, UT 84116–0650
801/538–6165
Contact: George Delavan, Director

Office of Rehabilitation
State Board of Education
250 E. 5th, South
Salt Lake City, UT 84111
801/538–7530
Contact: Judy Ann Buffmire, Exec. Dir.

Div. of Services to the Handicapped
120 N. 200, West, Rm. 201
Salt Lake City, UT 84103
801/538–4199
Contact: Theron Olsen, Director

Div. of Mental Health
Dept. of Social Services
120 N. 200, West, 4th F.
P.O. Box 45500
Salt Lake City, UT 84145–0500
801/538–4270
Contact: Bill Geurts, Children & Adolescent Program Specialist

Utah Council for Handicapped & Developmentally Disabled Persons
120 N. 200, West
P.O. Box 1958
Salt Lake City, UT 84110
801/538–4184
Contact: Frances Morse, Exec. Dir.

Legal Center for the Handicapped
455 E. 400 South, Suite 201
Salt Lake City, UT 84111
801/363–1347; 800/662–9080
Contact: Phyllis Geldzahler, Exec. Dir.

Developmental Center for Handicapped Persons
Utah State University
Logan, UT 84322–6800
801/750–1981
Contact: Dr. Marvin Fifield, Director

Utah Parent Center
4984 South 300 West
Murray, UT 84107
801/265–9883; 800/468–1160
Contact: Stevia Bowman, Director

Parent-to-Parent
455 E. 400, South, Ste. 300
Salt Lake City, UT 84111
801/364–5060; 800/662–4058

Autism Society of Utah
Autism Society of America
668 S. 13th East
Salt Lake City, UT 84102
801/263–8317
Contact: Kathy Kirkman, Pres.

Weber/Davis Chapter
Autism Society of America
c/o 1292 North 700 East
Bountiful, UT 84010
801/292–5868
Contact: Candace Robinson, Pres.

Association for Retarded Citizens of Utah
455 E. 400, South, Ste. 300
Salt Lake City, UT 84111
801/364–5060
Contact: Ray Behle, Exec. Dir.

VERMONT

Div. of Special Education
Dept. of Education
State Capitol Office Building
120 State St.
Montpelier, VT 05602–3403
802/828–3141
Contact: Marc E. Hull, Director

Special Education Unit [Ages 3–5]
Dept. of Education
120 State St.
Montpelier, VT 05602–2703
802/828–3141
Contact: Kathy Sollace, Preschool Coordinator

Special Education Unit [Ages 0–2]
Dept. of Education
120 State St.
Montpelier, VT 05602–2703
802/828–3141
Contact: Kim Keiser, 0–3 Coordinator

Vocational Rehabilitation Div.
Dept. of Social & Rehabilitative Services
103 S. Main St.
Waterbury, VT 05676
802/241–2196
Contact: Richard Douglas, Director

Div. of Mental Retardation Programs
Dept. of Mental Health
103 S. Main St.
Waterbury, VT 05676
802/241–2636
Contact: Charles Mosely, Director

Dept. of Mental Health
103 S. Main St.
Waterbury, VT 05676
802/241–2732
Contact: Linda Taft, Mental Health Children's Specialist

Vermont Developmental Disabilities Council
103 S. Main St.
Waterbury, VT 05676
Contact: Thomas Pombar, Director

Vermont Developmentally Disabilities Law Project
12 North St.
Burlington, VT 05401
802/863–2881
Contact: Judy Dickson, Director

Vermont Information & Training Network (VITN)
Vermont/ARC
Champlain Mill, No. 37
Winooski, VT 05404
802/655–4016
Contact: Joan Sylvester, Director

Vermont Chapter
Autism Society of America
3 Bedford Oven
South Burlington, VT 05403
802/769–1140; 802/658–3374
Contact: Paul & Anne Bakeman, Presidents

Vermont Association for Retarded Citizens
Champlain Mill, No. 37
Winooski, VT 05404
802/655–4014
Contact: Joan Sylvester, Exec. Dir.

VIRGIN ISLANDS

Div. of Special Education
Department of Education
P.O. Box 66400
Charlotte Amalie
St. Thomas, VI 00801
809/776–5802
Contact: Priscilla Stridiron, Director

Div. of Special Education [Ages 3–5]
Dept. of Education
44–46 Kongens Gade
St. Thomas, VI 00802
809/776–5802
Contact: Dana Fredebaugh, ECSE Supervisor

Div. of Maternal & Child Health/Crippled Children's Services [Ages 0–2]
Dept. of Health
Kund Hansen Complex
St. Thomas, VI 00802
809/776–3580
Contact: Patricia Adams, Program Dir.

Developmental Disabilities Council
P.O. Box 2671

Kings Hill
St. Croix, VI 00850
809/772–2133
Contact: Mark Vinzant, Director

Committee on Advocacy for the Developmentally Disabled
Apartment No. 2, 31A New St.
Fredericksted, St. Croix VI 00840
809/772–1200
Contact: Russell Richards, Director

VI Coalition of Citizens with Disabilities
St. Thomas Chapter
P.O. Box 9500
St. Thomas, VI 00801
809/776–1277

VI Coalition of Citizens with Disabilities
St. Croix Chapter
P.O. Box 5156 Sunny Isles
St. Croix, VI 00820
809/778–7370

VI Parent Support Group
P.O. Box 11868
St. Thomas, VI 00801
809/776–4303
Contact: Don Laird, Director

VIRGINIA

Office of Special & Compensatory Education
Dept. of Education
P.O. Box 6Q
Richmond, VA 23216–2060
804/225–2402
Contact: William Helton, Director

Div. of Special Education Programs [Ages 3–5]
Dept. of Education
P.O. Box 6Q
Richmond, VA 23216–2060
804/225–2873
Contact: Andrea Lazzari

Children & Youth Services [Ages 0–2]
Office of Mental Retardation Services
P.O. Box 1797
Richmond, VA 23233
804/786–3710
Contact: Michel Fehl, Director

Dept. of Rehabilitative Services
State Board of Vocational Rehabilitation
P.O. Box 11045
Richmond, VA 23230
Contact: Altamont Dickerson, Commissioner

Office of Mental Retardation Services
P.O. Box 1797
Richmond, VA 23214
804/786–1746
Contact: Stanley Butkus, Director

Virginia Autism Resource Center
134 W. Piccadilly St.
Winchester, VA 22601
703/667–7771
Contact: S. Gail Mayfield, Project Director

Developmental Disabilities Planning Council
Dept. for Rights of the Disabled
Monroe Building, 17th Fl.
101 N. 14th St.
Richmond, VA 23219
804/225–2042
Contact: James Rothrock, Exec. Dir.

Dept. for Rights of the Disabled
James Monroe Building, 17th Floor
101 N. 14th St.
Richmond, VA 23219
804/225–2042; 800/552–3962 (TDD & Voice)
Contact: Carolyn W. Hodgins, Director

Virginia Institute for Developmental Disabilities
Virginia Commonwealth University
301 W. Franklin St., Box 3020
Richmond, VA 23284–3020
804/225–3876
Contact: Dr. Howard Garner, Director

Parent Education Advocacy Training Center (PEATC)
228 S. Pitt St., Room 300
Alexandria, VA 22314
703/836–2953
Contact: Winifred Anderson, Director

Parent-to-Parent of Virginia
VA Inst. for Dev. Disabilities
VA Commonwealth University
301 W. Franklin St., Box 3020
Richmond, VA 23284
804/225–3875; 800/344–0012
Contact: Mary Cunningham, Coordinator

Virginia State Society
Autism Society of America
1209 Lawrence Grey Dr.
Virginia Beach, VA 23455
804/464–6493
Contact: Dolores Bartel, Pres.

Blueridge Society
Autism Society of America
134 W. Piccadilly St.
Winchester, VA 22601
703/667–7771
Contact: Charlotte Crane, President

Central Virginia Chapter
Autism Society of America
4808 Monumental St.
Richmond, VA 23226
804/358–3745
Contact: Bonnie Atwood, President

Northern Virginia Chapter
Autism Society of America
2903 Hideaway Road
Fairfax, VA 22031–1310
703/532–6391
Contact: Suzanne and Larry Butcher

Peninsula Society
Autism Society of America
158 Coventry Lane
Newport News, VA 23602
804/872–9553
Contact: Cathy Odom, President

Roanoke Valley Chapter
Autism Society of America
803 Red Lane
Salem, VA 24153
703/389–9603
Contact: Patricia Buckley, Pres.

Tidewater Chapter
Autism Society of America
3523 Wellington Street
Norfolk, VA 23513
Contact: Barbara Dixon, Pres.

Association for Retarded Citizens of Virginia
6 N. 6th St.
Richmond, VA 23219
804/649–8481
Contact: Chris Rowe, Exec. Dir.

WASHINGTON

Special Education Section
Superintendent of Public Instruction
FG–11 Old Capitol Building
Olympia, WA 98504–0001
206/753–6733
Contact: Dr. Gregory Kirsch, Director

Superintendent of Public Instruction [Ages 3–5]
FG–11 Old Capitol Building
Olympia, WA 98504–0001
206/753–0317
Contact: Joan Gaetz, ECSE Coordinator

DSHS/Birth to Six Planning Project [Ages 0–2]
12th & Franklin Sts.
MS: OB–33J
Olympia, WA 98604–0095
206/586–2810
Contact: Susan Baxter

Div. of Vocational Rehabilitation
Dept. of Social & Health Services
State Office Bldg. No. 2
MS: OB–21C
Olympia, WA 98504
206/753–2544

Contact: Sharon Stewart–Johnson, Director

Div. of Developmental Disabilities
Dept. of Social & Health Services
P.O. Box 1788, OB–42C
Olympia, WA 98504
206/753–3900
Contact: Susan Elliott, Director

Children & Adolescent Services
Mental Health Div.
MS: OB–42F
Olympia, WA 98504
206/753–5414
Contact: Jann Hoppler, Administrator

Developmental Disabilities Planning Council
Ninth & Columbia Bldg.
MS: GH–52
Olympia, WA 98504–4151
206/753–3908
Contact: Sharon Hansen, Exec. Dir.

Washington Protection & Advocacy System
1550 W. Armory Way, Ste. 204
Seattle, WA 98119
206/284–1037
Contact: Barbara Oswald, Co–Director

Child Development & Mental Retardation Center
University of Washington
Seattle, WA 98195
206/543–3224
Contact: Dr. Michael Guralnick, Dir.

Parents Advocating Vocational Education (PAVE)
6316 S. 12th St.
Tacoma, WA 98645
206/565–2266; 800–5–PARENT (In WA)
Contact: Martha Gentili, Director

Specialized Training of Military Parents (STOMP)
12208 Pacific Hwy., S.W.
Tacoma, WA 98499
206/588–1741
Contact: Heather Hebdon, Project Manager

Pierce County Parent-to-Parent
12208 Pacific Hwy., S.W.
Tacoma, WA 98499
206/588–1741
Contact: Betty Johnson, Coordinator

Washington State Chapter
Autism Society of America
1207 South 45th Ave.
Yakima, WA 98908
509/966–0625
Contact: Jerri Jacobs, Pres.

Clark County Chapter
Autism Society of America
12208 N.E. 72nd St.
Vancouver, WA 98662
206/254–6339
Contact: John Weber, President

Pierce/Tacoma Chapter
Autism Society of America
1508 S. MacArthur
Tacoma, WA 98465
206/564–7409
Contact: Beth Evans, Pres.

Spokane Area Chapter
Autism Society of America
W. 704 23rd
Spokane, WA 99203
Contact: Patricia Garvin, Pres.

Association for Retarded Citizens of Washington
1703 E. State St.
Olympia, WA 98506
206/357–5596

WEST VIRGINIA

Office of Special Education
Dept. of Education
B–304, Building 6
Capitol Complex
Charleston, WV 25305
304/348–2696
Contact: Nancy Thabet, Director

Preschool Handicapped [Ages 3–5]
Office of Special Education
Dept. of Education
B–304, Building 6
Capitol Complex
Charleston, WV 25305
304/348–2696
Contact: Pam George, Coordinator

Dept. of Health [Ages 0–2]
1800 Washington St., East
Capitol Complex, Rm. 461
Charleston, WV 25305
304/348–2276; 304/348–0627
Contact: Wanda Radcliff, Early Intervention Coordinator

Div. of Rehabilitation Services
State Board of Rehabilitation
State Capitol
Charleston, WV 25305
304/766–4601
Contact: Earl Wolfe, Director

Developmental Disabilities Services
Div. of Behavioral Health
Dept. of Health
1800 Washington St., East
Charleston, WV 25305
304/348–0627
Contact: Sharon Sturm, Director

Children's Mental Health
Office of Behavioral Health
1800 Washington St., East
Charleston, WV 25305
304/348–0627
Contact: David Saenz, Acting Dir.

Developmental Disabilities Planning Council
c/o Dept. of Health
625 D. St.
Charleston, WV 25303–3111
304/348–2276
Contact: Richard Kelly, Director

W.V. Advocates for the Developmentally Disabled, Inc.
1200 Brooks Medical Building
Quarrier St., Suite 27
Charleston, WV 25301
304/346–0847; 800/642–9205
Contact: Vicky Smith, Exec. Dir.

University Affiliated Center for Developmental Disabilities
West Virginia University
509 Allen Hall/P.O. Box 6122
Morgantown, WV 26506–6122
304/293–4692
Contact: Ashok Dey, Director

Project STEP
116 E. King St.
Martinsburg, WV 25401
304/263–HELP
Contact: Carol Tamara, Director

Huntington Area Chapter
Autism Society of America
104 Leisure Lane
Huntington, WV 25705
Contact: Elaine Harvey, Pres.

N. Central WV Chapter
Autism Society of America
104 Steiner Blvd.
Barboursville, WV 25504
Contact: Roselyn Barker, Pres.

N. Central WV Chapter
Autism Society of America
306 Davis St.
Clarksburg, WV 26301
304/624–6085
Contact: Polly Dennison, Pres.

Association for Retarded Citizens of West Virginia
Market Square Bldg., Rm. 400
700 Market St.
Parkersburg, WV 26101
304/485–5283
Contact: Nancy Lipphardt, Exec. Dir.

WISCONSIN

Div. of Handicapped Children & Pupil Services
Dept. of Public Instruction
125 S. Webster St.

P.O. Box 7841
Madison, WI 53707–7841
608/266–1649
Contact: Victor J. Contrucci, Director

Early Childhood Sensory & Language Impaired Programs [Ages 3–5]
Dept. of Public Instruction
P.O. Box 7841
Madison, WI 53707
608/266–6981
Contact: John Stadtaueller, Chief

Bureau of Planning [Ages 0–2]
Dept. of Health & Human Services
P.O. Box 7850
Madison, WI 53707
608/266–3405
Contact: Ken Streit, Senior Planning Analyst

Div. of Vocational Rehabilitation
Dept. of Health & Social Services
1 W. Wilson St., Rm. 830
P.O. Box 7852
Madison, WI 53707
608/266–5466
Contact: Judy Norman-Nunnery, Administrator

Developmental Disabilities Office
Dept. of Health & Human Services
P.O. Box 7851
Madison, WI 53707
608/266–9329
Contact: Dennis Harkins, Director

Office of Mental Health
Dept. of Health & Human Services
P.O. Box 7851
Madison, WI 53707
608/266–3249
Contact: Deborah Allness, Director

Wisconsin Council on Developmental Disabilities
P.O. Box 7851
Madison, WI 53707
608/266–7826
Contact: Jayn Wittenmyer, Exec. Dir.

Wisconsin Coalition for Advocacy, Inc.
16 N. Carroll St., Suite 400
Madison, WI 53703
608/251–9600; 800/328–1110
Contact: Lynn Breedlove, Exec. Dir.

Waisman Center University Affiliated Facility
1500 Highland Ave.
Madison, WI 53705–2280
608/263–5940
Contact: Terrence Dolan, Director

Parent Education Project
United Cerebral Palsy of S.E. Wisconsin
230 W. Wells St.
Milwaukee, WI 53203
414/272–4500
Contact: Liz Irwin, Director

Parent-to-Parent
5522 University Ave.
Madison, WI 53705
608/231–3335
Contact: Sara Pedersen, Coordinator

Wisconsin State Society
Autism Society of America
4317 S. Packard Ave.
Cudahy, WI 53110
414/481–5094
Contact: Patti Meerschaert, Pres.

Fox Valley Area Chapter
Autism Society of America
1301 East Pershing
Appleton, WI 54911
Contact: Della Young, Pres.

Madison Chapter
Autism Society of America
6622 Greenbriar Rd.
Middleton, WI 53562
Contact: Fran Bicknell, Pres.

Milwaukee Chapter
Autism Society of America
6900 Horizon Dr.
Greendale, WI 53129
414/425–0763
Contact: Bob Serak, President

Association for Retarded Citizens of Wisconsin
5522 University Ave.
Madison, WI 53705
608/231–3335
Contact: Merlen Kurth, Exec. Dir.

WYOMING

Special Programs Unit
Dept. of Education
Hathaway Building
Cheyenne, WY 82002–0050
307/777–7414
Contact: Ken Blackburn, Director

Div. of Community Programs [Ages 3–5]
Dept. of Health & Social Services
354 Hathaway Building
Cheyenne, WY 82002
307/777–7115
Contact: Wayne Johnson, Program Manager

Div. of Vocational Rehabilitation
Dept. of Health & Social Services
Hathaway Building, Room 327
Cheyenne, WY 82002
307/777–7389
Contact: Joan Watson, Director

Div. of Community Programs
355 Hathaway Building
Cheyenne, WY 82002–0170
307/777–6488
Contact: Steve Zimmerman, Administrator

Council on Developmental Disabilities
Barrett Bldg., Rm. 408
Cheyenne, WY 82003–0001
307/777–7230
Contact: Sharron Kelsey, Exec. Dir.

Wyoming Protection & Advocacy System, Inc.
2424 Pioneer Ave., No. 101
Cheyenne, WY 82001
307/632–3496; 800/328–1110
Contact: Jeanne Kawcak, Exec. Dir.

Parent-to-Parent
Council on Developmental Disabilities
Barrett Bldg., Rm. 408
Cheyenne, WY 82002
307/777–7230
Contact: Brett Wilson, Program Manager

Association for Retarded Citizens of Wyoming
P.O. Box 1205
Cheyenne, WY 82003
307/632–7105
Contact: Lorinda Vetter, Exec. Dir.

Index